THE LORD OF
THE GOSPELS

THE LORD OF THE GOSPELS

The 1990 Sperry Symposium
on the New Testament

Edited by
Bruce A. Van Orden and
Brent L. Top

Deseret Book Company
Salt Lake City, Utah

Library of Congress Cataloging-in-Publication Data

Sperry Symposium on the New Testament (1990 : Brigham Young
    University)
    The Lord of the Gospels / the 1990 Sperry Symposium on the New
Testament ; edited by Bruce A. Van Orden and Brent L. Top.
      p. cm.
    Papers prepared for the symposium held 20 Oct. 1990 on Brigham
Young Univ. campus.
    Includes bibliographical references and index.
    ISBN 0-87579-479-3
    1. Bible. N.T. Gospels – Criticism, interpretation, etc. –
Congresses. 2. Jesus Christ – Mormon interpretations – Congresses.
I. Van Orden, Bruce A. II. Top, Brent L. III. Title.
BS2555.2.S64 1990
226'.06 – dc20   91-141
                                                    CIP

Printed in the United States of America

10   9   8   7   6   5   4   3   2   1

Contents

Preface

The beloved apostle John had a clear agenda when he wrote the fourth Gospel. Throughout his book he cited the multiple witnesses of the Lord Jesus Christ's divinity as a testimony:

"And many other signs truly did Jesus in the presence of his disciples, which are not written in this book:

"But these are written, that ye might believe that Jesus is the Christ, the Son of God; and that believing ye might have life through his name" (John 20:30–31).

Each Gospel writer likewise wished to testify through the works of their Lord that they had found their Messiah and Master, so that through their writings others might also be led to know that Jesus is the Lord.

Three Gospel writers—Matthew, Mark, and Luke—recorded an account of Jesus' interview with one of the scribes who asked, "Which is the first commandment of all?" Jesus answered by citing the Sh'ma (see Deuteronomy 6:4): "The first of all the commandments is, Hear, O Israel; The Lord our God is one Lord" (Mark 12:29). Then he added what it means to *hear* the Lord: "And thou shalt love the Lord thy God with all thy heart, and with all thy soul, and with all thy mind, and with all thy strength: this is the first commandment" (Mark 12:30).

All of our standard works testify that Jesus is the Christ and that we must obey his gospel to obtain eternal life. The New Testament, illustrating as it does events in the mortal ministry of Jesus, is especially suited to help us become better acquainted with the Lord, to know him for what he really is—our Redeemer, our Savior, our Friend. He himself said in his intercessory prayer: "And this is life eternal, that they might know thee the only true God, and Jesus Christ, whom thou has sent" (John 17:3).

Coming to know the Master requires diligent study of the scriptures. "Search the scriptures," Jesus commanded; "they are they which testify of me" (John 5:39). Elder Howard W. Hunter of the Quorum of the Twelve Apostles counsels us:

"Scriptures contain the record of the self-revelation of God, and through them God speaks to man. Where could there be more profitable use of time than reading from the scriptural library the literature that teaches us to know God and understand our relationship to him? Time is always precious to busy people, and we are robbed of its worth when hours are wasted in reading or viewing that which is frivolous and of little value" (in Conference Report, Oct. 1979, p. 91).

Brigham Young University and the LDS Church Educational System are honored to sponsor the annual Sidney B. Sperry Symposium for the benefit of gospel students the world over. The nineteenth annual Sperry Symposium with the theme "The Lord of the Gospels" was held 20 October 1990 on the Brigham Young University campus. This volume contains the written versions of many of the presentations made at that symposium.

The insights, instruction, and inspiration contained in this volume are offered to Latter-day Saints everywhere, particularly to Gospel Doctrine teachers and class members, to help in grasping some of the central and most inspiring themes of the four Gospels in the New Testament. Elder James E. Faust of the Quorum of the Twelve Apostles shares his apostolic witness of the Lord Jesus Christ and his holy word in the new covenant, or the New Testament. Twelve other gospel scholars and religious educators have compiled the fruits of recent research and their own insights about Jesus and the four Gospels.

May the words contained herein inspire as well as instruct and motivate us to use the holy scriptures to strengthen our individual testimonies of Christ, that we may feel as earlier disciples felt: "Did not our heart burn within us, while he talked with us by the way, and while he opened to us the scriptures?" (Luke 24:32). And may we follow the example of the Berean converts recorded in the New Testament: "they received the word with all readiness of mind, and searched the scriptures daily, whether those things were so" (Acts 17:11).

Bruce A. Van Orden
Brent L. Top
Editors

CHAPTER ONE

A Surety of a Better Testament

Elder James E. Faust
Quorum of the Twelve Apostles

It is an honor and a pleasure to be invited by Donald Q. Cannon, acting dean of Religious Education, to participate in the nineteenth annual Sidney B. Sperry Symposium at this great university. Brother Cannon suggested in his formal invitation that my assignment with the BYU Jerusalem Center and the Holy Land might be a helpful background against which to discuss some phase of the life and ministry of the Lord Jesus Christ. I hope this is true. He also reminded me that my calling places upon me a responsibility to witness concerning the reality of the Savior and his mission. I know this to be true.

I take my text from Paul to the Hebrews: "By so much was Jesus made a surety of a better testament" (Hebrews 7:22). What is "a surety"? We find in turning to the dictionary that *surety* is the state of being sure; it is an undertaking or a pledge; it also refers to one who has become legally liable for the debt, default, or failure in duty of another (*Webster's New Collegiate Dictionary,* 1977 ed.). Do not the Savior and his mission have claim upon all these meanings?

What is a testament? The primary meaning of *testament* is a covenant with God. It is also holy scripture, a will, a witness, a tangible proof, an expression of conviction (*Webster's New Collegiate Dictionary,* 1977 ed.). So the Savior as a surety is a guarantor of a better covenant with God.

We all know that moving from the Old Testament to the New Testament is moving from the rigid formality of the letter of the law to the spirit. It is a better testament because the intent of a person alone becomes part of the rightness or wrongness of human action. So our intent to do evil or our desire to do good will be a free-standing element of consideration of our actions. We are told we will be judged in part by the intent of our hearts (D&C 88:109). An example of being convicted by free-standing intent is found in Matthew:

"Ye have heard that it was said by them of old time, Thou shalt not commit adultery:

"But I say unto you, That whosoever looketh on a woman to lust after her hath committed adultery with her already in his heart" (Matthew 5:27–28).

This New Testament is harder doctrine. In the old English common law, a formality and rigidity developed in the administration of the law to the point where, for justice to obtain, the law of equity developed. One of my favorite maxims in equity is, "Equity does what ought to be done." The New Testament goes further. In a large measure we will be judged not only by what we have done but what we should have done in a given situation.

Much of the spirit of the New Testament is found in the Sermon on the Mount. The New Testament requires a reconciliation of differences. "Therefore if thou bring thy gift to the altar, and there rememberest that thy brother hath ought against thee;

"Leave there thy gift before the altar, and go thy way; first be reconciled to thy brother, and then come and offer thy gift" (Matthew 5:23–24).

In the New Testament, swearing becomes completely prohibited:

"Again, ye have heard that it hath been said by them of old time, Thou shalt not forswear thyself, but shalt perform unto the Lord thine oaths:

"But I say unto you, Swear not at all; neither by heaven, for it is God's throne:

"Nor by the earth; for it is his footstool: neither by Jerusalem; for it is the city of the great King.

"Neither shalt thou swear by thy head, because thou canst not make one hair white or black.

"But let your communication be, Yea, yea; Nay, nay: for whatsoever is more than these cometh of evil" (Matthew 5:33–37).

Then follows more of the hard doctrine of the New Testament:

"But I say unto you, That ye resist not evil: but whosoever shall smite thee on thy right cheek, turn to him the other also.

"And if any man will sue thee at the law, and take away thy coat, let him have thy cloke also.

"And whosoever shall compel thee to go a mile, go with him twain.

"Give to him that asketh thee, and from him that would borrow of thee turn not thou away.

"Ye have heard that it hath been said, Thou shalt love thy neighbour, and hate thine enemy.

"But I say unto you, Love your enemies, bless them that curse you, do good to them that hate you, and pray for them which despitefully use you, and persecute you" (Matthew 5:39–44).

The New Testament suggests a new form and content of prayer. It is profoundly simple and uncomplicated:

"And when thou prayest, thou shalt not be as the hypocrites are: for they love to pray standing in the synagogues and in the corners of the streets, that they may be seen of men. Verily I say unto you, They have their reward.

"But thou, when thou prayest, enter into thy closet, and when thou hast shut the door, pray to thy Father which is in secret; and thy Father which seeth in secret shall reward thee openly.

"But when ye pray, use not vain repetitions, as the heathen do: for they think that they shall be heard for their much speaking.

"Be not ye therefore like unto them: for your Father knoweth what things ye have need of, before ye ask him.

"After this manner therefore pray ye: Our Father which art in heaven, Hallowed be thy name.

"Thy kingdom come, Thy will be done in earth, as it is in heaven.

"Give us this day our daily bread.

"And forgive us our debts, as we forgive our debtors.

"And lead us not into temptation, but deliver us from evil: For thine is the kingdom, and the power, and the glory, for ever. Amen" (Matthew 6:5–13).

The New Testament suggests that the doing of our good works ought to be in secret:

"But when thou doest alms, let not thy left hand know what thy right hand doeth.

"That thine alms may be in secret: and thy Father which seeth in secret himself shall reward thee openly" (Matthew 6:3–4).

But the greatest challenge, the hardest doctrine, is also found in the Sermon on the Mount:

"Be ye therefore perfect, even as your Father which is in heaven is perfect" (Matthew 5:48).

The Savior as "the mediator of the new testament" (Hebrews 9:15) introduced a higher law of marriage:

"And the Pharisees came to him, and asked him, Is it lawful for a man to put away his wife? tempting him.

"And he answered and said unto them, What did Moses command you?

"And they said, Moses suffered to write a bill of divorcement, and to put her away.

"And Jesus answered and said unto them, For the hardness of your heart he wrote you this precept.

"But from the beginning of the creation God made them male and female.

"For this cause shall a man leave his father and mother, and cleave to his wife;

"And they twain shall be one flesh: so then they are no more twain, but one flesh.

"What therefore God hath joined together, let not man put asunder" (Mark 10:2–9).

The challenge of Jesus was to replace the rigid technical "thou shalt not" of the law of Moses needed by the spiritually immature children of Israel with the spirit of the "better testament." How was that to be done? Time was short. He had only three years. How should he begin? Obviously he must begin with the apostles and the small group of disciples around him who would have the responsibility to carry on the work after his death. President J. Reuben Clark, Jr., describes this challenge as follows: "This task involved the overturning, the virtual outlawing, of the centuries-old Mosaic law of the Jews, and the substitution therefor of the Gospel of Christ" (*Why the King James Version,* Classics in Mormon Literature Series [Salt Lake City: Deseret Book Co., 1979], p. 51).

It was not easy for even the apostles to understand, Doubting Thomas being a good example. Thomas had been with the Savior when the Savior, on several occasions, foretold of his death and resurrection. Yet when Thomas was told that the resurrected Christ lived, he said, "Except I shall see in his hands the print of the nails, and put my finger into the print of the nails, and thrust my hand into his side, I will not believe" (John 20:25). Perhaps Thomas can be forgiven because so great an event had never happened before.

What about Peter's conversion to the great principle that the gospel of Jesus Christ is for everyone? He had been an eyewitness, as he stated in 2 Peter, that "we have not followed cunningly devised fables, when we make known unto you the power and coming of our Lord Jesus Christ, but were eyewitnesses of his majesty" (2 Peter 1:16). To what had Peter been an eyewitness? He had been an eyewitness to everything in the Savior's ministry. He had seen the Savior welcome the Samaritans, who were loathed by the Jews, following the encounter with the Samaritan at the well of Jacob (see John 4). Peter had seen a vision and heard the voice of the Lord, "What God hath cleansed, that call not thou common" (Acts 10:15). Finally, fully converted and receiving a spiritual confirmation, Peter opened his mouth, and said, "Of a truth I perceive that God is no respecter of persons:

"But in every nation he that feareth him, and worketh righteousness, is accepted with him" (Acts 10:34–35).

It is strengthening to review the testimonies of the apostles that Jesus is, in fact, the Christ. These testimonies are also a surety of a better testament. The first recorded testimony of the divinity of the Savior is the occasion of Jesus walking on the water, which is more fully recorded in Matthew 14:

"But the ship was now in the midst of the sea, tossed with waves: for the wind was contrary.

"And in the fourth watch of the night Jesus went unto them, walking on the sea.

"And when the disciples saw him walking on the sea, they were troubled, saying, It is a spirit; and they cried out for fear.

"But straightway Jesus spake unto them, saying, Be of good cheer; it is I; be not afraid.

"And Peter answered him and said, Lord, if it be thou, bid me come unto thee on the water.

"And he said, Come. And when Peter was come down out of the ship, he walked on the water, to go to Jesus.

"But when he saw the wind boisterous, he was afraid; and beginning to sink, he cried, saying, Lord, save me.

"And immediately Jesus stretched forth his hand, and caught him, and said unto him, O thou of little faith, wherefore didst thou doubt?

"And when they were come into the ship, the wind ceased.

"Then they that were in the ship came and worshipped him, saying, Of a truth thou art the Son of God" (Matthew 14:24–33).

The second is that of Peter. The fullest account appears in Matthew, with which we are all familiar:

"When Jesus came into the coasts of Caesarea Philippi, he asked his disciples, saying, Whom do men say that I the Son of man am?

"And they said, Some say that thou art John the Baptist: some, Elias; and others, Jeremias, or one of the prophets.

"He saith unto them, But whom say ye that I am?

"And Simon Peter answered and said, Thou art the Christ, the Son of the living God.

"And Jesus answered and said unto him, Blessed art thou, Simon Bar-jona: for flesh and blood hath not revealed it unto thee, but my Father which is in heaven.

"And I say also unto thee, That thou art Peter, and upon this rock I will build my church; and the gates of hell shall not prevail against it" (Matthew 16:13–18).

The third instance again involves Peter. After the great sermon on the bread of life, in which the Savior made clear to those who had been fed by the loaves and the fishes that he and his doctrine were the Bread of Life, John records:

"From that time many of his disciples went back, and walked no more with him.

"Then said Jesus unto the twelve, Will ye also go away?

"Then Simon Peter answered him, Lord, to whom shall we go? thou hast the words of eternal life.

"And we believe and are sure that thou art that Christ, the Son of the living God" (John 6:66–69).

The testimony of the divinity of the Savior given by God the Father and heard by Peter, James, and John is recorded in connection with the happenings on the Mount of the Transfiguration. The accounts of Matthew, Mark, and Luke all tell of the appearance of Moses and Elias talking to the Savior. Then Matthew records:

"Then answered Peter, and said unto Jesus, Lord, it is good for us to be here: if thou wilt, let us make here three tabernacles; one for thee, and one for Moses, and one for Elias.

"While he yet spake, behold, a bright cloud overshadowed them: and behold a voice out of the cloud, which said, This is my beloved Son, in whom I am well pleased; hear ye him.

"And when the disciples heard it, they fell on their face, and were sore afraid.

"And Jesus came and touched them, and said, Arise, and be not afraid.

"And when they had lifted up their eyes, they saw no man, save Jesus only.

"And as they came down from the mountain, Jesus charged them, saying, Tell the vision to no man, until the Son of man be risen again from the dead.

"And his disciples asked him, saying, Why then say the scribes that Elias must first come?

"And Jesus answered and said unto them, Elias truly shall first come, and restore all things.

"But I say unto you, That Elias is come already, and they knew him not, but have done unto him whatsoever they listed. Likewise shall also the Son of man suffer of them.

"Then the disciples understood that he spake unto them of John the Baptist" (Matthew 17:4–13).

We are grateful for these profound statements of the "eyewitnesses of his majesty" (2 Peter 16). They form part of the footings of our faith. But the miracles performed by the Savior and the testimonies of those who saw and heard were far from convincing to everyone, perhaps because a testimony is such a personal, spiritual conviction.

The New Testament is a surety of better testament because so much is left to the intent of the heart and of the mind. The refinement of the soul is part of the reinforcing steel of a personal testimony. If there is no witness in the heart and in the mind, there can be no testimony. The Sermon on the Mount produces deep, spiritual reinforcing that moves us up to higher spiritual attainment.

I leave with you my blessing. May the Lord watch over you and strengthen you. I invoke a blessing upon the institutions sponsoring this great seminar to be powerful in instructing faith and witness and testimony. And I witness to you in the authority of the holy apostleship of the divinity of the calling and mission of the Savior and of the restoration of the gospel by Joseph Smith. To this, I bear witness and testimony in the name of the Lord Jesus Christ, amen.

CHAPTER TWO

A Message of Judgment from the Olivet Sermon

Arthur A. Bailey
Brigham Young University

Matthew 24 and 25 are Jesus' last public discourse, the Olivet sermon. Most of the sermon consists of four parables related to the activities of the members of the kingdom and the judgments that will befall them at the time of the Second Coming. The focus of this study is on the declarations made to the wicked or evil servants in each parable. The statements made to the wicked servants in the parables are about the punishment that will be meted to those who participate in the types of wickedness that will prevail in the kingdom before Jesus comes to end all unrighteousness. Admittedly, some theorizing will be essential because these parables relate to a time yet future; and given our present circumstances, we may have difficulty comprehending the wickedness of a time when, if possible, even the very elect of the kingdom could be deceived (JST Matthew 24:21).

THE SETTING

The Olivet message is delivered two days before the Last Supper, when the hatred toward Jesus has never been more intense. His betrayal is imminent, and he knows it. Leaving the city, he seeks solitude on the Mount of Olives. Later his disciples come seeking answers to these questions: "When shall these things be which thou hast said concerning the destruction of the temple, and the Jews; and what is the sign of thy coming; and of the end of the world or the destruction of the wicked?" (JST Matthew 24:4). His response to their questions is the Olivet sermon. The four parables that conclude the discourse are of the faithful and the evil servant (at the end of chapter 24), the ten virgins, the talents, and the sheep and the goats (all in chapter 25). Each parable is presented and identified as a likeness of the kingdom of heaven.[1]

These parables explicitly compare the righteous and the unrighteous within the kingdom.[2] Parables are effective for teaching because they can obscure meaning and yet make it so vivid it is impossible to misunderstand (compare Matthew 21:45). Elder Bruce R. McConkie taught that only those who knew the doctrines of the gospel could understand the lessons of the parables.[3] Thus Jesus' hearing audience was quite exclusive, for only those who had the Holy Spirit could have the mysteries unfolded to them (compare 1 Nephi 10:19), and even for them, thoughtful reflection was required for a proper interpretation.[4]

Joseph Smith declared that a key to understanding parables was to find out what the question was that "caused Jesus to utter the parable."[5] The questions that help us understand the parables in the Olivet sermon are the questions asked by the disciples at the beginning of Matthew 24. The judgment upon the wicked servant in Matthew 24:47–51, who received his portion with hypocrites for his oppressive tactics toward his fellow servants and for other acts of apostasy, indicates a kind of wickedness that will exist among members of the kingdom before the Second Coming. Jesus' revelation of this truth to his disciples is obviously a warning as well as a sign of events that will transpire before he comes again. The end of the wicked will be when the Lord of the servants comes and assigns them a fate with other pretenders (compare JST Matthew 24:56).

THE PARABLE OF THE TEN VIRGINS

Immediately after the parable in Matthew 24 that relates specifically to the Second Coming and the end of the wicked, chapter 25 begins with the statement, "at that day before the Son of man comes, the kingdom of heaven shall be likened to ten virgins" (JST Matthew 25:1). Elder McConkie stated that the kingdom of heaven is the church and the ten virgins are a specific group who are pure, clean, active, faithful members anticipating the second coming of Christ.[6] The Savior declared that when he comes in glory, the parable of the ten virgins would be fulfilled (see D&C 45:56).

The ten virgins took their lamps and went to participate in a wedding celebration. These events were very popular in Palestinian villages. Everyone participated. Some religious duties were excused and the study of the Torah was suspended in favor of these festivities. One function of bridal attendants was to await the arrival of the groom and welcome him when he came to receive his bride and take her to their new home. His companions, the bridal attendants, and other invited guests then escorted them there.[7] In this account, however, no bride accompanies the party, because the bridegroom represents Christ and the ten virgins represent his Church.[8]

But the bridegroom delayed his arrival, and as the evening wore on the maidens slept. Finally, at midnight the cry was raised announcing his arrival. All the maidens arose and trimmed their lamps, but only five could give light. The other five lamps, though trimmed, could not. They appeared to be able to give light but could produce none because they lacked oil. The Greek verb *sbennumi*[9] used in this passage suggests that though the lamps may at one time have been able to give light, they could not now be rekindled. Jesus declared, "At that day, when I shall come in my glory, shall the parable be fulfilled which I spake concerning the ten virgins. For they that are wise and have received the truth, and have taken the Holy Spirit for their guide, and have not been deceived—verily I say unto you, they shall not be hewn down and cast into the fire" (D&C 45:56–57). The oil in this parable, then, represents the Holy Spirit.

The judgment in the New Testament against the five foolish virgins was the shut door. From Doctrine and Covenants 45:57 we learn that this judgment is tantamount to being cast into the fire. The motif of the shut door is fascinating. The door obviously represents a barrier of some kind, a state of isolation or separation from various influences, and whichever side of the door one is on determines what one hears or experiences.

Luke reports that the kingdom of heaven is within each individual (Luke 17:21), suggesting that whether or not the door is opened or closed is really an individual decision. John records these words of the Savior, "I stand at the door, and knock: if any man hear my voice, and open the door, I will come in to him, and will sup with him, and he with me" (Revelation 3:20). Luke explains that once the door of the kingdom is shut the Lord's only answer to their plea is, "I will not receive you, for ye know not from whence ye are" (JST Luke 13:25).

The Greek word translated "shut" in Matthew 25:10 is *kleio*. It is the same word Josephus uses to describe the state of mind of the Jews who came to Jerusalem for the Passover and for refuge two years before the city was destroyed.[10] Although the city at that time was rampant with indescribable wickedness and civil strife, the people refused to leave. It was as though they denied the very obvious evidence of their impending destruction, and they suffered severe consequences. They could have left any time they chose, because the Romans had not yet arrived to surround the city, but the Jews simply would not leave. Josephus implies that their ability to think clearly had become debilitated. They had deluded themselves to such an extent that they were oblivious to their impending annihilation.[11]

Furthermore, Doctrine and Covenants 45:57 implies that the foolish virgins were deceived. Matthew says they took their lamps but no oil. The wise virgins, on the other hand, took not only their lamps but also "oil in their vessels with their lamps" (Matthew 25:4). Because we know that the wise maidens took vessels for oil (v. 4), it is probable that the foolish ones did the same,[12] though the King James Version says only that the foolish virgins "took their lamps, and took no oil with them" (v. 3). They must have had some kind of vessels capable of carrying the oil, for it would have done them no good even "to go and buy" without vessels in which to carry the oil. So, it appears that the foolish virgins may have taken empty vessels. They may have had a purpose for their actions, but whatever their reason, to carry an empty vessel and to be unaware of it or to be unwilling to admit that it is empty is severe self-delusion. Such self-delusion is apparently the kind of deception that creates spiritual blindness to the realities of the Judgment Day.

Moreover, consider the wise virgins' answering the foolish virgins' plea of "give us of your oil" by telling them to go and buy. Was it possible to buy oil at midnight? Could that be a further illustration of how foolish the five really were? Surely, they knew that what they needed could not be borrowed or bought at such an hour. President Spencer W. Kimball declared: "The kind of oil which is needed to illuminate the way, light up the darkness is not share-able. How can one share a tithing receipt; a peace of mind from righteous living; an accumulation of knowledge? How can one share faith or testimony? How can one share attitudes or chastity, or a mission? How can one share temple privileges and security? Each must obtain that kind of oil for himself."[13] In our quest for life in the eternal kingdom we must be aware that there are no substitutes for devoted service, righteous living, and a proper attitude of humility. What a great risk we take anytime we ignore the Savior's injunction to "watch . . . for ye know neither the day nor the hour" (Matthew 25:13).

After their attempt to buy oil, they returned to the wedding feast but the door was shut. In response to their request to be admitted, the bridegroom declared, "I know you not" (Matthew 25:12). In the Joseph Smith Translation the bridegroom's response is rendered, "Ye know me not" (JST Matthew 25:11). Other New Testament references that contain this same phrase or imply it include Joseph Smith's translation of Matthew 7:33, wherein the Lord declares to those who claim to have prophesied in his name and to have done many mighty works, "Ye never knew me; depart from me ye that work iniquity." Luke 13:25–27 records that the Lord responded to those who come pleading to the shut door: "I will not receive you for ye know not from whence ye are . . . depart from me all workers of iniquity. There shall be weeping and gnashing of teeth among you, when you shall see Abraham, and Isaac, and Jacob, and all the holy prophets in the kingdom of God and you are thrust out." Evidently, those whom the foolish virgins represent must feel they belong in the kingdom.

The Book of Mormon says of those who know not the Lord: "And it shall come to pass that when the second trump shall sound then shall they that never knew me come forth and shall stand before me. And then shall they know that I am the Lord their God, that I am their Redeemer; but they would not be redeemed. And then will I confess unto them that I never knew them; and they shall depart into everlasting fire prepared for the devil and his angels" (Mosiah 26:25–27). Doctrine and Covenants 112:25–26 declares that those of the Savior's house who have professed to know but who have not known Christ are guilty of blasphemy against him.

The harshness of these statements pronounced upon those who know him not indicates that they are in a state of rebellion. In some instances, perhaps, the rebellion is similar to that of the devil and his angels in the premortal life. The refusal to be redeemed while yet claiming membership in his Church implies that the claimants are guilty of grievous iniquity that will separate them from the power of redemption, and they will weep and wail and gnash their teeth when they recognize their Lord and are then thrust out of his kingdom (JST Luke 13:27–28).

The Savior's response to their appeal to "open to us" is appropriate, not because he does not want the door to be opened but because he cannot open it. The opening of the door seems to involve a personal, conscious act of moral agency on the part of the one desiring admittance to the wedding feast—that is, repentance (compare Revelation 3:20).

Those who refuse to repent are shut out of the Savior's presence by their own volition (compare 2 Nephi 26:23–28).

THE TALENTS

In the parable of the talents (Matthew 25:14–30), one man is given five, which he doubles; another is given two, which he also doubles; the third is given one, but he refuses to use it properly. The emphasis here is on the actions of these servants in the kingdom before the return of their master, or the Second Coming.

Originally a talent was a weight of measure; in this context it could represent the weight of responsibility for fulfilling a particular commission in the kingdom.[14] In a modern revelation, the Lord declared that improving our talents is directly related to how we conduct ourselves in our stewardship responsibilities (D&C 82:19–21).

The narrative focuses on the servant who received one talent and then failed in the charge given him. We have commonly interpreted the parable as being about refusing to develop the abilities or capabilities God may have blessed us with—that is, abilities to sing, to write, to act, to paint, and so forth. And yet, refusing to cultivate these talents does not appear to be such a serious offense as to merit being cast "into outer darkness: there shall be weeping and gnashing of teeth" (Matthew 25:30).

This aspect of seriousness is reflected also in the parable of the marriage feast, where one man came improperly dressed. When he was discovered by the king, he was bound hand and foot and "cast . . . away into outer darkness; there shall be weeping and gnashing of teeth" (JST Matthew 22:13). The Lord declares that "the children of the wicked one shall be cast into outer darkness" (JST Matthew 8:12). Furthermore, in Matthew 13:43 we read that the offenders in the kingdom are cast out among the wicked and there shall be weeping and gnashing of teeth. This theme of weeping and gnashing of teeth is also reported in Luke 13:28 in connection with those who come to the closed door and are told to depart. And, in Matthew 24:51, the unfaithful steward is appointed his portion with the hypocrites and "there shall be weeping and gnashing of teeth."

Additional information about the state of some souls who fall under this damning indictment is found in the Book of Mormon:

"And then shall it come to pass, that the spirits of the wicked, yea, who are evil—for behold, they have no part nor portion of the Spirit of the Lord; for behold, they chose evil works rather than good; therefore the spirit of the devil did enter into them, and take possession of their house—and these shall be cast out into outer darkness; there shall be weeping, and wailing, and gnashing of teeth, and this because of their own iniquity, being led captive by the will of the devil" (Alma 40:13).

These individuals have no part nor portion of the Spirit of the Lord because they chose evil works and the spirit of the devil possessed them. Their own iniquity condemned them to outer darkness.

In the Book of Mormon we also read about a time of judgment when the wicked "shall have cause to howl, and weep, and wail, and gnash their teeth; and this because they would not hearken unto the voice of the Lord; therefore the Lord redeemeth them not" (Mosiah 16:2). In Doctrine and Covenants 85:9 those "who are not found written in the book of remembrance . . . shall be cut asunder, and their portion shall be appointed them among unbelievers, where are wailing and gnashing of teeth." In Doctrine and Covenants 101:90 the Lord declares that he "will cut off those wicked, unfaithful, and unjust stewards," who oppress the saints, "and appoint them their portion among hypocrites, and unbelievers." The Book of Mormon references imply a fulness of suffering in outer darkness, but the Doctrine and Covenants indicates that some may be afflicted with only a portion of that torment. It appears, however, that those who remain in a state of hypocrisy and disbelief will not be redeemed to a reward of glory hereafter.

King Benjamin declared: "For behold, there is a wo pronounced upon him who listeth to obey that [evil] spirit; for if he listeth to obey him, and remaineth and dieth in his sins, the same drinketh damnation to his own soul; for he receiveth for his wages an everlasting punishment, having transgressed the law of God contrary to his own knowledge" (Mosiah 2:33; compare 36–39). The reason for such terrible condemnation comes because an individual knowingly transgresses the laws of the kingdom. For example, the man who came by invitation to the wedding feast in Matthew 22:2–14 but who was improperly dressed must have known that he was inappropriately attired. Unlike the servant who received the one talent, the wedding guest made no excuse for his behavior; nevertheless, it was still a serious offense and the king ordered his servants to "bind [the guest] hand and foot, and take him away, and cast him into outer darkness" (Matthew 22:13).[15]

"Outer darkness" and its attendant suffering are mostly related to judgments for members of the kingdom, particularly for those who are in some state of apostasy. From Moses 1:22, it appears that Satan and his servants suffer the same type of torment. Passages in the Doctrine and Covenants imply that others besides members could fall under this condemnation in certain circumstances (see D&C 101:81–91) and indicate that many people (D&C 76:109) will be saved in the telestial kingdom who have been guilty of committing serious sins (D&C 76:103). Joseph Smith explained that the torment inflicted upon people for their sins is "as exquisite as a lake burning with fire and brimstone," but if they repent they can still be saved.[16] Thus, "outer darkness" and exquisite torment "as a lake burning with fire and brimstone" are descriptive of how people suffer for their sins as the devil himself is tormented. In some instances the judgment appears to be permanent; in others, only temporary. That is, some receive only a portion of the decreed judgment (D&C 85:9; JST Matthew 24:55), while others suffer a fulness (JST Matthew 8:12; compare Luke 13:25–28). The issue seems to be the amount of knowledge one possesses, the application of it to stewardship responsibility, and whether one in transgression chooses to repent.

There are those who refuse to repent. These, of course, are the sons of perdition (D&C 76:44). The type of suffering implied by the scriptural terms appears to be the same in intensity for all, but one's willingness or unwillingness to repent may determine the duration of the suffering. Repentance requires temporary suffering. Those who refuse to accept this requirement will be doomed to eternal torment. The wickedness being punished here seems to be something apart from, or in addition to, slothfulness, which is a sin the servant who received one talent was guilty of.

THE PARABLE OF THE SHEEP AND GOATS

The parable of the sheep and the goats begins with the Son of Man present in glory with his twelve apostles, probably the angels of the parable of the wheat and the tares (Matthew 13:39–42; D&C 86:1–7). In the other parables it is quite obvious that the judgments rendered are upon members of the Church and not upon the world generally. Because of the reference to "all nations" in the parable of the sheep and the goats (Matthew 25:32), it is not so evident that the pronounced judgments are limited to Church members. It is recorded elsewhere that the Twelve are judges of "the whole house of Israel, even as many as have loved me and kept my commandments, and none else" (D&C 29:12).[17] This statement, if applied to the parable of the sheep and the goats, may be taken to mean that the sheep and goats are members of the kingdom of heaven. Concerning this Elder McConkie stated: "That the words here spoken by Jesus are directed to the Church and not to all men is implicit in the whole conversation. Those in the account who are being judged by the King, are people who believed in Christ, who professed to know him and his laws, and who therefore were expected to recognize him whether he appeared in person or manifest himself through his lowly and suffering mortal brethren."[18] Also, the Savior's statement "inasmuch as ye have done it unto one of the least of these my brethren" (Matthew 25:40) suggests discipleship in the kingdom, even for the goats.

As the people are gathered for judgment, the sheep, or the righteous, are on the right hand and the goats, the unrighteous, are on the left hand. The motifs of the sheep and the goats are similar in many ways. Both animals provided milk and meat; they were used as sacrificial animals; they could be trained to follow their shepherd. One basic difference is that goats are more difficult to control than sheep. Fences that will hold sheep will not necessarily hold goats, and because goats have some peculiar eating habits, once they escape they can do severe damage to more than just plants.[19]

The reaction of the goats to the declaration, "depart into everlasting fire," seems to be one of surprise, or perhaps disappointment: "When saw we thee an hungred, or athirst, or a stranger, or naked, or sick, or in prison, and did not minister unto thee?" (Matthew 25:44). The Savior's response that "inasmuch as ye did it not to one of the least of these [my brethren], ye did it not to me" (v. 45) indicates that the issue here is how they treated their fellow members of the kingdom.

Another reference to the left hand in relation to judgment in the New Testament is in Mark 10:37–40. The disciples asked to sit beside the Savior on his right hand and on his left hand in his glory. He declared that he could not grant that request, for "it shall be given to them for whom it is prepared" (v. 40; compare Matthew 20:20–23). There are several statements of judgment from the Book of Mormon about those on the left hand. Mosiah 5:10 says that whoever will not take upon him the name of Christ will find himself on the left hand of God. King Benjamin further exhorted the people to retain always the name written in their hearts that they be "not found on the left hand of God" (Mosiah

5:12). The people undoubtedly knew the implication of his statements, but the theme is not expounded in other places in the Book of Mormon.[20]

The Lord declared in the Doctrine and Covenants: "I revoke not the judgments which I shall pass, but woes shall go forth, weeping, wailing and gnashing of teeth, yea, to those who are found on my left hand" (D&C 19:5). And in Doctrine and Covenants 29:26–29, speaking of the final judgment, Jesus claims that he will be ashamed before the Father to own those on his left hand. To them he will declare, "Depart from me, ye cursed, into everlasting fire, prepared for the devil and his angels," a place from which they cannot return because they have no power (vv. 28–29). Verses 41–45 in this same section indicate that those to whom the Lord speaks the words "Depart from me, ye cursed, into everlasting fire, prepared for the devil and his angels" (compare Matthew 25:41), are those who cannot be redeemed from the last death (v. 41) or their "spiritual fall, because they repent not" (v. 44). Obviously, this judgment is reserved for those who refuse to be redeemed. Thus, it appears that the goats in the parable are those who, because of their failure to repent, can qualify as sons of perdition.

This refusal to repent may indicate that they are guilty of the works of the devil. Therefore, they are unrepentant liars, deceivers, false accusers, and oppressors of mankind. Such behavior is evident all around us. Each of us is susceptible to these or similar characteristics and must be constantly on guard against practicing them. Oppressiveness can be manifest in anyone. For example, fathers and mothers may permit the cares of the world to interfere with family duties; divorced fathers and mothers may neglect their legal and ethical family obligations; family members, friends, casual acquaintances, and even strangers who verbally, emotionally, or sexually abuse others are all guilty of similar offenses. We would surely be shocked at the suggestion that we would do such things to our Redeemer. Can you imagine our own reaction and how we would deny ever doing anything so shameful to the Savior of the world? Yet, by his own words, "Inasmuch as ye have done it unto one of the least of these my brethren, ye have done it unto me," we stand condemned. Yes — even of deeds like those just mentioned and more.

To repent of such atrocious actions requires suffering, perhaps even the torment of "outer darkness." Alma described his suffering for his abuses of the Saints as "eternal torment" (Mosiah 27:29). Those who repent will be redeemed from their suffering, as Alma was. There are those who, having made positive virtues part of their character and having achieved a high degree of light and knowledge within the kingdom, will revert to their own means of exercising power over the children of God. Then, their refusal to repent will elicit the declaration "depart from me, ye cursed, into everlasting fire, prepared for the devil and his angels" (Matthew 25:42).

The Greek word translated as "devil" is *ho diabolo.* It means the slanderer. To slander means to utter false charges and misrepresent the truth with the intent to defame and damage other individuals. It also means to accuse unjustly.[21] So, although the goats give the impression of not knowing the effect of their neglect of others, they are in effect liars and false accusers. Otherwise, it would be unjust to prescribe for them the punishment reserved for the liar of liars (compare Moses 4:4), the great accuser (Revelation 17:10), and his diabolical servants. But the punishment is just, precisely because they are his servants and act contrary to what they know to be true (compare Mosiah 2:33). Therefore, Jesus "saves all except them — they shall go away into everlasting punishment, which is endless punishment, which is eternal punishment to reign with the devil and his angels in eternity" (D&C 76:44).

They will not be redeemed from the last death, even the second death that shall be invoked when the Lord says, "Depart, ye cursed" (D&C 29:41), "for they cannot be redeemed from their spiritual fall, because they repent not" (D&C 29:44). The refusal to be redeemed, as the Lord says elsewhere, will prevent their being resurrected to everlasting life and assures their rise in the resurrection of damnation, the two "being on a parallel the one on the one hand and the other on the other hand, according to the mercy, and the justice, and the holiness which is in Christ" (3 Nephi 26:5).

OBSERVATIONS AND CONCLUSIONS

The five foolish virgins who lacked oil, or the Spirit of the Lord, could not know Christ without that influence in their lives. Thus, he said to them, "Ye know me not." They are shut out of his presence and he commands them to depart, because they are workers of iniquity. They weep and gnash their teeth, apparently in outer darkness. And Jesus declared that at the Judgment those who have known him not will then know "that I am their Redeemer; but they would not be redeemed" (Mosiah 26:26). Since they are in the kingdom, they must have deliberately chosen not to know the Lord. Their iniquity separates them from the powers of salvation, and because many will not repent, even after suffering the torment of weeping and gnashing their teeth, they must "depart into everlasting fire prepared for the devil and his angels" (Mosiah 26:27).

The servant who received one talent was cast into outer darkness where, according to the parable, the wicked of the kingdom suffer. They weep and wail and gnash their teeth, apparently in company with the devil who suffers in the same way (Moses 1:22). The outer darkness spoken of here does not appear to be a permanent state. That is, the wicked are tormented there, but then those who repent, after receiving their portion of punishment, are judged to come forth to some kingdom of glory (Alma 41:6–7; compare D&C 76:85). The unrepentant must depart into "everlasting fire prepared for the devil and his angels" (Matthew 25:41; D&C 29:28). That is the fate of those on the left hand, the goats. They cannot be redeemed because they hearken not to the voice of the Lord. Of them Jesus said he will be ashamed, and he will command them to depart into everlasting fire, which appears to be comparable to the lake of fire and brimstone referred to in Doctrine and Covenants 76:36, Revelation 19:20, and 2 Nephi 9:16.

So, whether the individual in the kingdom is guilty of behavior like that of the unfaithful steward, or of those who know not Christ, like the ten virgins, or of the servant who received one talent, their placement in outer darkness to suffer with the devil and his angels may be meant to encourage them to repent so that at the final judgment they are not found on the left hand. These three parables may represent the types of people whose misdeeds will lead them to suffer the torment of weeping and wailing and gnashing of teeth, a large group from whom the sons of perdition will emerge.

Thus the type of wickedness that Jesus comes to put an end to is that perpetrated by the sons of perdition, and those who, being deceived by them, choose works of darkness rather than light. No proportion is specified for the number of those on the left hand who cannot be redeemed. The fifty percent implied in the parable of the ten virgins and the thirty-three percent in the parable of the talents may indicate the extent that members of the kingdom will participate in extremes of wickedness. For in "outer darkness" some will suffer only a portion of the torment because of their willingness to repent, whereas those who refuse to repent must endure it all, a torment which is everlasting.

It seems that the Savior intended to teach that as a sign of his coming (compare D&C 45:39) not only would apostates be at work within the kingdom to deceive many (compare D&C 50:7; see also JST Matthew 24:21–22) but also their actions would be so clever that many apostates would not be discovered until the Lord himself comes with the Twelve Apostles to sit in judgment upon them. The lesson should be poignant for all Church members: hypocrisy, or spiritual wickedness in the name of Christ, will be exposed in his presence. The guilty must then depart into everlasting fire reserved for the devil and his children. In regard to the unpardonable sin, Paul declared that God "hath made it impossible for those who were once enlightened, and have tasted of the heavenly gift, and were made partakers of the Holy Ghost, and have tasted the good word of God, and the powers of the world to come, if they shall fall away, to be renewed again unto repentance; seeing they crucify unto themselves the Son of God afresh and put him to an open shame" (Hebrews 6:4–7).

The judgment to receive one's portion with the hypocrites, the shut door, to be cast into outer darkness, and to go into everlasting fire, suggests a particular type of suffering for specific types of sin. This suffering is described as "eternal torment" or "damnation" to work more expressly on the minds of men (D&C 19:7). Thus, until the final judgment, or the words, "depart, ye cursed," are uttered upon those who deserve it, any who are willing and believe in repentance can be redeemed if they so choose.

NOTES

1. The phrase "kingdom of heaven" is used in the introduction to the parable of the ten virgins, but it does not appear in the Greek account of the parable of the talents; note the italics in KJV Matthew 25:14. Joseph Smith did not include the phrase in the JST, vv. 13–14. The use of *hosper gar* in the Greek text implies a comparison or contrast, and the content of the parable suggests a relationship to the kingdom of heaven. W. F. Arndt, W. Bauer, and F. W. Gingrich, ed. *A Greek-English Lexicon of the New Testament* (Chicago: University of Chicago Press, 1957). The phrase does not appear in the introduction to the parable of the sheep and goats.

2. The English term *parable* originates from the Greek *parabole*, which means "type," "figure," and "illustration." The word appears seventeen times in Matthew, thirteen times in Mark, and eighteen times in Luke. It does not appear in the Greek account of John. For example, in the Greek version of John 10:6 (the parable

of the lost sheep), the word *paroimia* is used. It means "proverb" but has been translated *parable* in the KJV. The term itself comes from the combination of *para*, meaning "alongside," "side by side," and *ballo*, which means to "throw," "cast," or "put down"; the combined words, *para* and *ballo*, mean "to compare." Arndt, Bauer, Gingrich, ed., *A Greek-English Lexicon of the New Testament.*

3. Bruce R. McConkie, *Doctrinal New Testament Commentary*, 3 vols. (Salt Lake City: Bookcraft, 1965–73), 1:283–84.

4. This disconcerting aspect about parables is seen in Ezekiel 17:2, where he is instructed to "put forth a riddle and speak a parable unto the House of Israel." The Hebrew word *hedah* means "riddle," "an enigmatic or perplexing saying or question." Francis Brown, S. R. Driver, and Charles A. Briggs, ed., *A Hebrew and English Lexicon of the Old Testament* (Oxford: Clarendon Press, n.d.).

5. Joseph Smith, *Teachings of the Prophet Joseph Smith*, sel. Joseph Fielding Smith (Salt Lake City: Deseret Book Co., 1979), pp. 276–77.

6. McConkie, *Doctrinal New Testament Commentary*, 1:685.

7. Matthew, in *The Anchor Bible*, ed. W. F. Albright (Garden City, N.Y.: Doubleday, 1971), p. 302. See also *The Interpreters Bible*, ed. George A. Butterich, et al. (New York: Abingdon Press, 1951), 7:556. Some New Testament manuscripts (Bezae and Kordiethi) include the phrase "and the bride." Nestle, *Novum Testamentum Graece* (Stuttgart: Deutsche Bibelstiftung, n.d.), p. 68, note.

8. In the Greek New Testament the five wise virgins go with the bridegroom into *tous gamous* (the marriages). Although this is a plural form, not much can be suggested by its use because singular and plural forms are used interchangeably with little or no difference in meaning. See Arndt, Bauer, and Gingrich, *A Greek-English Lexicon of the New Testament*, Chicago: University Press, 1957.

9. The KJV translates the Greek phrase *hoti hai lampades hemon sbennuntal* "for our lamps are gone out" (Matthew 25:8). Some other modern translations render it "our lamps are going out." *Eight Translation New Testament* (Wheaton: Tyndale House Publishers, 1974). The verb *sbennumi* means "to extinguish," "put out," or "quench." It is the same term Herodotus uses to describe how the fire was extinguished that had been set to burn the pyre of Croesus and his companions after their capture by Cyrus. He reports that when the fire had been burning for some time, Cyrus had a change of heart and ordered his men to extinguish the fire. After all human efforts failed to put it out, Croesus prayed and a cloud appeared in a clear sky and a deluge of rain quenched the fire. The KJV translators preserve this "totally out" meaning of the term. *Herodoti Historiae*, Carolus Hude, ed. (Oxford: University Press, 1979), 1:86–87.

10. Josephus, *Jewish War*, trans. L. Feldman, Loeb Classical Library, vol. 3, 6.428.

11. H. G. Liddell and Robert Scott, *A Greek-English Lexicon*, rev. by Sir Henry Stuart Jones and Roderick McKenzie (Oxford: Clarendon Press, 1977). *Thura* ("door") can be used as a metaphor for access to the soul or mind of man.

12. *Novum Testamentum Graece*, p. 68, note T. One manuscript, the Bezae, says that the foolish virgins also took vessels for oil with them. The earthen jars

in which they kept their oil were opaque, so only the one carrying the container would know it was empty.

13. See address given by Spencer W. Kimball to Monument Park 2d Ward, Salt Lake City, 22 Dec. 1965, p. 14.

14. A talent was originally a measure of weight varying from fifty-eight to eighty pounds. By New Testament times it was used as a unit of coinage. Its value fluctuated according to the type of metal used in the minting. For example, the silver talent of Aegina in modern values could be as much as $1,600. *A Greek-English Lexicon of the New Testament.*

15. The Greek word *exoteros* used to describe the darkness is a superlative and means that which is farthest out. The term for "darkness" is *skotos,* and it is the same word for the darkness of chaos in Genesis 1:2. It is also used to refer to the domain of evil spirits and to designate the place of punishment for those who violate the mystery rites. Arndt, Bauer, Gingrich, *A Greek-English Lexicon of the New Testament.* See also Liddell, Scott, *A Greek-English Lexicon,* Clarendon Press, 1977.

16. Smith, *Teachings of the Prophet Joseph Smith* (Salt Lake City: Deseret Book Co., 1979), p. 357.

17. Although this parable is reported in a context of the Second Coming, it may be a type of the final judgment at the end of the millenium after the little season of wickedness (compare D&C 29:27).

18. Elder McConkie also says that "the latter-day revelations which deal with the same subject all speak in terms of members of the church and not the world in general." *Doctrinal New Testament Commentary,* 1:691.

19. *Encyclopaedia Judaica,* 16 vols. (Jerusalem), 7:539; 11:1333.

20. "The right hand or side is called the dexter and the left the sinister. *Dexter* connotes something favorable; *sinister,* on the other hand, suggests something unfavorable or unfortunate. The Lord has frequently utilized this distinction to contrast the blessed state of those who are loyal to him and keep the commandments (those on his right hand) and the pitiable condition of those who come to know his wrath and displeasure (those on his left hand)." Joseph Fielding McConkie and Robert L. Millet, *Doctrinal Commentary on the Book of Mormon,* 2 vols. (Salt Lake City: Bookcraft, 1987–present), 2:178.

21. *Webster's Third New International Dictionary* (Springfield: G. & C. Merriam Co.), 1969.

CHAPTER THREE

Miracles: Meridian and Modern

Donald Q. Cannon

Acting Dean of Religious Education
Brigham Young University

I appreciate the opportunity to participate at the Sperry Symposium on the New Testament. The Sperry Symposium provides a unique and useful service to the LDS community. In almost every case, the lectures provide supplemental information for the Gospel Doctrine course of study for the following year. Thus, teachers and students have an opportunity to increase their knowledge of the course of study for the following year. This paper is an effort to link New Testament studies with LDS Church history studies. Miracles are the common ground. They were performed in both eras.

There are several good definitions of the word *miracle.* The *American Heritage Dictionary* definition is "an event that appears unexplainable by the laws of nature and so is held to be supernatural in origin or an act of God."[1] *The Interpreter's Dictionary of the Bible* says a miracle is "an event, whether natural or supernatural, in which one sees an act or revelation of God."[2] The *Study of Miracles* defines miracles as "something that we do not understand because it transcends our experience, and lies beyond the scope of the laws of nature so far ascertained by us."[3] From the perspective of the restored gospel, Elder Bruce R. McConkie wrote: "Miracles are those occurrences wrought by the power of God which are wholly beyond the power of man to perform."[4]

It is helpful to examine the reactions to miracles and the attempts to explain them since the time of Christ. Augustine thought of miracles as contrary to what we know about nature. Thomas Aquinas agreed with Augustine but stressed the incapacity of nature to produce miracles. With the advent of modern science, people stressed that miracles violate the laws of nature. This set of circumstances caused Spinoza to try to find natural explanations for miracles that were recorded in the Bible.[5] C. S. Lewis represented a return to a position closer to

Augustine's with his statement that a miracle is "an interference with Nature by supernatural power."[6]

In his book *Miracles,* Lewis contends that—

1. Naturalists believe in nature only.
2. Supernaturalists believe in nature and something beyond nature.
3. Naturalists do *not* believe in miracles.
4. Supernaturalists *do* believe in miracles.

He goes on to say that miracles do not break the laws of nature. Although miracles may interrupt the laws of nature, they do not break or change the laws. Finally, Lewis states that if you believe in God, you believe in miracles.[7]

Through the centuries, scientists, philosophers, and theologians have debated the subject of miracles, failing to come to a unified view of the subject. From a unique vantage point, Elder James E. Talmage, a scientist and an apostle of the Lord, explained the relationship between natural laws and miracles:

"Miracles are commonly regarded as occurrences in opposition to the laws of nature. Such a conception is plainly erroneous, for the laws of nature are inviolable. However, as human understanding of these laws is at best but imperfect, events strictly in accordance with natural law may appear contrary thereto."[8]

To develop a doctrinal framework for understanding miracles, we must turn to the scriptures and learn the role of miracles in God's work:

"For behold, I am God; and I am a God of miracles; and I will show unto the world that I am the same yesterday, today, and forever; and I work not among the children of men save it be according to their faith" (2 Nephi 27:23).

This scripture is, in a real sense, the heart of my presentation. It declares emphatically that God is a God of miracles. It further declares that God is the same yesterday, today, and forever, thus supporting the proposition that God is the same in every generation and that the modern Church is as capable of producing miracles as was the Church when Christ was here on the earth. Moroni, another Book of Mormon prophet, expanded on the ideas introduced by Nephi:

"For do we not read that God is the same yesterday, today, and forever, and in him there is no variableness neither shadow of changing?

"But behold, I will show unto you a God of miracles, even the God of Abraham, and the God of Isaac, and the God of Jacob; and it is that same God who created the heavens and the earth, and all things that in them are.

"And now, O all ye that have imagined up unto yourselves a god who can do no miracles, I would ask of you, have all these things passed, of which I have spoken? Has the end come yet? Behold I say unto you, Nay; and God has not ceased to be a God of miracles.

"Who shall say that it was not a miracle that by his word the heaven and the earth should be; and by the power of his word man was created of the dust of the earth; and by the power of his word have miracles been wrought?

"And who shall say that Jesus Christ did not do many mighty miracles? And there were many mighty miracles wrought by the hands of the apostles.

"And if there were miracles wrought then, why has God ceased to be a God of miracles and yet be an unchangeable Being? And behold, I say unto you he changeth not; if so he would cease to be God; and he ceaseth not to be God, and is a God of miracles.

"And the reason why he ceaseth to do miracles among the children of men is because that they dwindle in unbelief, and depart from the right way, and know not the God in whom they should trust" (Mormon 9:9, 11, 15, 17–20).

Several significant ideas are presented in these verses. First, God is unchanging. Second, he is a God of miracles. Third, the creation of the earth is a miracle. Fourth, Christ worked many miracles. Fifth, if there are no miracles, that lack results from the unbelief of the people.

Later, Moroni included another doctrinal discourse on miracles given by his father, Mormon:

"Wherefore, my beloved brethren, have miracles ceased because Christ hath ascended into heaven, and hath sat down on the right hand of God, to claim of the Father his rights of mercy which he hath upon the children of men?

"For he hath answered the ends of the law, and he claimeth all those who have faith in him; and they who have faith in him will cleave unto every good thing; wherefore he advocateth the cause of the children of men; and he dwelleth eternally in the heavens.

"And because he hath done this, my beloved brethren, have miracles ceased? Behold I say unto you, Nay; neither have angels ceased to minister unto the children of men.

"For behold, they are subject unto him, to minister according to the word of his command, showing themselves unto them of strong faith and a firm mind in every form of godliness" (Moroni 7:27–30).

These verses testify that the Savior still performs miracles, even though he is no longer living on earth. These miracles are performed by his servants, acting under his direction. These scriptures from the Book of Mormon help us understand the relationship of miracles to God. They also help us see that faith is necessary in order to have miracles.

There is one other matter related to miracles that must be considered. Elder James E. Talmage wrote a thoughtful statement on the purpose of miracles in which he relates them to proving the power of God: "Miracles are not primarily intended, surely they are not needed, to prove the power of God; the simpler occurrences, the more ordinary works of creation do that. But unto the heart already softened and purified by the testimony of the truth, to the mind enlightened through the Spirit's power and conscious of obedient service in the requirements of the Gospel, the voice of miracles comes with cheering tidings, with fresh and more abundant evidences of the magnanimity of an all-merciful God."[9]

In his book *The Miracles of Jesus the Messiah,* E. Keith Howick sets forth four major purposes for miracles:[10]

1. "To witness his identity as the Messiah." In a real sense, the miracles were the credentials presented by Jesus Christ to authenticate his divinity.

2. "To witness his authority and power." Many times the Savior was challenged about his authority. His miracles solidified and established his claims to authority.

3. "To evidence and confirm his teachings." The miracles were almost always accompanied by instructions. His miracles illustrated sacred truths he was trying to teach.

4. "To express his compassion." Through the performance of his miracles Jesus gave a positive example of his compassionate teachings, such as "do unto others," "love your enemies," "go the extra mile," and so forth. His miracles were acts of mercy that relieved human suffering. Miracles, then, are not merely a display of supernatural power. They are acts carried out by God's power to serve a definite purpose.

Related to the purpose of miracles is a further application that goes well beyond the obvious interpretation. The best example of such an application is taken from the sermons of Martin Luther. Commenting on the healing of the deaf man described in Mark 8:31–37, Luther said in a sermon given in 1538:

"That Christ hath healed this man—over this they are amazed. But that they themselves can hear, over this they do not wonder. Through this small miracle God will stir us up to recognize the greatest of miracles. The whole world is deaf, that they do not comprehend this."[11]

People, Luther contended, have their physical hearing, yet they are spiritually deaf. They need to have their spiritual ears opened.

Having studied miracles from an historical and scriptural framework, I have concluded that miracles are selective. They are *not* universal. Not everyone will be healed; not everyone will be protected. There is simply a randomness and selectivity that characterizes miracles. This, I believe, is due to the various purposes of miracles.

In the Gospels and commentaries on the life and works of the Savior, we have record of Jesus performing thirty-six miracles. In the course of my research, I have found records of some thirty-six hundred miracles performed during this dispensation. And certainly there are many, many more miracles recorded in individual journals as well as in the privacy of our hearts. The evidence of this being an age of miracles is indeed impressive.

Turning first to the miracles of the Messiah, we discover that many systems of classification have been created; however, I have elected to develop my own system of classification. I have developed six categories of miracles, performed by the Savior in the meridian of time. Similar miracles in each category have been performed in our dispensation.

1. Healings
2. Raising the dead
3. Casting out devils or evil spirits
4. Miracles of nature
5. Providing food
6. Passing unseen

HEALINGS

Let us begin with the healing of the nobleman's son described in John 4:46–54. While Jesus was at Cana, a nobleman asked Jesus to come to Capernaum and heal his son. Jesus told him if he had faith his son would be healed and He didn't need to go with him. As the nobleman traveled home his servants met him, telling him the glad news "thy son liveth." This miracle is often compared to the healing of the centurion's servant (Matthew 8:5–13). Both miracles are similar in the sense that the healing was accomplished while Jesus was some distance from the afflicted person.

This same kind of "long-distance" miracle occurred also in our dispensation. John Henry Smith, son of George A. Smith, loved to go boating in the Provo River when he was a boy. One day when the water was very high, he and his companions capsized. John's friends made it to the bank, but John Henry sank, came up and sank again. Suddenly a great wave arose, lifted John out of the water, and deposited him on the river bank. At the time of this event, George A. Smith was in Salt Lake. While thinking about his son and being concerned about his welfare, he hastened to a secret place and prayed for his son. At that moment his son was miraculously saved.[12]

Jesus healed Peter's wife's mother when she was sick with a fever. This healing is recorded in three of the Gospels—Matthew, Mark, and Luke.

"And when Jesus was come into Peter's house, he saw his wife's mother laid, and sick of a fever.

"And he touched her hand, and the fever left her: and she arose, and ministered unto them" (Matthew 8:14–15).

Numerous miracles are recorded in LDS Church history about those who suffered from fever. One such miracle involved Parley P. Pratt: "21st—Rode thirty-five miles and dined at the Bishop's, Unionville, and arrived home at sundown; found all my family in tolerable health except my little daughter Isabel, who had been sick with a fever and cold on the lungs. I ministered to her and she speedily recovered."[13]

One of the major medical problems at the time of Christ was leprosy. Lepers were common in the Holy Land of that time, and for Jesus to heal them was a positive good. The first three Gospels contain references to the healing of lepers by Jesus Christ:

"And it came to pass, when he was in a certain city, behold a man full of leprosy: who seeing Jesus fell on his face, and besought him, saying, Lord, if thou wilt, thou canst make me clean.

"And he put forth his hand, and touched him, saying, I will: be thou clean. And immediately the leprosy departed from him" (Luke 5:12–13).

In my view, the modern-day counterpart of leprosy may be cancer. In terms of the extent to which it exists, the suffering involved, and the number of deaths, cancer is like leprosy of old. Consequently, I present a miracle involving cancer in the twentieth century. It concerns a girl named Suzanne Shakespeare, who tells the story in her own words:

"I was nine years old before I realized there was hurt and unhappiness in the world because of one word — cancer. . . .

"Earlier that winter my lower left leg had been bruised while ice skating. . . . When the pain became constant, my parents took me to the doctor. An X-ray sent me to the local hospital and further diagnosis found me in the Primary Children's Hospital in Salt Lake City, Utah, with things ahead of me I still can hardly understand.

"Ewing Sarcoma is the name for a type of bone cancer, a type so rare and with so little research available that one hardly knew where to begin. I hated the needles, the doctors, the nurses that came with the needles, the pain in my leg, the wanting to go home when I couldn't. How was I to understand that my parents had been given only a sliver of hope. . . .

"My parents prayed for a miracle; I prayed that it must be a bad dream and it wasn't really happening to me. I knew prayers were answered, but I wanted mine answered right now!

"Five long, painful, learning years later, the miracle had happened. I was alive, I was fourteen, and life was beginning all over again. I still remember the day the doctors told me I wouldn't have any more medicine and I was free of the disease. It's true I had a limp and one leg was several times smaller than the other, but I had a beautiful head of my OWN hair and life. Could anything stand in my way now?"[14]

At the pool of Bethesda Jesus healed a man who had been sick for thirty-eight years. As it reads in John 5:9: "And immediately the man was made whole, and took up his bed, and walked."

In our dispensation, many people have been healed who had been ill for several years. One such healing occurred in France, soon after the mission was opened by William Howells. Ann Browse had a lingering illness, which had plagued her for many years. Her friends and family told her not to be baptized for fear of her life (they baptized in the ocean in those days). Because of her faith she went through with the baptism. After she emerged from the icy water, her illness was completely gone. This event caused such an excitement in the area that the report was rampant that a ducking in the sea on a cold morning was a sure cure.[15]

Several miracles in the New Testament concern sight being restored or the blind being made to see. One such example, the healing of the blind man at Bethsaida, is recorded in Mark 8:22–26. To accomplish this miracle, the Savior, in a sense, administered to the man, or at least laid hands on him in a manner similar to our administering to the sick.

In our dispensation the blind have also received their sight. One example is Lucy Mack Smith:

"In the afternoon, I went with my husband to a blessing meeting; I took cold, and an inflammation settled in my eyes, which increased until I became entirely blind. The distress which I suffered for a few days surpasses all description. Every effort was made by my friends to relieve me, but all in vain. I called upon the elders, and requested them to pray to the lord, that I might be able to see, so as to be able to read without even wearing spectacles. They did so, and when they took their hands off my head, I read two lines in the Book of Mormon; and although I am now seventy years old, I have never worn glasses since."[16]

The Savior had the power to restore hearing to those who were deaf. We referred briefly to the miracle recorded in Mark 7. In the region around the Sea of Galilee, Jesus healed a man who was deaf. As the scripture says, they were astonished by his healing power (Mark 7:31–37).

In May 1833 Noah Packard, a Mormon missionary, healed a child who was deaf. He tells of being invited into a home near Seneca Lake in New York. He laid his hands on the head of a boy who had no power of hearing, and immediately the boy was healed.[17] The power that was with the Messiah was with this missionary.

A most interesting and remarkable miracle performed by the Lord involved the simple act of touching his clothing. In Mark 5:28–34 we read about a woman who had an issue of blood for about twelve years. Many physicians had treated her, but the illness persisted. She had such great faith that she believed just touching the Savior's robe could heal her. In the crowd surrounding the Lord she managed to touch his garment. Immediately he noticed that someone had touched him. The disciples were astonished that he would notice a particular person in such a multitude. He told the woman, "Daughter, thy faith hath made thee whole."

Similar miracles have transpired in this dispensation. George Halliday, when he was working as a missionary in Bristol, England, tells about a woman who approached him and asked him to heal her son, who was gravely ill. He gave her his handkerchief and told her to place it on her son and he would be healed. When she arrived home, she was told her son was dead. She reiterated the promise Elder Halliday had given and ran in and placed his handkerchief on her son. The next morning the son came down to breakfast and soon regained his health.[18]

RAISING THE DEAD

Three accounts of Jesus Christ's raising people from the dead are recorded in the Gospels. As an example I have chosen to use the raising of the daughter of Jairus. This miracle is recorded in all three synoptic Gospels. Jairus asked the Savior to come and heal his daughter who was near death. While they were en route to his house, the news came that she was dead. When they entered the house Jesus took her by the hand and asked her to arise. "Straightway the damsel arose, and walked" (Mark 5:42).

Instances of people being raised from the dead since 1820 are not very numerous; however, they have occurred. A modern miracle of raising the dead is one involving Lorenzo Snow. This event occurred in Brigham City, Utah, in 1891 and involved Lorenzo Snow's niece, Ella Jensen. She came down with scarlet fever, became progressively more ill, and even announced to her nurse that she was going to die. She did die—they could not find any pulse. Her parents decided to notify her uncle, Elder Lorenzo Snow. They found him in a meeting at the Brigham City tabernacle. Lorenzo Snow left the meeting and took Rudger Clawson, the stake president, with him to the Jensen home. To the astonishment of her parents, Elder Snow asked for consecrated oil. He then invited President Clawson to anoint her, following which he sealed the anointing. As he did so he said: "Dear Ella, I command you, in the name of the Lord, Jesus Christ, to come back and live; your mission is not ended." Ella remained lifeless for about an hour after they left. Then, she suddenly opened her eyes and asked for Brother Snow. She said he had called her back. Ella lived for sixty-five years beyond that time. She wrote a detailed account of her experience. This miracle was also recorded by Rudger Clawson. It is a well-documented event.[19]

CASTING OUT EVIL SPIRITS

Several instances are recorded in the New Testament of demons or evil spirits being cast out. Both the Lord Jesus Christ and his apostles did this. Mark and Luke record the same incident, where Jesus encountered the one possessed of a demon in the synagogue at Capernaum.

"And there was in their synagogue a man with an unclean spirit; and he cried out,

"And Jesus rebuked him, saying, Hold thy peace, and come out of him.

"And when the unclean spirit had torn him, and cried with a loud voice, he came out of him" (Mark 1:23, 25–26).

In the dispensation of the fulness of times have been recorded several miracles in which evil spirits were cast out. The first miracle of the Church, the one involving Newell Knight, is perhaps the best-known miracle of this type in LDS Church history. Rather than use this well-known account, let me illustrate this point with one that is less well-known.

This miracle occurred in Tazewell County, Virginia, in 1844. The missionary is identified only as H. G. B. (Henry Green Boyle).[20] He was called upon to administer to a young girl who was very sick. He began to perform the ordinance and found himself praying that a devil be cast out of her. The evil spirit left her, but within ten minutes entered another girl in the house. He blessed her; the spirit departed and then possessed a third person. This process went on for nearly thirty-six hours, when the evil spirit finally left the house.[21]

MIRACLES OF NATURE

One of the larger categories of miracles performed by Jesus is miracles of nature. The so-called first miracle, changing water into wine, fits comfortably into this category. There are also numerous references to catching fish where the Savior directed fishermen to cast their nets. Perhaps one of the most significant New Testament miracles of nature is the incident on the Sea of Galilee in which Jesus calmed the storm. This event was recorded in all three synoptic Gospels:

"And when he was entered into a ship, his disciples followed him.

"And, behold, there arose a great tempest in the sea, insomuch that the ship was covered with the waves: but he was asleep.

"And his disciples came to him, and awoke him, saying, Lord, save us: we perish.

"And he saith unto them, Why are ye fearful, O ye of little faith? Then he arose, and rebuked the winds and the sea; and there was a great calm.

"But the men marvelled, saying, What manner of man is this, that even the winds and the sea obey him!" (Matthew 8:23–27).

In the modern period are also recorded miracles of nature that show the power of the Lord over the elements. One occurred when the Mormon pioneers began their exodus from Nauvoo. In February 1846 when they first started across the Mississippi, the river was not frozen and some wagons capsized when they tried to float them across. This difficulty soon ended, however, when the river suddenly froze over, and before long the Saints could travel over the ice without any loss of life or property.[22]

PROVIDING FOOD

Closely related to the miracles of nature are the miracles wherein the Savior provided food. The gospel writers record the feeding of crowds of four thousand and five thousand, who gathered to listen to the Lord, without sufficient provisions. Interestingly, the feeding of the five thousand is the only specific miracle recorded by all four Gospel writers, and there are only slight variations in the details reported regarding this miracle. The account found in John is the most complete:

"After these things Jesus went over the sea of Galilee, which is the sea of Tiberias.

"And a great multitude followed him, because they saw his miracles which he did on them that were diseased.

"And Jesus went up into a mountain, and there he sat with his disciples.

"And the passover, a feast of the Jews, was nigh.

"When Jesus then lifted up his eyes, and saw a great company come unto him, he saith unto Philip, Whence shall we buy bread, that these may eat?

"And this he said to prove him: for he himself knew what he would do.

"Philip answered him, Two hundred pennyworth of bread is not sufficient for them, that every one of them may take a little.

"One of his disciples, Andrew, Simon Peter's brother, saith unto him,

"There is a lad here, which hath five barley loaves, and two small fishes: but what are they among so many?

"And Jesus said, Make the men sit down. Now there was much grass in the place. So the men sat down, in number about five thousand.

"And Jesus took the loaves; and when he had given thanks, he distributed to the disciples, and the disciples to them that were set down; and likewise of the fishes as much as they would.

"When they were filled, he said unto his disciples, Gather up the fragments that remain, that nothing be lost.

"Therefore they gathered them together, and filled twelve baskets with the fragments of the five barley loaves, which remained over and above unto them that had eaten.

"Then those men, when they had seen the miracle that Jesus did, said, This is of a truth that prophet that should come into the world.

"When Jesus therefore perceived that they would come and take him by force, to make him a king, he departed again into a mountain himself alone" (John 6:1–15).

In the dispensation of the fulness of times, many instances of food being provided in a miraculous manner are known to us. One of the best-known and best-documented is the miracle of the quail. This event took place in October 1846 when the last group of Saints left Nauvoo. They did not have the necessary provisions for the trip. When they arrived on the Iowa side of the river, a miracle occurred. Following are the words of Thomas Bullock, an eyewitness:

"This morning we had a direct manifestation of the mercy and goodness of God, in a miracle being performed in the camp. A large, or rather several large flocks of Quails, flew into camp—some fell on the wagons—some under—some on the breakfast tables—the boys and brethren ran about after them and caught them alive with their hands—men who were not in the church marvelled at the sight—the brethren and sisters praised God and glorified his name, that what was showered down upon the children of Israel in the wilderness is manifested unto us in our persecution. The boys caught about 20 alive and as to the number that were killed—every man, woman and child had quails to eat for their dinner—after dinner the flocks increased in size—

Captain Allen ordered the brethren not to kill when they had eaten and were satisfied. (A steam boat passed within 5 or 6 rods of our wagons at the time we were catching the quails with our hands)."[23]

A few years later a similar miracle transpired in Provo. It is called the Provo sugar miracle. The early settlers of Provo faced numerous problems in 1854 and 1855. Grasshoppers, frost, and floods all took their toll, and they almost ran out of food by July 1855. Having prayed for a miracle they experienced a miraculous event. The pioneers discovered a sticky substance on the leaves of the Cottonwood trees along the Provo River. They called it honey dew or sugar manna. They gathered the leaves, placed them in water and boiled them until they produced a sugary syrup. Between three thousand and four thousand pounds of sugar was produced. Their lives were spared.[24]

PASSING UNSEEN

One unusual category of miracles is identified as passing unseen. There are three separate instances of Jesus Christ passing unseen or unrecognized. Such events occurred both before and after the resurrection. One is described in Luke.

"And all they in the synagogue, when they heard these things, were filled with wrath,

"And rose up, and thrust him out of the city, and led him unto the brow of the hill whereon their city was built, that they might cast him down headlong.

"But he passing through the midst of them went his way" (Luke 4:28–30).

In modern times the miracle of passing unseen also provided protection, just as when the Lord was protected by the miracle. During the antipolygamy crusade in the 1880s in Utah, President Wilford Woodruff experienced the same type of miracle. While meeting with other Church leaders in the Historian's Office in Salt Lake City, Wilford Woodruff noticed that the building had been surrounded by federal marshals. Realizing that they had warrants for his arrest, he prayed that the Lord would help him escape. He walked out of the Historian's Office, crossed the street, and "passed unseen." As he noted in his journal, "the eyes of all the marshals was closed by the power of God."[25] This miracle was recorded in the journals of numerous eyewitnesses.

OTHER TYPES OF MODERN MIRACLES

Many other kinds of miracles have occurred among Latter-day Saints in the nineteenth and twentieth centuries. Miracles involving temple garments, other kinds of healings, the prolonging of life, and responding to promptings of the Spirit have taken place. Truly it can be said that we live in an age of miracles.

It would be impossible in this brief paper to examine all of these miracles, but let us consider a few examples, which should illustrate the frequency with which miracles have occurred and still take place among Latter-day Saints.

On a cold January afternoon during wartime in 1943, Hack Severson, a thirteen-year-old boy who worked on the docks, was warming himself in the guard shack at the changing of the guards. Hack, watching the two marines unload their weapons, was seated six feet away, half leaning and half sitting on the edge of a desk. In all of the times that he had watched this procedure nothing had gone awry, but today one of the marines was talking to his buddy and neglected to point the barrel toward the ceiling before pulling the trigger. Suddenly Hack heard a clear voice say distinctly, "Move." He was startled and confused, but immediately the voice came again more firmly, "Move!" And at that precise moment it was as if someone picked him up and bodily moved him two or three inches to the right. As he shifted he heard the deafening roar of the shell exploding from the pistol.

Immediately the shack came alive, and the offending guard was arrested. Everyone else began searching for the bullet. After clearing the heavy beam inside the shack the slug had blasted a hole in a worker's lunchbox and come to rest in a roast beef sandwich. One of the marines remembered that Hack had been seated right in the path of the bullet. Upon close examination the marine noticed a hole in Hack's jacket. Hack did not remember the hole being there before. They ripped off his jacket and found a second hole under the sleeve. Holes were likewise found in his shirt. Hack tore off his shirt, and there were three ragged, bullet-size tears in his undershirt. The bullet had moved between Hack's ribs and his left arm so precisely that he hadn't been aware of its passing. From then on Hack was called the "miracle kid" far and wide.[26]

Permit me to recount a miracle from my own family. When I was only sixteen years old, Mother had become seriously ill. Medical diagnosis revealed that she had cancer. Furthermore, if the malignant cells were not removed she would die. The only chance was an operation that had only rarely been performed before. My father called the family together and asked if my brothers and sisters and I would be willing to pray and fast for our mother. Of course we agreed and began an extended period of fasting. During the fast Mother was administered to and promised that she would live to rear her children. The operation was a success. When my mother died in 1969, my youngest sister was twenty years old.[27]

Just a few weeks ago, while I was in southern Utah attending the dedication of the new monument at Mountain Meadows, I personally witnessed another miracle. This miracle was identified by President Gordon B. Hinckley, who spoke and offered the dedicatory prayer in the Centrum at Southern Utah State University in Cedar City. President Hinckley said that the coming together and reconciliation between descendants of the Latter-day Saints involved in the massacre and descendants of the survivors from Arkansas constituted a genuine miracle. It was truly remarkable to see and feel the spirit of healing in that building as decades of hatred, pain, and bitterness were overcome by the power of love and the gospel of Jesus Christ.

This is indeed an age of miracles! As President Howard W. Hunter said: "Yes, there will always be plenty of miracles if we have eyes to see and ears to hear."[28] God is a God of miracles!

NOTES

1. *The American Heritage Dictionary of the English Language,* new college ed. (Boston, Massachusetts: Houghton Mifflin Co., 1976), p. 837, s.v. "miracle."

2. *The Interpreter's Dictionary of the Bible,* vol. 3 (Nashville, Tennessee: Abingdon Press, 1962), p. 392, s.v. "miracle."

3. Ada Habershorn, *The Study of Miracles* (Grand Rapids, Mich.: Kregel Publishing, 1975), p. 1.

4. Bruce R. McConkie, *Mormon Doctrine,* 2d ed. (Salt Lake City, Utah: Bookcraft, 1958), p. 506.

5. *The International Standard Bible Encyclopedia,* vol. 3 (Grand Rapids, Mich.: William B. Eerdmans Publishing Co., 1986), p. 372.

6. C. S. Lewis, *Miracles: A Preliminary Study* (New York: Macmillan, 1953), p. 15.

7. Ibid., pp. 15, 128.

8. James E. Talmage, *Articles of Faith,* (Salt Lake City, Utah: The Church of Jesus Christ of Latter-day Saints: 1988), p. 220.

9. Ibid, p. 219.

10. E. Keith Howick, *The Miracles of Jesus the Messiah* (Salt Lake City, Utah: Bookcraft, 1985), pp. 10–11.

11. Ernst and Marie-Luise Keller, trans. Margaret Kohl, *Miracles in Dispute: A Continuing Debate* (Philadelphia: Fortress Press, 1969), p. 248.

12. Kenneth W. Godfrey, Audrey M. Godfrey, and Jill Mulvay Derr, *Women's Voices: An Untold History of the Latter-day Saints, 1830–1900* (Salt Lake City, Utah: Deseret Book Co., 1982), pp. 266–67.

13. *The Autobiography of Parley P. Pratt,* ed. Parley P. Pratt, Jr. (Salt Lake City, Utah: Deseret Book Co., 1976), p. 430.

14. Suzanne Shakespeare, "Courageous Daughter of Zion," *Voices from the Past: Diaries, Journals, and Autobiographies* (Provo, Utah: Campus Education Week Program, Brigham Young University, 1980), pp. 151–52.

15. *Supporting Saints: Life Stories of Nineteenth-Century Mormons,* ed. Donald Q. Cannon and David J. Whittaker (Provo, Utah: Religious Studies Center, Brigham Young University, 1985), p. 61.

16. Lucy Mack Smith, *History of Joseph Smith* (Salt Lake City, Utah: Bookcraft, 1958), pp. 237–38.

17. Noah Packard, "The Life and Travels of Noah Packard," *Voices from the Past* (Provo, Utah: Campus Education Week Program, Brigham Young University, 1980), p. 3.

18. "Miracles in the Mormon Church," *Magazine of Western History,* vol. 13 (1891), p. 766.

19. Thomas Romney, *The Life of Lorenzo Snow* (Salt Lake City, Utah: Deseret Book Co., 1955), pp. 385–97; and Francis Gibbons, *Lorenzo Snow: Spiritual Giant, Prophet of God* (Salt Lake City, Utah: Deseret Book Co., 1982), pp. 192–96.

20. This information was provided by Susan Easton Black from her forthcoming publication, *Biography of the Mormon Battalion Members,* vol. 1.

21. "Miracles in the Mormon Church," *Magazine of Western History,* vol. 13 (1891), pp. 765–66.

22. David E. Miller and Della S. Miller, *Nauvoo: The City of Joseph* (Santa Barbara, Calif.: Peregrine Smith, 1974), p. 198.

23. Thomas Bullock Journal, 9 Oct. 1846, LDS Historical Department, Salt Lake City, Utah.

24. Donald Q. Cannon, "The Grasshopper War of 1855 and the Provo Sugar Miracle," *Ensign,* Feb. 1986, pp. 60–61.

25. *Wilford Woodruff's Journal: 1833–1898,* ed. Scott G. Kenney, vol. 8 (Midvale, Utah: Signature Books, 1985), pp. 376. See also Keith W. Perkins, "Andrew Jenson: Zealous Chronologist" (Ph.D. diss., Brigham Young University, 1974), pp. 70–71.

26. Kris Mackay, *Gift of Love* (Salt Lake City, Utah: Bookcraft, 1990), pp. 107–112.

27. For the context of this story, see Donald Q. Cannon, "Who Is Jesus Christ?" *New Era,* Mar. 1978, pp. 10–12.

28. Howard W. Hunter, in Conference Report, Apr. 1989, pp. 18–21.

CHAPTER FOUR

He Has Risen:
The Resurrection Narratives
As a Witness of
a Corporeal Regeneration

Richard D. Draper

Brigham Young University

JEWISH ANTAGONISM

Jewish antagonism toward the early Christians was both intense and active. Justin Martyr accused the Jews of having chosen "selected men from Jerusalem" whom they sent into all parts of the Mediterranean world to say "that a godless sect, namely the Christians, had appeared and recounting what all who know us not are wont to say against us."[1] This propagation of slander appears to have been a longstanding tradition persisting from the days of Saul down to the time when Justin wrote, about A.D. 160. That Origen made the same reproach suggests the enmity persisted well into the third century.[2] Eusebius, in his *Ecclesiastical History*, corroborated Martyr and Origen's testimonies. He stated that "we found in the writings of former days that the Jewish authorities in Jerusalem sent round apostles to the Jews everywhere announcing the emergence of a new heresy hostile to God, and that their apostles, armed with written authority, confuted the Christians everywhere."[3] Because the center of this activity was Jerusalem, all the writings likely reflected conditions before the fall of Jerusalem in A.D. 70.

The Jewish confutation denigrated the reputation of the Savior. From ancient sources, we gain some idea of the character of the propaganda used against him: "Jesus was born, they said, in a village, the illegitimate child of a peasant woman and soldier named Panthera. The woman was divorced by her husband who was a carpenter, for adultery. Jesus himself emigrated to Egypt, hired himself out as a labourer there, and after picking up some Egyptian magic, returned to his own country and full of conceit because of his powers proclaimed himself God. His so-called miracles were unauthenticated, his prophesies were proved false and in the end he was not helped by the Father, nor could he help himself. His disciples had taken his body and pretended that he had risen again and was Son of God."[4] This assault struck against the historical witnesses of the Lord's divinity: the conditions of his conception, his miracles and prophecies, and, important for this study, his resurrection. The latter was the most necessary to discredit and, fortunately for the Lord's detractors, the easiest.

THE DIFFICULTY IN ACCEPTING THE IDEA OF A PHYSICAL RESURRECTION

The Hellenistic mind-set found the idea of a resurrection strange indeed. Many a Greek or Roman would have had little difficulty believing that a god had sired a son. Their mythology abounded with stories of gods consorting with mortal women and having children by them.[5] Further, the belief in prophecy and portents was wide-spread.[6] Publications that commonly reported miracles and miracle mongers appeared frequently.[7] Even the idea that a mortal man could become as the gods was not difficult for many to accept.[8] There were even precedents for both men and gods dying and coming back to life.[9] But the idea that a mortal could rise from the dead and enter eternal life with a *physical body* had little precedent. Much of the Hellenistic world denied the reality of any kind of resurrection, let alone a physical one. There were those who believed that mortals had been resuscitated—even brought back from the world of spirits—but these events had occurred only in isolated incidents and merely postponed eventual death.[10] In addition, the Hellenistic cosmology found the belief in any kind of a general resurrection at the end of world history totally foreign.[11]

Accordingly, it is easy to understand the Athenian reaction to Paul when "he preached unto them Jesus, and the resurrection" (Acts 17:18). The crowd responded by calling him "a babbler" who set forth "strange gods" (v. 18). Later he gave his "unknown god" sermon (vv. 22–31) to which the people listened intently until he got to the resurrection. "And when they heard of the resurrection of the dead, some mocked: and others said, We will hear thee again of this matter" (v.

32), but in the end few accepted the witness.[12] Certainly, the idea of a resurrection found no popular response from the Greeks.

Samaritan and Jewish belief, especially the Sadducees', followed suit. There was biblical precedent for people dying and being resuscitated. Elijah had raised a boy from the dead (1 Kings 17:17–23) as had Elisha (2 Kings 4:18–37), but most people rejected the notion of a corporeal and eternal resurrection. The Pharisees were the exception to this line of thinking. Basing their interpretation of the Old Testament on the oral tradition handed down by their leaders, they made belief in a literal resurrection a point of doctrine. Indeed, most Pharisees believed that the coming Messiah would hold the key to life and when he came he would exercise that power.[13] Because of the popularity of this sect, many Jews began to accept the idea of a corporeal resurrection; however, the belief never became universal, and a strong contingent continued to reject it.

Paul's frustration in trying to teach both Jews and Gentiles about the death and resurrection of Christ shows in his statement: "we preach Christ crucified, unto the Jews a stumbling-block, and unto the Greeks foolishness" (1 Corinthians 1:23). Paul's statement, though centered on the Crucifixion, has direct bearing on the Jewish reaction to the Christian witness of the resurrection of the Lord.

THE IMPORTANCE OF THE CRUCIFIXION TO JEWISH ANTAGONISTS

The Jewish rulers deliberately contrived and carefully engineered the Savior's execution. They could have stoned him as they later did Stephen and received little more than a slap on the wrist. But stoning would not do. Their purpose was insidious and ingenious — they aspired to both discredit and shame the Lord. Their plan was inspired by a popular interpretation of Deuteronomy 21:22–23: "He that is hanged [upon a tree] is accursed of God" (cf. Gal. 3:13). The Hebrew word *qelalah,* translated "accursed," denotes something or someone delivered up to divine wrath, or dedicated to destruction.[14] God removed those under this indictment from his favor and protection and delivered them over to the powers of hell.[15]

Both the Pharisees and the Sadducees believed that a crucified person fell under that condemnation. The Jewish rulers desperately needed to discredit the belief in the Lord's divinity and specifically engineered his death so that he appeared to fall under the anathema of God. Thus, the manner of the Lord's death was designed to witness that hades, not paradise, claimed him. Paul's statement that Jesus' crucifixion was a stumbling block to the Jews suggests that the message which the Jewish rulers wanted to give rang loud and clear in the ears of the Circumcision.

The witness of the Resurrection, however, subverted the Sanhedrin's carefully contrived and skillfully developed plot. The Christian proclamation of the Resurrection meant that despite appearances, God never abandoned his Son. For that reason, it is not surprising that the apostolic witness within earliest Christianity held, as an article of faith, a belief in the physical resurrection. By this doctrine, the early Christians refuted the charges of the Jewish authorities. The Lord himself emphasized this teaching.

THE SAVIOR TAUGHT A CORPOREAL RESURRECTION

From the outset of his ministry, the Lord made it clear that there would be a resurrection and that it would involve his physical body. Soon after beginning his ministry, Jesus cleared the temple of the profane. When challenged by the rulers to show some sign to demonstrate his authority, he declared: "Destroy this temple, and in three days I will raise it up. Then said the Jews, Forty and six years was this temple in building, and wilt thou rear it up in three days? But he spake of the temple of his body. When therefore he was risen from the dead, his disciples remembered that he had said this unto them; and they believed the scripture, and the word which Jesus had said" (John 2:18–22).

Only after the Savior's death the disciples came to understand the meaning of his words. During the period in which they traveled with him, although he introduced the subject a number of times, the disciples pondered and struggled, never comprehending the Resurrection. For instance, during his discourse on the bread of life, he "knew in himself that his disciples murmured at it, [therefore] he said unto them, Doth this offend you? What and if ye shall see the Son of man ascend up where he was before?" If they could not accept his doctrine, they would not be prepared to accept his resurrection.

In another public discourse he hinted strongly at the Resurrection: "Therefore doth my Father love me, because I lay down my life, that I might take it again. No man taketh it from me, but I lay it down of myself. I have power to lay it down, and I have power to take it again.

This commandment have I received of my Father." At this many cried out: "He hath a devil, and is mad; why hear ye him?" (John 10:17–18, 20). His claims sounded at best like those of a deranged mind, at worst like one possessed of a demon.

When he attempted to prepare his disciples for his death and resurrection, they did not comprehend. "He took unto him the twelve, and said unto them, Behold, we go up to Jerusalem, and all things that are written by the prophets concerning the Son of man shall be accomplished. For he shall be delivered unto the Gentiles, and shall be mocked, and spitefully entreated, and spitted on: And they shall scourge him, and put him to death: and the third day he shall rise again." His statement could not be more straightforward, yet his disciples "understood none of these things: and this saying was hid from them, neither knew they the things which were spoken" (Luke 18:31–34). Mark's version helps us understand one of the reasons why the disciples did not comprehend: "He taught his disciples, and said unto them, The Son of man is delivered into the hands of men, and they shall kill him; and after that he is killed, he shall rise the third day. But they understood not that saying, and were afraid to ask him" (Mark 9:30–32). Matthew's account suggests there was at least limited understanding: "Jesus said unto them, The Son of man shall be betrayed into the hands of men: And they shall kill him, and the third day he shall be raised again. And they were exceeding sorry" (Matthew 17:22–23).[16]

On another occasion when the Lord taught about his forthcoming death and resurrection, Peter grasped part of the message. "From that time forth began Jesus to shew unto his disciples, how that he must go unto Jerusalem, and suffer many things of the elders and chief priests and scribes, and be killed, and be raised again the third day. Then Peter took him, and began to rebuke him, saying, Be it far from thee, Lord: this shall not be unto thee" (Matthew 16:21–22). Peter clearly understood that the Lord was to die but totally missed the idea of a resurrection.

All four gospel narratives agree that before Christ's resurrection the disciples did not comprehend the doctrine. They did understand that he would go to Jerusalem and die there, but they do not seem to have understood what would happen beyond that point. With such a stress in the Gospels on this idea, it seems that there were a number of converts to primitive and early Christianity who were willing to accept Christ as the Messiah but could not accept the doctrine of the resurrection.

THE PHYSICAL RESURRECTION REJECTED BY SOME EARLY CHRISTIANS

The apostles continually battled against antiresurrection thinking that kept pushing its way into the Church. Paul asked the Corinthians: "Now if Christ be preached that he rose from the dead, how say some among you that there is no resurrection of the dead?" (1 Corinthians 15:12). A few years later, John warned that "many deceivers are entered into the world who confess not that Jesus Christ is come in the flesh" (2 John 1:7).[17]

Paul found it necessary to cite multiple witnesses of the Resurrection to combat the growing heresy. He stated that the resurrected Lord "was seen of Cephas, then of the twelve: After that, he was seen of above five hundred brethren at once; of whom the greater part remain unto this present, but some are fallen asleep. After that, he was seen of James; then of all the apostles. And last of all he was seen of me" (1 Corinthians 15:5–8).

The apostolic fathers, writing at the close of the first century, fought the same tendency. Ignatius bore forceful testimony to both the Smyrnaeans and the Trallians that Christ rose with a real body. "I know," he cried, "that Christ had a body after the resurrection, and I believe that he still has."[18] But such doctrine was not popular. Many of the second-century converts to Christianity were Hellenists, and more especially Platonists. They could not imagine a God contaminated by association with the flesh. Origen was one of the most vocal of these. He completely rejected the idea that Christ could have risen with a corporeal body. The Father, Son, and Holy Ghost, he insisted, live without bodies. "That being the case, bodies will be dispensed with in eternity, there being no need for them. . . . To be subject to Christ is to be subject to God, and to be subject to God is to have no need of a body."[19] Jerome, who wrote a century and a half later, reported that the debate was still raging.[20]

By the time of Augustine the doctrine had become a major point of contention within the Christian community. "There is no article of the Christian faith," he wrote, "which has encountered such contradiction as that of the resurrection." Further, "nothing has been attacked with the same pertinacious, contentious contradiction, in the Christian faith, as the resurrection of the flesh. On the immortality of the soul many Gentile philosophers have disputed at great length, and in many books they have left it written that the soul is immortal: when they come to the resurrection of the flesh, they doubt not indeed, but they most openly deny it, declaring it to be absolutely impossible that this earthly flesh can ascend to Heaven."[21]

Greek philosophy, especially Neoplatonism, was the main contributor to the rejection of this belief so central to the apostolic witness. Many of the Greek philosophers had a deep and abiding distrust of things of the flesh, and that distrust has continued into modern Christianity.

MANY MODERN CHRISTIANS REJECT THE IDEA OF A CORPOREAL RESURRECTION

To this day a large number of Christians reject the doctrine of the physical resurrection.[22] For example, a popular college text used in many introductory New Testament classes in the United States proclaims: "We need to keep in mind that the empty tomb was an ambiguous witness to the resurrection. It attests the absence of the body, but not necessarily the reality or presence of the risen Jesus."[23] Therefore, the reports of his appearance are more important in establishing the reality of a physical resurrection.

"[These] traditions present a varied picture insofar as they portray the mode of Jesus' resurrection. Jesus ate with the disciples — they could see and touch the marks of the nails; but he could go through closed doors and vanish from their sight. It is a misnomer to speak of the 'physical' resurrection. Paul claimed that the appearance to him was of the same nature as the appearances to Peter, the twelve, and so on (see Acts 9:1–9; 22:4–11; 26:9–18), but how could that be a physical appearance? Indeed, in the same chapter of 1 Corinthians, he describes the resurrected body as a spiritual, not a physical, body and says that flesh and blood (that is, the physical body) cannot inherit the kingdom of God (1 Cor. 15:50; cf. 15:35–58)."[24]

The authors completely ignore the statement in Luke "handle me and see; for a spirit hath not *flesh and bones,* as ye see me have" (24:39; emphasis added), nor do they discuss what Paul meant when he stated that the resurrected body was "spiritual."

THE SPIRITUAL BODY

Paul used the word *pneumatikos* for "spiritual" in 1 Corinthians 15:44, 46. As a rule the term was used in reference to items revealed from heaven, such as the Mosaic law (Romans 7:14); gifts of the spirit (Romans 1:11); and general blessings from God (Ephesians 1:3). Its use connects strongly with physical things. In such cases it referred to the inner life of man. He who was filled with the spirit of God (the spiritual man, *pneumatikos anthropos*) could understand the things of God while the natural man (*psuchikos anthropos*) could not (1 Corinthians 2:14–15). Thus, Paul contrasted the spiritual member of the church with the uninspired person of the world. The point is, the term *spiritual* does not preclude either physical or mortal association. Paul, however, made a distinction between the resurrected and the natural, or mortal, body. He taught that the resurrected body possessed the divine spirit (*pneuma*), having given up the mortal soul (*psucha*). But his words in no way suggest an absence of physical matter associated with the resurrected body. In fact, Paul's use of *spiritual* strongly parallels Alma's statement, "I say unto you that this mortal body is raised to an immortal body, that is from death, even from the first death unto life, that they can die no more; their spirits uniting with their bodies, never to be divided; thus the whole becoming spiritual and immortal, that they can no more see corruption" (Alma 11:45).

ALL THINGS WERE DONE "ACCORDING TO THE SCRIPTURES"

The writers of the Gospels strove to remove the anathema of the cross by bearing witness of the Resurrection. They made the Old Testament their ally, demonstrating that the Savior had died and rose again "according to the scriptures" (1 Corinthians 15:3–4).[25] They taught that definite historical events would transpire to fulfill Old Testament prophecy before the coming end (Matthew 24; Luke 21:22; 22:37; 24:25–27, 32). They stressed that these events were according to God's bidding; he designed the whole operation and set all things in order (Luke 21:18; cf. 12:7). The Father had determined that the Son of man would be betrayed and suffer for all (Luke 22:22) and then triumph through the Resurrection. Of the Gospel writers, Luke especially emphasized the latter point. He quoted the Savior, saying, "*It is written,* and *thus* it behoved Christ to suffer, and to rise from the dead the third day" (Luke 24:46; emphasis added). Luke underscored the divine hand directing all things with the Lord's question: "Ought not Christ to have suffered these things, and to enter into his glory?" followed by the answer, "And beginning at Moses and all the prophets, he expounded unto them in all the scriptures the things concerning himself" (Luke 24:26–27). On another occasion after the resurrection "he said unto them [his disciples], These are the words which I spake unto you, while I was yet with you, that all things must be fulfilled, which were written in the law of Moses, and in the prophets, and in the psalms, concerning me. Then opened he their understanding, that they might understand the scriptures" (Luke 24:44–45).

Further, not only did the prophesied events have to occur, but they also had to be witnessed, especially by the apostles who were then to bear testimony of their reality (Luke 21:12–13; Mark 13:9–10). They were to share that witness only after all had been fulfilled: "Jesus charged them, saying, Tell the vision to no man, until the Son of man be risen again from the dead" (Matthew 17:9). After the resurrection he proclaimed "ye are witnesses of these things" (Luke 24:48). Therefore, the Gospel writers carefully noted that the apostles and others constantly accompanied the Savior during the final hours before his death, at the crucifixion, and at his subsequent appearances (Mark 14:17; Luke 22:14; cf. Acts 1:21–26). At the crucifixion "all his acquaintance, and the women that followed him from Galilee, stood afar off, beholding these things" (Luke 23:49). Here we see the emphasis of the Gospel writers on eyewitness reports of the Crucifixion. The same is also true of his interment and postresurrection appearances.

WITNESSES TO THE INTERMENT OF THE LORD

Each Gospel writer stressed that the Savior truly died. Matthew noted that three women were present with Joseph of Arimathaea when the Lord was buried. These same witnesses carefully wrapped the body in preparation for burial and placed it in the tomb. Joseph then personally rolled a large rock over the opening, and some of the women lingered for a long period (Matthew 27:56–61).

The next day a delegation of Jewish rulers asked Pilate for permission to set a guard around the tomb, "saying, Sir, we remember that that deceiver said, while he was yet alive, After three days I will rise again. Command therefore that the sepulchre be made sure until the third day, lest his disciples come by night, and steal him away, and say unto the people, He is risen from the dead: so the last error shall be worse than the first. Pilate said unto them, Ye have a watch: go your way, make it as sure as ye can. So they went, and made the sepulchre sure, sealing the stone, and setting a watch" (Matthew 27:63–66).

This passage clearly indicates that these men remembered well and correctly interpreted the prophecies of the Lord concerning his resurrection.[26] Matthew's account shows us two things: first, no one could have tampered with the body nor removed it; second, the Lord did not somehow resuscitate and escape from the tomb on his own.

The accounts of both Mark and Luke parallel Matthew's version, even to the point of identifying Joseph's rolling a large stone across the entrance to the tomb after the women had witnessed "where he [the Lord] was laid" (Mark 15:42–47; Luke 23:50–56).

John's account varies somewhat. He noted that before the Savior was taken from the cross, a soldier speared Jesus in the side to assure his death. Joseph procured the body from Pilate and then, with the help of Nicodemus, wound the body in spiced linen and placed it in a sepulchre "nigh at hand" (John 19:38–42). John did not mention the presence of any women nor Joseph's rolling a stone over the entrance to the tomb. Nonetheless, John satisfied the divine mandate for more than one witness by identifying Nicodemus as a member of the party.

Taken together, the Gospels leave no doubt that the Savior actually died and was buried. The spear thrust, the wrapping of the body, the sealing of the tomb, the presence of more than one person at the time of and after the burial—all attest the actual death of the Lord.

THE EMPTY TOMB

Only two specific details connected with the resurrection are common to all four Gospel narratives: the tomb was empty, and Mary Magdalene was either the first or among the first to see it. According to Matthew, Mary and a woman he calls "the other Mary" came to the tomb near dawn. Before their arrival an angel had descended in glory, frightened the guards into a state of immobility, and rolled back the stone. The angel remained until the women arrived to assure them that "he is not here: for he is risen, as he said. Come, see the place where the Lord lay. And go quickly, and tell his disciples that he is risen from the dead; and, behold, he goeth before you into Galilee; there shall ye see him: lo, I have told you" (Matthew 28:1–8).

The gospel of Mark adds additional information to the narrative. He identified the other Mary as the mother of James, and stated that another woman, Salome, came with them. Finding the tomb open, the women entered and there saw "a young man sitting on the right side, clothed in a long white garment; and they were affrighted." He reassured them, saying, "Be not affrighted: Ye seek Jesus of Nazareth, which was crucified: he is risen; he is not here: behold the place where they laid him. But go your way, tell his disciples and Peter that he goeth before you into Galilee: there shall ye see him, as he said unto you" (Mark 16:1–7).[27]

Luke's account noted that three women—Mary Magdalene, Mary the mother of James, and Joanna—probably the same as Salome—along with others came to the tomb early Sunday morning to finish the burial procedures. Finding the tomb open they went inside, "and found not the body of the Lord Jesus. And it came to pass, as they were much perplexed thereabout, behold, two men stood by them in shining garments." This frightened the women, but the angels quickly reassured them with the words: "Why seek ye the living among the dead? He is not here, but is risen: remember how he spake unto you when he was yet in Galilee, Saying, The Son of man must be delivered into the hands of sinful men, and be crucified, and the third day rise again." These women then reported what they had seen and heard to the apostles (Luke 24:1–10).

John's account differs the most. He said that Mary came alone while it was yet dark to the sepulchre. Having found the stone rolled away, she quickly ran to find Peter and John (John 20:1–2). John mentioned neither any other women nor an angelic visitation. He focused on Mary's experience. The Joseph Smith Translation (John 20:1) indicates that the angels were present when Mary arrived; however, she apparently did not converse with them nor recognize their angelic nature, suggesting that she arrived some moments before the other women and left too early to hear the divine witness.

At any rate, her report brought an immediate response from Peter and John. Both ran to the sepulchre. John outran Peter but stooped outside the tomb and saw the grave clothes lying therein. Peter, on the other hand, did not pause at the opening but ran into the tomb. John then followed and "saw, and believed. For as yet they knew not the scripture, that he must rise again from the dead. Then the disciples went away again unto their own home" (John 20:5–10).

With the exception of John, the disciples reacted with bewilderment to the empty tomb. According to Luke, Peter, after viewing the tomb, "departed, wondering in himself at that which was come to pass" (Luke 24:12). Even the witness of the women, who arrived soon after, did not alleviate the disciples' perplexity, for "their words seemed to them as idle tales, and they believed them not" (Luke 24:11).

Though differing somewhat in detail, each Gospel narrative insists that the physical body of the Lord was missing from the tomb. The message of the empty sepulchre is clear: the physical body of Jesus played an actual part in the Resurrection. Each account stands as an independent witness with its own details; all agree that the tomb was empty of Christ's physical body.

THE LORD'S APPEARANCE TO MARY MAGDALENE AND THE OTHER WOMEN

Not only were women the first to know of the resurrection, but they were also the first to see the risen Lord. Mary of Magdala was the first to see the Savior (Mark 16:9–10; John 20:1). Drawn back to the tomb, the troubled Mary stood outside for a time weeping. After a few moments, she looked into the tomb and there saw divine beings, likely the same angels who had testified to the other women. Mary did not recognize them as celestial. When they inquired why she wept, she expressed her fears and left before they could respond. Within moments the Lord Jesus Christ appeared to her. Initially, she did not recognize him but when he spoke her name, "She turned herself, and saith unto him, Rabboni; which is to say, Master. Jesus saith unto her, Touch me not; for I am not yet ascended to my Father: but go to my brethren, and say unto them, I ascend unto my Father, and your Father; and to my God, and your God" (John 20:16–17).

This account does not directly witness a corporeal resurrection; Mary was forbidden to embrace the Lord, "for," said he, "I am not yet ascended to my Father" (v. 17). Why she was not allowed to touch him is not clear, but that there was no physical contact between them is certain.[28] Nevertheless, the Savior's explanation intimates that the injunction was temporary.

Shortly thereafter he appeared to the other women who were on their way to see the disciples "saying, All hail. And they came and held him by the feet, and worshipped him. Then said Jesus unto them, Be not afraid: go tell my brethren that they go into Galilee, and there shall they see me" (Matthew 28:9–10). The scriptures do not explain why these women were permitted to touch the Lord whereas Mary had been forbidden. The word "held" correctly translates the Greek *krateo,* showing that they did not merely touch his feet but actually held fast to them.[29] Most important, they could see and feel and hold something. The testimony of the women rested on a double foundation: divine testimony and tactile witness. They saw and heard from angels that the Lord had risen, and then they actually saw the Lord and held his feet in worship.

Even in light of these sure testimonies, the male disciples refused to believe the women. Mary's personal witness, probably given not long after the other women's story, fared no better: "And they, when they had heard that he was alive, and had been seen of her, believed not" (Mark 16:11). The writer of each Gospel affirms that the women's combined testimony did not convince the men. Throughout that Sunday morning the men were downhearted and frightened. They didn't know what to believe. Thus their eventual conversion to the reality of the Resurrection makes their witness more credible.

THE LORD'S APPEARANCES TO HIS DISCIPLES

The first of Jesus' many postcrucifixion appearances to the early brethren occurred Sunday afternoon. The Lord met Cleopus and an unnamed disciple walking to Emmaus but did not disclose his identity. He asked them why they were troubled, and the disciples recounted the startling events of the day, especially the empty tomb and the witness of the women, concluding with an admission of their own perplexity. "O fools and slow of heart to believe all that the prophets have spoken," exclaimed the yet unrecognized Lord. "Ought not Christ to have suffered these things, and to enter into his glory? And beginning at Moses and all the prophets, he expounded unto them in all the scriptures the things concerning himself" (Luke 24:25–27; cf. 3 Nephi 23:9–14). The hearts of both disciples burned for joy as he spoke to them. Arriving at Emmaus a little before sundown, they constrained the Lord to "abide with us." He agreed and "went in to tarry with them" (Luke 24:29). Graciously, the Lord blessed and began to serve the food. As he did so, the disciples recognized him. But before their astonished minds could formulate a question, he vanished.

The Lord may not have eaten before disappearing, although he did handle the food, for "he took bread, and blessed it, and brake, and gave to them" (Luke 24:30). The disciples knew that he was substantial, real, and alive.

The two disciples quickly returned to Jerusalem and found where the other disciples were gathered. Their story met with the same skepticism, however, as that of the sisters' earlier: "neither believed they them" (Mark 16:13). While these two witnesses were yet trying to persuade their brethren, the Lord appeared to the assembled company. This initially caused panic, but Jesus reassured them:

"Why are ye troubled? and why do thoughts arise in your hearts? Behold my hands and my feet, that it is I myself: handle me, and see; for a spirit hath not flesh and bones, as ye see me have. And when he had thus spoken, he shewed them his hands and his feet. And while they yet believed not for joy, and wondered, he said unto them, Have ye here any meat? And they gave him a piece of a broiled fish, and of an honeycomb. And he took it, and did eat before them" (Luke 24:38–43).

Jesus' eating appears to have been a critical factor in convincing the disciples of the reality of the physical resurrection. Although they felt the nail prints in his hands and his feet, "they yet believed not for joy" (Luke 24:41). Only when the Savior requested something to eat did they fully believe. Perhaps they then remembered his statement from the Last Supper: "With desire I have desired to eat this passover with you before I suffer: For I say unto you, I will not any more eat thereof, until it be fulfilled in the kingdom of God" (Luke 22:15–16). The act of eating fully demonstrated that the Passover was fulfilled in Christ; moreover, he had overcome all things, including physical death.

After they believed, the Lord began to teach them "that they might understand the scriptures, And said unto them, Thus it is written, and thus it behoved Christ to suffer, and to rise from the dead the third day: And that repentance and remission of sins should be preached in his name among all nations, beginning at Jerusalem. And ye are witnesses of these things" (Luke 24:45–48). This passage reveals the apostles' purpose: to be personal witnesses to all of the Lord's ministry and teachings, and most significantly, to the corporeal resurrection.

Here John's narrative teaches an important lesson. He explained that the apostle Thomas was absent from the initial appearance. Although Thomas received ample testimony from the others, he still refused to believe. He reacted in the same way as the others had when they had heard the witness of the women and the two disciples from

Emmaus. Nothing short of tangible proof would suffice. As Thomas said, "Except I shall see in his hands the print of the nails, and put my finger into the print of the nails, and thrust my hand into his side, I will not believe" (John 20:25–29). A week later all the disciples, including Thomas, were together. Once again the Lord appeared. "Reach hither thy finger," he commanded Thomas, "and behold my hands; and reach hither thy hand, and thrust it into my side: and be not faithless, but believing." Thomas's reaction was immediate and sincere; he simply exclaimed: "My Lord and my God" (v. 28). Because of Thomas, we now have additional evidence of the Lord's physical resurrection.

One other lesson may be learned from this narrative. The Lord said: "Thomas, because thou hast seen me, thou hast believed: blessed are they that have not seen, and yet have believed." The Lord's words suggest that henceforth others would be required to believe in the resurrection based on the testimony of the disciples, not through tangible proofs. John alone among the disciples realized the significance of the empty tomb. He had not seen the Lord, yet he believed. Jesus asked the others to follow his example.

CONCLUSION

Each Gospel writer suggested that the early disciples found it most difficult to accept the reality of the resurrection. However, they also showed that through irrefutable proofs the disciples came to know the truth. Those proofs came primarily through a demonstration of the physical reality of the risen Lord. The disciples were commanded to bear witness of that reality. That is the context of the testimony of John: "That which was from the beginning, which *we have heard*, which *we have seen* with our eyes, which *we have looked upon*, and *our hands have handled*, of the Word of life" (1 John 1:1; emphasis added). Those who deny the literal resurrection do so not by misinterpreting this testimony but by rejecting it.

NOTES

1. Justin Martyr, *Dialogue with Trypho*, 17. 1 in *P.G.* 6:512–13; cf. 47. 4; 96. 1–3; 108. 2; 117. 3; W. H. C. Frend, *Martyrdom and Persecution in the Early Church: A Study of a Conflict from the Maccabees to Donatus* (Grand Rapids, Mich.: Baker, 1965), p. 192.

2. *Contra Celsum*, 6. 27; cf. 4. 32; Frend, *Martydom and Persecution*, p. 192.
3. Eusebius, *In Isaiah*, 18. 1 in *P.G.* 24:213A; Frend, *Martyrdom and Persecution*, p. 192.
4. Frend, *Martyrdom and Persecution*, pp. 192–93. For primary text see Origen, *Contra Celsum* 1. 27, 29, 32, 41, and Justin Martyr, *Dialogue*, 108.2. For the same tactic being used at the end of the second century in Carthage, see Tertullian, *Apolology*, 21. 22.

For *Panthera* as the name of a soldier from Sidon in Phoenicia in the beginning of the first century after Christ, see A. Deissmann, *Light from the Ancient Near East*, trans. L. R. M. Strachan, 4th ed. (Grand Rapids, Mich.: Baker, 1978), pp. 73–74 and fig. 8.]

5. For examples from the Hellenistic culture, see Ovid, *Metamorphoses*, 1. 589–94; 5. 301–519.
6. See, for the Romans, Cicero, *De Divinationa*, 1. 1–38; 2. 64, 70; Tacitus, *Histories*, 1. 3, 18, 86; 4. 81; for the Jews, Josephus, *Jewish Wars*, 6. 285–95.
7. For healings, see Tacitus, *Histories*, 4. 81; Suetonius, *Lives of the Caesars*, "Vespasian," 7; Dio Cassius, 65. 271.
8. See e.g. Ovid, *Metamorphoses*, 14. 800–828.
9. Among the orientals were a number of dying and rising savior-gods: Tammuz, Bel-Marduk, Adonis, Sandan-Heracles, Attis, Osiris, the Cretan Zeus, and Dionysus, for example. But these were never really mortal and, thus, had no bearing on the New Testament witness.
10. A number of Greek authors (e.g. Homer, *Iliad*, 24. 551; Herodotus, 3. 62; Aeschylus, *Agamemnon*, 1360 f.) simply state that resurrection is impossible. Others accepted the idea but only as an isolated miracle (e.g. Plato, *Symposium*, 179c; Lucian, *De Saltatione*, 45).
11. Gerhard Kittel, ed., *Theological Dictionary of the New Testament*, trans. Geoffrey W. Bromiley (Grand Rapids, Mich.: Wm. B. Eerdmans, 1964), s.v. *anastasis*. (Hereafter cited as *TDNT*).
12. Apparently Paul had a little success. Luke notes that "certain men clave unto him," as well as a woman (Acts 17:34).
13. The Sadducees and Samaritans, in many instances, rejected the idea while the Pharisees accepted it (Matthew 22:23; Acts 23:6–8). For discussion see *TDNT*, s.v. *egeiro*.
14. The LXX uses *katara*, "to curse," to translate *qelalah*. A closely related concept comes from the Greek word *anathema* and carries the idea of being separated or cut off from God. Out of this grew the idea that to be crucified was to be anathematized, or damned from the presence of God. *TDNT*, s.v. *anatithami*, and *ara*.
15. In a real way, this aptly described the condition of the Savior both in the Garden of Gethsemane and on the cross. He descended below all things, suffering the pains of damnation for all. Cf. D&C 19:17–19; 88:6.
16. Other accounts (Matthew 20:17–19; Mark 10:32–34) mention this teaching but do not give the disciple's reaction.
17. This phrase may have been used to offset a docetic heresy entertained

by some early Christians. According to this view the Savior only appeared to have a physical body and to suffer on the cross. Such a view disallows a corporeal resurrection.

18. Ignatius, *Epistle to the Smyrnaeans*, 3, in *P.G.* 5:709; cf. *Epistle to the Trallians*, 9; in *P.G.* 5:681.

19. Origen, *Peri Archon*, 2. 6. 2, in *P.G.* 11:210.

20. Ibid., 2. 3, in *P.G.* 11:188–91.

21. Augustine, *On the Psalms*, Psalm 89. 32, in *P.L.* 37:1134.

22. For examples, see R. H. Fuller, *The Formation of the Resurrection Narratives*, 2d ed. (New York: Macmillan, 1980); P. Perkins, *Resurrection: New Testament Witness and Contemporary Reflection* (Garden City, N.Y.: Doubleday, 1948); G. O'Collins, *Jesus Risen: An Historical, Fundamental, and Systematic Examination of Christ's Resurrection* (New York: Paulists Press, 1987).

23. Robert A. Spivey, and D. Moody Smith, *Anatomy of the New Testament: A Guide to Its Structure and Meaning* (New York: Macmillan, 1988), p. 239.

24. Ibid.

25. There are a number of scriptures the Lord could have used, for example, Job 19:25; Ezekiel 37:12; Hosea 13:14; Isaiah 25:8; 26:19: 53:12.

26. At the beginning of his ministry the Savior stated to the Jewish leaders: "Destroy this temple, and in three days I will raise it up" (John 2:19; cf. Mark 14:58). It would be remarkable but not impossible that they remembered this statement. Certainly the conditions under which the Lord uttered it were of a singular and noteworthy nature.

27. The Joseph Smith Translation (Mark 16:3–6) corrects these verses noting that there were two angels present and that the women entered the sepulchre and saw that it was empty before they departed.

28. The Greek verb *hapto* carries the idea of clinging, embracing, and holding—often for the purpose of reassurance and affection. The object of such an embrace is often friendship, even intimacy.

29. The Greek word *krateo* used by Matthew stands in contrast to the word *hapto* used by John noted in footnote 28. The word *krateo* means to hold, seize, grasp, and restrain. The shared meaning element is to take hold and keep hold of something or someone.

CHAPTER FIVE

The Surprise Factors in the Teachings of Jesus

Kenneth W. Godfrey

Director, Logan Institute of Religion

Since the beginning of time people have enjoyed a good story, and Jesus was the master storyteller. His stories, often told as parables, differed markedly from the allegorical stories of the rabbis of his day, even "as the fresh air of the fields differs from the dust of the study."[1] The majority of Rabbinic parables reinforced traditional Jewish values. Jesus, however, often subverted meaningless or harmful traditions while teaching the higher law of his gospel at the same time. Indeed, many of his parables challenge the social norms even of our day. Bad servants are rewarded, and good servants seem to be punished. His heroes are sometimes unsavory characters—an unjust judge, neighbors who do not want to be neighborly, a man who pockets someone else's treasure by purchasing his fields, a steward who cheats his master, a sinful woman, and other socially unacceptable characters.

In addition, many of the Christ's parables demonstrate behavior that is unusual in its cultural setting but which is unarguably better, leaving the audience wondering why most people do not perform just that way. Several others feature themes that conflict with daily life, challenging the natural reason of the hearer.[2]

Jesus did not tell stories merely to entertain or shock his audience. Each parable had a purpose. Some atypical features were used to arouse attention and stimulate thought. Some details surprisingly contradict commonly held beliefs, and still others appear in the stories strictly for their literary value. One scholar concluded that the Master's atypical approach to many subjects "cleverly led the listeners along by degrees," until they clearly understood that God's way of looking at people is different from that of man.[3] The surprise factor in the teachings of Christ has often been overlooked or disregarded by scholars, perhaps because his teachings are so familiar to the twentieth-century world.

If we were to place ourselves in a Palestinian audience at the meridian of time, however, perhaps we would gasp in astonishment at many of his stories.

The parables of Jesus contain unusual, or shocking elements when examined in their oriental or peasant setting. Moreover, the Savior used exaggeration and hyperbole to heighten their effect and to raise "the issue set in mundane terms to ultimate seriousness."[4] He wanted to teach his followers as well as his detractors that many of their social and religious norms were short-sighted and offensive to God. By using atypical parables to illustrate his teachings, Christ showed a more excellent way.

THE PARABLES OF THE LOST SHEEP, THE LOST COIN, AND THE PRODIGAL SON

If we assume, as do many Biblical scholars[5] that the parables of the lost sheep, the missing piece of silver, and the prodigal son were intended for the Pharisees, then we can conclude that they begin with a shock to pharisaic sensitivities. In the oriental world the social status assigned to a particular profession was a very serious matter. Even today, a camel driver, for example, is very careful not to be known as a fisherman, and if he is seen fishing, he will quickly point out to the visitor that he is a camel driver, not a fisherman. Shepherds, though glorified in allegories, were despised socially. Herding sheep was clearly considered an unclean occupation. One authority believed shepherds were despised because their flocks grazed on private property. Furthermore, Joachim Jeremias tells us that shepherds were also known for their dishonesty and thievery.[6] Thus, even though the metaphor of sheep and shepherds as symbols of Israel and her leaders, including God, were well known from Old Testament and intertestamental times, the average Jew generally despised shepherds.[7] And, though it is difficult to see how rabbis managed to revere the Shepherd of the Old Testament and despise the one who herded the neighbor's sheep, that nevertheless was the case.[8]

Knowing full well this pharisaic attitude toward shepherds, Jesus began the parable of the lost sheep by asking, "What man of *you* having an hundred sheep . . . " (Luke 15:4; emphasis added). If the Master had wanted to defer to pharisaic feelings, "he would have had to begin the parable something like this: 'Which man of you owning an hundred sheep, if he heard that the hired shepherd had lost one, would he not summon the shepherd and demand that the sheep be found under threat of fine?' "[9] Any man who believed shepherds were unclean would naturally be offended to be addressed as one. According to the Lucan text, Jesus further insulted his audience by deliberately blaming the shepherd for the loss of the sheep. Thus, Jesus forced the Pharisees to see themselves as being responsible for having lost the wandering sheep.

Another anomaly in this parable is often overlooked because of its sentimental appeal. The extravagance of joy over finding one lost sheep contrasts sharply with the apparent lack of concern over the ninety-nine. The shepherd's joy seems an overreaction. After all, he took the risk of leaving the flock in the wilderness while he searched for the one missing sheep and then celebrated with his neighbors over one percent of his flock. As Bible scholar C. G. Montefiore pointed out, surely this action introduced a new kind of shepherd. A communal celebration over a lost sheep would have been extraordinary among Palestinian shepherds and may emphasize the nonliteral referent of the parable. It is, however, the climactic center and a detail not always brought out in analysis of the narrative.[10]

Immediately following the parable of the lost sheep is the parable of the lost coin, in which a woman was the central figure. Once again the Savior challenged pharisaic and scribal attitudes toward less favored groups of people in society. Thus, when understood in its cultural setting, elements of this parable were also calculated to be disturbing to the Pharisees.

Additional surprises awaited Jesus' audience as he then expounded what is perhaps the greatest of all parables. The parable of the prodigal son is loaded with elements atypical of first-century Palestine. The goodness of the father stood out — especially considering the disgraceful conduct of the son. But today's reader is ready to accept such behavior because he knows the father really represents God. To Jesus' audience, however, the conduct of the father was hardly a matter of course. A first-century Jewish son would not have dared ask his father for his share of his inheritance while the father was still alive and in good health. And the typical father would hardly have capitulated so quickly.[11] The son's request was equivalent to wishing his father's death, for there was no law or custom among either the Jews or the Arabs that entitled a son to share the father's wealth while the father was still alive.[12] The son's insulting request was magnified by the father's apparent good health. No historical document ever recorded any father having divided his inheritance under pressure from a son, especially a younger son.[13] In fact, aside from this parable, scholars have been unable to find in all Middle Eastern literature, from ancient times to the present, a case of any son, older or younger, asking his inheritance from a father who was still in good health.[14] The prodigal's request was even more surprising because he not only requested his inheritance but also the right to dispose of it as he pleased. In view of ancient literature and customs, Jesus obviously intended to illustrate a profound break in the relationship between the father and the son. The son was truly lost.[15]

In light of the implications of the request, it is even more remarkable that the father agreed. Had Jesus been telling a typical Middle Eastern story, the father would have exploded and disciplined the son because of the cruel nature of his demand. Instead, he acquiesed to the son's request. Bible scholar, Kenneth Bailey, thoughtfully remarked that it is "difficult to imagine a more dramatic illustration of the quality of love, which grants freedom even to reject the lover, than that given in this opening scene."[16] In fact, Bailey goes on to quote the scholar Derrett who wrote "that no father would have granted such a request without making a tacit but certain reservation in his own favor. . . . If the father does grant this request, he is jeopardizing his own 'living.' "[17] Perhaps Jesus meant to imply that fathers should treat their sons with greater love and compassion. His notion of familial love was much broader and far more moving than that expected in Palestine.

Jesus' Jewish audience must have been especially amazed and attentive as they then learned that the young son squandered his inheritance and was reduced to taking a job as a pig herder. His pride completely broken, the prodigal son resolved to return home. Then comes another surprise. If the story reflected true oriental customs, a crowd would have gathered around the returning prodigal and subjected him to mocking, taunting songs, and perhaps even physical abuse. The father, however, in a series of dramatic actions, protected the boy from the hostility of the village and restored him to fellowship within the community. For instance, the father ran down the road to greet his lost child. Yet "an Oriental nobleman with flowing robes never runs anywhere."[18] To do so is humiliating. Great men are not seen running in public. Such an action of itself would have drawn a crowd. But instead of experiencing the ruthless hostility he deserved and anticipated, the son was overwhelmed with an unexpected, visible demonstration of love and forgiveness. The father's actions spoke eloquently as he kissed his son again and again.[19] By such an unusual and unmerited response, Jesus adeptly illustrated God's amazing patience and love for even his ungrateful children.

THE PARABLE OF THE TWO DEBTORS

Jesus, known for his wisdom and intellectual prowess, was invited to eat with a group of learned Pharisees. Naturally, the Pharisees expected a discussion of theological or spiritual matters. They could not have anticipated the dramatic surprises that awaited.[20] Upon arriving, Jesus met with an insult. Simon, in a serious breach of courtesy, failed to provide water for guests, or at least Jesus, to wash their feet. This failure implied that the visitor was of inferior rank. Furthermore, Simon gave Jesus no kiss — a marked sign of contempt, or at least a further claim on Simon's part to a much higher social position.[21] The other guests must have noticed these intentional snubs and waited expectantly for the Master's response. Perhaps he would say something about not being welcome and withdraw. Instead, to everyone's surprise, he ignored the obvious insults. Preparing to eat, the guests stretched out their feet behind them away from the food. Then a woman, a known sinner, quietly entered, bathed Jesus' feet with her tears, and wiped them with her hair. By custom, a peasant woman let down her hair only in the presence of her husband. The Talmud indicates that a husband could divorce his wife for letting down her hair in the presence of another man.[22] In addition, the words *to touch* in biblical language sometimes depicted sexual intercourse. Clearly, such usage is not intended here, but Simon employed the word in this context to imply that this close contact was very improper and if Jesus were a prophet, he would know and refuse such attention, especially from a woman.[23] Furthermore, because she was a sinner, Christ would have been considered defiled by her touch.

Knowing full well that the woman's expressions of love were judged unrighteously by Simon and his friends, Jesus began another parable, which would be disconcerting for the host and his guests. "Simon," the Master began, "I have something to say to you." This phrase, used everywhere in Palestine, was the introduction to a blunt speech the listener probably did not want to hear.[24]

Jesus then related the parable of the two debtors, illustrating that love is the natural response to unmerited forgiveness. Moreover, Jesus praised the sinful woman while condemning Simon's thoughtless behavior. Not only was praising a woman in male company considered inappropriate but in the Middle East the visitor was expected, almost required, to say again and again that he was undeserving of the courtesies extended. In the final blow, Jesus turned to the woman, his voice taking on a tone of gentleness as he expressed gratitude to the daring woman in desperate need of a kind word. It was a stunning rebuke to Simon and a confirmation of the inherent worth of women.[25] But most astonishing of all, Christ then forgave her sins, thus assuming an authority his audience did not believe any mortal possessed. The gospel of love once again transcended the tyranny of tradition.

THE PARABLE OF THE GOOD SAMARITAN

Along with the parable of the prodigal son, the parable of the good Samaritan is generally thought to be the greatest story in all literature. This story, too, when understood in its cultural context has several surprises that emphasize the radical doctrines of Christ. A man who went down from Jericho was beaten, robbed, stripped naked, and left "next to death." A man thus wounded could not be identified by either his speech or the manner of his dress. A priest, the first to pass by, could not have been certain whether the man was a gentile and hence, unclean, or a Jew. But even if the man were a Jew, he might be dead, and mere contact with him would defile the priest. If a priest defiled himself he could not collect, distribute, or eat the tithes, and thus his family and servants would suffer. So, rather than risk defilement, he passed by on the other side of the road and continued his journey. The Levite who came next at least approached the victim. Though not bound by the stricter regulations the priest was governed by, a Levite could only eat the "wave offering" and wear his phylacteries when in a state of ritual purity. Contact with a corpse was at the top of the list of sources of defilement. Thus the Levite could render aid, and if the man were dead or died while he cared for him, the repercussions for the Levite would not be quite so serious as for the priest. Perhaps because he belonged to a lower social class than the priest and might well have had no way of taking the man to safety and because he also may have feared that the robbers still lurked around, the Levite, too, chose to continue on his way.

After hearing about the priest and the Levite, the audience probably expected the next character to be a Jewish layman. "Not only is

priest-Levite-layman a natural sequence," but these same three classes
of people officiated at the temple. "Even as delegations of priests and
Levites went up to Jerusalem" and returned after two weeks of service,
so "also the delegation of Israel went up to serve them." Thus Jesus'
listeners probably expected this logical sequence of travelers on the
road. But to their surprise, Jesus announced that the third man to come
along the road was a hated Samaritan. In the Jewish mind, Samaritans
were classed with the Philistines and Edomites. "He that eats the
bread of the Samaritans," the Mishna declares, "is like to one that eats
the flesh of swine." Jesus could more easily have told a story about a
noble Jew helping a hated Samaritan and found ready acceptance by
the audience. By giving the hero's role to the Samaritan, however,
Jesus confronted a deep hatred in his listeners and "painfully exposes
it."[26]

The Greek word for "compassion" that the Master used to convey
the feelings of the Samaritan has its roots in the word for innards,
which is a very strong statement in both Greek and Semitic imagery.
The Samaritan had a deep, gut-level reaction to the wounded man. The
Samaritan was not a gentile. He was bound by the same Torah that
taught that a neighbor was a countryman and kinsman; however, the
Samaritan was traveling in Judea, which made it even less likely for
him than for the priest and the Levite that the anonymous wounded
man could be considered a neighbor. "In spite of this, he is the one
who acts."[27]

The Samaritan would also have been aware that if the wounded
man regained consciousness, he would probably insult him for his
kindness because "oil and wine are forbidden objects if they emanate
from a Samaritan."[28] So, not only had the oil and wine come from an
unclean person but the tithe on them had not been paid. The wounded
man would incur an obligation to pay the tithing. The Samaritan, too,
ran the "grave risk" of having the family of the wounded man seek
him out to take vengeance upon him. Still, fully aware of the risks and
having far more to lose than the priest or the Levite, he took the man
to town. Kenneth Bailey suggests this cultural equivalent in America:
A Plains Indian in 1875 walks into Dodge City with a scalped cowboy
on his horse, checks into a room over the local saloon, and spends the
night caring for the injured man. "Any Indian so brave would be fortunate to get out of the city alive even if he had saved the cowboy's
life."[29]

"The courage of the Samaritan," Bailey informs us, "is demonstrated first when he stops in the desert (for the thieves are still in the area). But his real bravery is seen in this final act of compassion at the inn." The real point is not his courage, however, but rather the price he was willing to pay to complete his act of compassion.[30]

Finally, according to Bible scholar Charlesworth, it is almost impossible to overstress the sheer magnitude of the social crisis caused "by Jesus's rejection of the Jewish, especially Essene, rules of purification. The Parable of the Good Samaritan, perhaps, best symbolizes Jesus's exhortation that one should be willing to be defiled in the attempt to help another, even those of questionable beliefs and ancestry."[31] B. B. Scott writes that this "parable can be summarized as follows: To Enter the Kingdom one must get in the ditch and be served by one's mortal enemy."[32] Once again Christ exposed the fallacy of adhering to a seemingly sacred and time-honored tradition at the expense of the higher law of love.

THE PARABLE OF THE WORKERS IN THE VINEYARD

The parable of the workers in the vineyard seems incongruous to audiences everywhere. It began with an ordinary scene. The owner of a vineyard hired day laborers early in the morning. One denaris was the wage agreed upon. The scene was repeated at the third hour when the owner saw idle men in the *agora* (the marketplace where people waited to be hired). He hired them with the promise of a fair wage. Nothing unusual so far. Similar action was taken at the sixth and the ninth hours. At the eleventh hour yet other unemployed men were idling away their time. So the humanitarian owner hired them, also.

It seems rather reasonable to employ workers at midday for half a day. Hiring at the ninth and the eleventh hours, however, appears purely gratuitous and unbusinesslike. Those hired later, especially at the eleventh hour, seem to have been employed on the basis of their plight, not upon their usefulness. Rudolf Bultmann argues that the contract between the first and the last groups had to be mitigated by the intermediate stages or the story would sound improbable.[33]

The surprise in this story, the part that seems incredible, is that no matter when they were hired, all the workers were given the same wage. "The employer is not merely unusual, he is unique." Jesus "deliberately and cleverly led the listeners along by degrees until they understood that if God's generosity was to be represented by a man,

such a man would be different from any men ever encountered."[34]
Christ seems to be teaching us that it may not be as important when
we come to him as it is that we come to him at all. Those who truly
have a change of heart late in life or even in the next life and who come
into the Church and become disciples of the Master receive the same
celestial reward as those who experience an earlier conversion. Here
Jesus used a very simple story with a very unlikely ending to teach an
extraordinary message.

THE PARABLE OF THE PHARISEE AND
THE TAX COLLECTOR

A group of men came to listen to the Lord. Luke described them
as "certain which trusted in themselves that they were righteous, and
despised others" (Luke 18:9). Accordingly, Jesus told them a parable
about a righteous Pharisee and a despised tax collector. The Pharisee
in the parable went up to attend the morning or the afternoon atonement
sacrifice. In a grand gesture of religious superiority, he stood apart
from the other worshippers. Some authorities believe he was praying
aloud, in a sense preaching to the less fortunate around him. After all,
they had few chances to look at a truly righteous man, as he was, and
he "graciously" offered them a few words of judgment along with some
instructions in righteousness.[35] Other scholars contend that the list of
characteristics selected by the "righteous" Pharisee were intended to
apply to the tax collector standing nearby.[36]

Then Jesus spoke of the the tax collector's simple but fervent
prayer. The image of the tax collector in the mind of the Pharisee
sharply contrasts with the reality of the broken, humble man who stood
some distance away from the assembled worshippers. The repentant
man did not stand aloof but afar off, for he felt he was not worthy to
mingle with God's people before the altar. As he came to voice his
petition, he, like the woman in Simon's home, broke into dramatic and
unexpected behavior. He beat upon his chest, crying, "God be merciful
to me a sinner" (Luke 18:13). This action was surprising to those
listening to Jesus because the accepted posture for prayer was hands
crossed over the chest and eyes cast down. An even more remarkable
feature of this gesture was that it was characteristic of women, not
men. Interestingly, in all of biblical literature we find this gesture
mentioned only in this story and at the cross (Luke 23:48). Perhaps
he was beating his heart as the source of all his evil thoughts or as a

spontaneous expression of his personal pain. In any case, Christ's description of the tax collector's humble behavior seems designed to expose the pompous, self-righteous actions of the Pharisee. Such a gesture clearly illustrated the depth of the tax collector's remorse.[37] The parable concludes dramatically as Christ declared, "I tell you, this man went down to his house justified rather than the other: for every one that exalteth himself shall be abased; and he that humbleth himself shall be exalted" (Luke 18:14).

THE PARABLE OF THE UNJUST STEWARD

The parable of the unjust steward is often described as the "most puzzling of all the stories of Jesus." The scholar Charles C. Tarry writes: "This [parable] brings before us a new Jesus, one who seems inclined to compromise with evil. He approves of a program of canny self-interest, recommending to His disciples a standard of life which is generally recognized as inferior. . . . This is not the worst of it. He bases the teaching of the story of a shrewd scoundrel who feathered his own nest at the expense of the man who trusted him; and then appears to say to his disciples, Let this be your model."[38]

This parable was addressed to disciples as well as Pharisees. Upon hearing that the steward in the story was condemned and fired, they would have expected a classic debate in which the steward loudly and insultingly protested his innocence. The steward could have used many standard ploys to defend himself and blame everybody else, including the master himself. But to the surprise of the listeners, the steward remained silent. His only reaction was a soliloquy delivered on the way to get the accounts. His silence was supremely significant in the oriental context because it affirmed at least four things: First, I [the steward] am guilty. Second, the master knows the truth; he knows I am guilty. Third, the master expects obedience; disobedience brings judgment. And fourth, I cannot get my job back. Thus, the steward resolves now to protect his future.[39]

The steward had, at this point in the story, realized something else about his master that was significant. He was fired but not jailed. In fact, he was not even scolded. The master was unusually merciful toward him.[40] While commentaries by western scholars worry about how Jesus could use a dishonest man as an example, the oriental peasant at the bottom of the economic ladder finds such a parable pure delight. The typical storyteller in the Orient relates a series of stories about the clever fellow who triumphs over the "Mr. Big" of his community. To the eastern mind the surprising feature of this parable is that the steward is criticized as unrighteous and called a son of darkness. An oriental story teller would not feel any compulsion to add such a corrective. Thus, the western reader is surprised at the use of a dishonest man as a hero whereas the eastern reader is surprised that such a hero is criticized. Though Christ goes on to explain the righteous application of such unrighteous behavior, this parable is an outstanding example of one of his unique and effective literary techniques—the use of unsavory characters as heroes.[41]

THE PARABLE OF THE GREAT BANQUET

The parable of the great banquet contains at least two remarkable details. A king prepared a banquet for a large number of guests, but oddly, all of the guests refuse to attend. It was very strange for everyone to refuse such an invitation. Perhaps this was exaggeration to emphasize a point. In any case, the parable assumed that the fault was the guests', not the host's.

The second surprise was the issuing of a general invitation throughout the city for those in the streets to come and fill the empty banquet hall. The people who assembled would not have been the kind of guests a great man usually invites to dine with him. In a more typical story about a banquet, a few of the invited guests might send their regrets and the host would then invite others of a similar social status to take their places. But here the Savior again employs hyperbole to show that the kingdom will bring about a "total reversal." The invited are absent, and the uninvited are present.[42]

CONCLUSION

Jesus, the master teacher, used unlikely characters, unusual and socially unacceptable behavior, and unexpected endings in many of his parables. He used these devices to engage his audience and to reveal the uniqueness of his message. In the parable of the good Samaritan, for example, by using a downtrodden hero who possesses uncommon altruism, Christ taught a radically better style of conduct in human relations. Other parables reveal a God whose mercy is extraordinary, unlike that of any person Christ's audience would have known. Still other parables prod those comfortable in their own righteousness while comforting and providing hope for those who believe they are unworthy of any place in the kingdom of God. Christ taught his audiences by using the element of surprise to stimulate thought and leave his listeners pondering his message. He taught them that the requirements of living the gospel far exceeded traditional ethical thought and behavior. God's mercy, they came to realize, far surpassed their own. Understanding the atypical features of the Master's message enables modern Latter-day Saints to more fully grasp the profundity of his gospel. As a result we are even more challenged to elevate our own conduct, love our enemies, forgive those who trespass against us, and seek to redeem the lost, regardless of risk or personal cost.

NOTES

1. Craig L. Blomberg, *Interpreting the Parables* (Downers Grove, Ill.: Intervarsity Press, 1990), p. 32.

2. Norman A. Huffman, "Atypical Features in the Parables of Jesus," *Journal of Biblical Literature* 97 (July 1978): 207–8.

3. Ibid., p. 209.

4. Paul Ricoueur, "Bible Hermeneutics," *Semeta* 4 (1975): 109, 112–18.

5. Kenneth E. Bailey, one-volume combined edition of *Poet and Peasant* and *Through Peasant Eyes: A Literary-Cultural Approach to the Parables of Luke* (Grand Rapids, Mich.: William B. Eerdmans Publishing Co., 1980), and Blomberg, *Interpreting the Parables*.

6. Joachim Jeremias, *The Parables of Jesus* (New York: Charles Scribner's Sons, 1963), p. 133.

7. Blomberg, p. 180.

8. Bailey, *Poet and Peasant,* p. 147.

9. Ibid.

10. Huffman, pp. 209, 211. Some scholars believe that a flock of one hundred sheep would have had more than one shepherd to care for them, hence the ninety-nine were in no danger; Blomberg, *Interpreting the Parables,* p. 151.

11. Blomberg, *Interpreting the Parables,* p. 176.

12. Bailey, *Poet and Peasant,* pp. 162–64.

13. Ibid.

14. Ibid.

15. Ibid., p. 165.

16. Ibid.

17. Ibid., p. 166.

18. Ibid., p. 181.

19. Ibid., pp. 182–83.

20. Bailey, *Through Peasant Eyes,* p. 4.

21. Ibid., pp. 4–5.

22. Ibid., p. 9.

23. Ibid., p. 11.

24. Ibid., p. 12.

25. Ibid., pp. 13–21.

26. Ibid., pp. 47–48.

27. Ibid.

28. Ibid., p. 50.

29. Ibid., p. 52.

30. Ibid., p. 53.

31. James H. Charlesworth, *Jesus within Judaism* (London: Doubleday, 1988), p. 74.

32. B. B. Scott, *Jesus, Symbol-Maker for the Kingdom* (Philadelphia: Fortress, 1981), pp. 45–46.

33. Huffman, "Atypical Features in the Parables of Jesus," p. 209.

34. Ibid.

35. Bailey, *Through Peasant Eyes,* p. 149.

36. Ibid., pp. 151–55.

37. Ibid.

38. Charles C. Tarry, *Our Translated Gospels* (New York: Harper, 1936), p. 59.

39. Bailey, *Poet and Peasant,* pp. 97–98.

40. Ibid., p. 98.

41. Ibid., p. 105.

42. Huffman, "Atypical Features in the Parables of Jesus," p. 214.

CHAPTER SIX

The Passion of Jesus Christ

Richard Neitzel Holzapfel
Director, Irvine Institute of Religion

For many years, students of the New Testament have used Gospel "harmonies" to study Jesus' ministry as described in the writings of Matthew, Mark, Luke, and John. A Gospel harmony, sometimes called a synopsis (from the Greek *synoptos*), endeavors to weave all the details of the Gospel tradition into a single chronological strand, one composite order, or sequence.[1] A Gospel harmony usually presents the Gospels in parallel columns in such a way that a reader sees all similarities in the texts at a single glance.[2] One Latter-day Saint author argues that Gospel "harmonies are based upon the Gestalt principle that the whole of anything is greater than the sum of its parts. Since each gospel represents a part, the greater message of the life of Jesus can only be seen when all four are arranged together."[3] Although it is true that any study of Jesus' life should examine all relevant texts (in particular the four Gospels), it is not necessarily true that the Gestalt principle applies totally to a study of Jesus' life. The unwise use of a Gospel harmony—taking the four Gospels as a whole—can distort the historical setting of each story. Undoubtedly each writer preserved a separate and distinct account of Jesus' life and ministry for a good reason.

Jesus proclaimed the gospel—the good news (the English word *gospel* derives from the Anglo-Saxon *godspell*, which means "good tidings").[4] Jesus declared the gospel that the kingdom of God had come through him, and the New Testament writers presented the good news about Jesus.[5] The title given to their work from the second century onwards is significant: the Gospel *according to* Matthew, the Gospel *according to* Mark, and so on. So, although Jesus proclaimed a single gospel, the evangelists presented the life of Jesus in accordance with what they understood. Each writer thus gave his particular testimony, and as a result we now have four Gospels.[6]

In those Gospels we have four separate and distinct viewpoints of the Jesus' suffering, betrayal, trial, and crucifixion. The "Passion narratives" include most of the material found in Matthew 26–27, Mark 14–15, Luke 22–23, and John 12–19. Each was written at a different time for a different audience. To maintain the integrity of the story of the Passion as a whole, we must examine each narrative independent of the others, instead of making one Gospel of them. Attempting to harmonize the four accounts may lead us away from the messages and insights that each Gospel writer intended to teach. The phrase "the Garden of Gethsemane" is an example of what can happen when we harmonize the Gospel narratives. The phrase "Garden of Gethsemane" does not exist anywhere in the New Testament text; rather, it is a hybrid term constructed from the "Garden," in the Gospel according to John (John 18:1) and "Gethsemane," in the Gospels according to Matthew and Mark (Matthew 26:36; Mark 14:32). Such blending of the narratives may create concepts and historical notions that have no basis in the New Testament text itself for, although each Gospel relates the historical events of the Passion, each has a particular tone.

The first three Gospels – Matthew, Mark, and Luke – are called the synoptic Gospels because they share similar material (the Greek word *synoptikos* means "to see the whole together, to take a comprehensive view").[7] John stands apart from the synoptic Gospels because his work has a significant amount of unique material. John's narrative contains several important discourses delivered by Jesus that are not recorded anywhere else (John 13–17).

MATTHEW'S PASSION NARRATIVE

In Matthew, the Passion narrative (Matthew 26:1–27:56) begins with Jesus' anointing in Bethany: "Now when Jesus was in Bethany, in the house of Simon the leper, There came unto him a woman having an alabaster box of very precious ointment, and poured it on his head, as he sat at meat. But when his disciples saw it, they had indignation, saying, To what purpose is this waste? . . . . When Jesus understood it, he said unto them, Why trouble ye the woman? for she hath wrought a good work upon me. . . . For in that she hath poured this ointment on my body, she did it for my burial" (Matthew 26:6–13).

Jesus' statement "She did it for my burial," can only mean that he already knows that he will be crucified and buried without the customary anointing.[8] Then we read of Judas' betrayal (Matthew 26:1–5); the disciples prepare for the Passover (Matthew 26:17–19); Jesus identifies the betrayer and institutes the Lord's Supper (Matthew 26:20–30);

Jesus ends the dinner in the upper room with a passover hymn, possibly Psalms 113–18 (Matthew 26:30).

Following his departure from the upper room, Jesus goes to Gethsemane, where he "saith unto the disciples, Sit ye here, while I go and pray yonder" (Matthew 26:36). Having separated himself, Jesus begins to be "sorrowful and very heavy" (Matthew 26:37). An alternative translation from the Greek for *sorrowful* and *very heavy* is "distressed and troubled" (see footnote 37a in the LDS edition of the KJV). Eventually Jesus "fell on his face" (Matthew 26:39). In Matthew's account, Jesus begins his prayer sorrowful, troubled, and prostrate, but ends on his feet, resolutely facing the mob that has approached. In Matthew 26:46 Jesus commands his disciples "Rise, let us be going; see, my betrayer is at hand."

Judas, the traitor, greets Jesus, "Hail, master," and then kisses him (Matthew 26:49). By using a kiss to show whom the soldiers should arrest, Judas perverts a gesture of friendship he has had with his former Master. Matthew adds "Hail" to the salutation as a further example of Judas' falseheartedness. After a brief skirmish between one of the disciples and the high priest's servant, "All the disciples forsook him, and fled" (Matthew 26:56).

Jesus is betrayed by one of his own, abandoned by the remaining disciples, and in the end accused by his own religious leaders. Deserted by his disciples and surrounded by his enemies, Jesus is taken before the Sanhedrin (Matthew 26:57–68). They take him finally to the gentiles for trial, mockery, and execution. In spite of these trials, Jesus is self-possessed when he confronts the Roman governor who can decree his death.

Only Matthew informs us of the custom of releasing a prisoner at the feast, thus giving Pilate a possible escape clause. Another overtly Matthean insight is the account of Pilate's wife, who as a gentile recognizes Jesus' innocence and seeks his release, while the Jewish leaders work the crowd to have the notorious Barabbas released and Jesus crucified. Some important manuscripts of Matthew compare Barabbas and Jesus in a unique way, for they phrase Pilate's question in 27:17 thus: "Whom do you want me to release to you, Jesus Barabbas or Jesus called Christ?" Since "Barabbas" probably means "Son of the Father," it would be a fascinating irony for Pilate to have faced two accused men named Jesus, one "Son of the Father," the other "Son of God."[9]

Presented with the choice between the two, the Jewish crowd seeks the release of Barabbas. Pilate then "took water, and washed his hands before the multitude" (Matthew 27:24). He "scourged Jesus, [and] delivered him to be crucified" (Matthew 27:26).

Crucifixion was an ancient and malicious form of punishment that the Romans used to kill an enemy. The first-century Jewish historian Josephus, who witnessed several crucifixions as an adviser to Titus during the siege of Jerusalem, tersely describes this form of Roman punishment as "the most wretched of deaths." He reports that a threat by the Roman besiegers to crucify a Jewish prisoner caused the garrison of Machaerus to surrender in exchange for safe conduct.[10]

The practice of crucifixion was remarkably widespread in the ancient world, not just among the Romans, but for the Romans it was a political and military punishment, inflicted primarily on the lower classes, slaves, violent criminals, and the unruly elements in rebellious provinces, not the least of which was Judea.[11] The dominant reason for its use seems to be its allegedly matchless efficacy as a deterrent. Crucifixions were, of course, carried out publicly. By publicly displaying a naked victim at a prominent place such as a crossroads, a theatre, high ground, or the place of his crime, the Romans also ensured a criminal's uttermost humiliation. Jews were particularly averse to this punishment in light of Deuteronomy 21:23, which specifically pronounces God's curse on the crucified individual.

Matthew identifies some of the participants in the actual crucifixion and gives the location as "Golgotha" (Matthew 27:33).[12] The name may have been given to a place that resembled a skull, or it may have been so named because it was a regular place of execution.

Matthew's allusions to the Old Testament underscore the emphasis laid on God's acts. One such parallel Matthew offers is the story of Judas' death. Judas "went and hanged himself" (Matthew 27:5), an echo of the story of King David. It reveals the similarity of David's own flight to the Kidron and the subsequent betrayal by Ahitophel, who also hanged himself (2 Samuel 15:12, 14, 23; 17:23).[14]

Matthew's repeated use of the Old Testament provides a clue to his unique purpose, namely demonstrating the fulfillment of God's purposes in and through Jesus.[15] Matthew is interested in themes rather than in history; the most superficial examination of his Gospel from a purely historical point of view reveals that a disproportionate amount of attention is devoted to the Passion narrative. Thus Old Testament quotations in the Passion narrative combined with the familiar Matthean formula "that it might be fulfilled which was spoken by the prophet" (Matthew 27:35), the Gospel of Matthew reemphasizes God's salvation proclaimed from the beginning of time. The emphasis on the Messiah is his redemption from the captivity of sin, not from military power as expected by the Jews.

MARK'S PASSION NARRATIVE

In Mark's Passion narrative (Mark 14:1–15:47), the death plot (Matthew 14:1ff) is followed by the anointing in Bethany (Mark 14:3–9), Judas' betrayal (Mark 14:10ff), the preparation of the last meal, announcement of the betrayal, and the institution of the sacrament of the Lord's Supper (Mark 14:12–25). Jesus leaves the upper room committed to the necessity that he must suffer and die.[16] In Gethsemane, the prostrate Jesus suffers in anguish (Mark 14:32–42). He is God's son, yet endowed with the human will to live, he does not want to die. The name that Jesus uses in his cry to God, "Abba" (Father), heightens the pathos of this tragic scene:

"He took with him Peter, James and John, and began to be horror-stricken and desperately depressed. 'My heart is breaking with a death-like grief,' he told them. 'Stay here and keep watch.' Then he walked forward a little way and flung himself on the ground, praying that, if it were possible, the hour might pass him by. 'Dear Father,' he said, 'all things are possible to you. Let me not have to drink this cup! Yet it is not what I want but what you want' " (Mark 14:33–36, Phillips's Translation).[17]

It is the Father's will that Jesus die. His disciples, however, have not yet accepted this reality. Jesus states, "The sheep shall be scattered" (Mark 14:27). Peter characteristically denies that (Mark 14:29), only to be told by the Master that he would yet deny the Lord three times (Mark 14:30). The disciples at first stand in firm opposition to Jesus' arrest, but finally they all forsake him and flee. Mark's account emphasizes the complete abandonment of Jesus by everyone, even one unnamed follower (Mark 14:52).

Peter's denial recorded in Mark 14:66–72 is really threefold. Peter at first pretends he does not understand what he has been asked. Next he endeavors to get away from the courtyard. Unable to leave, he then denies his status as a disciple. Peter swears an oath that he does not even know Jesus. Mark ends the scene with the statement, "And Peter recalled to mind the word that Jesus said to him, Before the cock crow twice, thou shalt deny me thrice" (Mark 14:72). Ironically, at the very moment when Jesus is mocked by the Sanhedrin's challenge to prophesy (Mark 14:65), his prophecies are coming true. Mark's account of the first trial ends at this point, and the second trial begins.

The first trial before the Jewish Sanhedrin is the more decisive one, though from a legal perspective the Roman trial is more important. Throughout both trials, Jesus remains almost entirely silent. At the first trial he is charged with threatening to destroy the temple at Jerusalem and committing blasphemy (Mark 14:58, 64). In the second trial, he is accused of claiming to be "King of the Jews," a title that carries revolutionary overtones for the Romans (Mark 15:2).

During the first trial, Caiaphas, the high priest, specifically questions Jesus about his claim to be the Savior Messiah. Jesus' affirmation gives the Jewish leaders the needed pretext to bring a charge of treason against him. This charge would then be dealt with by Roman law and power, just as the Jewish leaders expected it to be (Mark 14:61–62). Not only does Jesus give evidence to convict himself under Roman law but he also gives Caiaphas grounds to convict him of blasphemy, a capital crime under the law of Moses, as the claim of being a messiah is not.

New Testament scholar Joel Marcus argues that there must have been something different about Jesus' claim to be the Messiah: "Why should Jesus' claim to be 'the Messiah, the Son of God' [Mark 14:61, KJV: 'the Christ, the Son of the Blessed'] be considered blasphemous if 'Son of the God' is merely a synonym for 'Messiah'? . . . One searches Jewish literature in vain for evidence that a simple claim to be the Messiah would incur such a charge."[18] Mark's report of the first trial indicates that Jesus' claim to be God's literal son is more crucial and controversial for the Jewish leaders than his claim to be the Davidic Messiah. Marcus believes that this claim is "understood in a quite realistic, almost biological sense" by the Jewish leaders.[19] The Messiah-kingship issue is simply a ruse to get the Romans to take care of Jesus in the second trial.

Mark's presentation of the events after the second trial is a painful, albeit succinct and unadorned, account. Characteristically, Mark reports the events with a few vivid words and without elaborating the detail: "And so Pilate, willing to content the people, released Barabbas unto them, and delivered Jesus, when he had scourged him, to be crucified.

And the soldiers led him away into the hall, called Praetorium; and they call together the whole band. And they clothed him with purple, and platted a crown of thorns, and put it about his head, And began to salute him, Hail, King of the Jews! And they smote him on the head with a reed, and did spit upon him, and bowing their knees worshipped him" (Mark 15:15–19).

At the time of Christ, scourging (flogging) was done with a whip made of several strips of leather embedded near the ends with pieces of metal and bone. The victim was bound to a pillar and then beaten with the whip. While it is true that the Jews limited the number of stripes to a maximum of forty (thirty-nine in case of a miscount), no such limitation was recognized by the Romans. Victims often did not survive this punishment. Jesus survives, only to be executed by means of crucifixion.

Two incidents prior to Jesus' death are recorded by Mark in this climactic part of the Passion narrative: the mockery (Mark 15:16–20) and the actual crucifixion (Mark 15:21–31). Mark's story of brutality ends with the veil of the temple being "rent in twain from the top to the bottom" (Mark 15:38), a final act of disorder in a violent scene when Jesus is put to death at the hands of ruthless men agitated by a frenzied crowd incited by their leaders.

LUKE'S PASSION NARRATIVE

Luke begins his Passion narrative (Luke 22:1–23:56) with the betrayal of Jesus by Judas, the Last Supper, and the farewell discourse (Luke 22:7–38). The narrative continues with Jesus' arrival at the Mount of Olives, his arrest, the denial by Peter, the mocking of Jesus, and the hearing before the Sanhedrin, the hearing before Pilate, Jesus' going before Herod Antipas, Jesus' walk to Golgotha, his words to the women of Jerusalem, his crucifixion, and finally his burial (Luke 22:39–23:56).

Luke's account is marked by delicacy and tenderness. He cannot bring himself to report some details which were too distressing: Luke does not say that Jesus was scourged nor that Judas actually kissed Jesus. Luke does, however, make us aware of the magnitude of the terrible struggle between Jesus and the powers of evil. The Passion is the last decisive struggle. Jesus comes out of it as victor through his patience — a word that is not a good rendering of the Greek *hypomone*, which suggests the attitude of the believer enduring blows in his trial as he is sustained by God.[20]

The decisive struggle occurs in "the place" at the mount of Olives. Here in great agony, the Lord bled from every pore: "And he came out, and went, as he was wont, to the mount of Olives; and his disciples also followed him. And when he was at the place, he said unto them, Pray that ye enter not into temptation. And he was withdrawn from them about a stone's cast, and kneeled down, and prayed, Saying, Father, if thou be willing, remove this cup from me: nevertheless not my will, but thine, be done" (Luke 22:39–42).

Then, comforted by God, Jesus emerges victorious. Now at peace, held in his Father's arms, he can be wholly reconciled to his God.

Luke uses the Greek *agonia* in 22:44 to indicate Jesus' intense anxiety over what will happen to him. The Greek meaning of *agonia* is the "athlete's state of mind before the contest, agony, dread."[21] As a result, Luke reports, Jesus "prayed more earnestly: and his sweat was as it were great drops of blood falling down to the ground" (Luke 22:44). Although some ancient manuscripts omit 22:43–44 (Codex Vaticanus), it was known to Justin Marytr, Irenaeus, Tatian, and Hippolytus in the second century.[22]

Events happen swiftly in Luke. Judas arrives with his newfound allies and attempts to salute Jesus. Jesus reminds Judas that it is the Son of Man whom he thus betrays. Peter, anxious to do something, smites off the ear of the high priest's servant. Jesus "touched [the servant's] ear, and healed him" (Luke 22:47–51). He helps his opponent, even in the midst of his own danger. The physician Luke sees Jesus as the greatest healer. Whether for friend or foe, Jesus' mission is one of reconciliation and healing.

The tearing of the veil of the temple just before Jesus' death is another Lucan feature departing from the other Gospels (Luke 23:45).[23] After the curtain is rent, Jesus addresses God: "Father, into thy hands I commend my spirit" (Luke 23:46). This action symbolizes Jesus' communing with the Father, who may have been present in the temple, at the last moment before his death.

The cry Jesus utters on the cross is not a scream of human suffering before death; rather it is the evening prayer known to every Jew: "Into your hands I commend my spirit." Jesus, however, prefaces it with the term that marks his unparalleled intimacy with God: "Father" (see Luke 23:46). Jesus dies in peace, at one with God.

The crucifixion itself is the last violent act by men in the life of him who promised them life after death. Yet Jesus' promise to the thief and to all of us is not one of mere "survival" after death but, more accurately, a "glorious future" beyond death (Luke 23:43).

JOHN'S PASSION NARRATIVE

John wrote his Gospel some sixty years after Jesus' death, so he had meditated on the Passion for a long time before committing it to writing. In John's Passion account (John 12:1–19:42) he chooses the episodes that have the most significance to the faithful. He presents the Passion as the triumphal progress of Jesus towards the Father. Jesus knows that he is going to die, he knows what kind of a death it will be, and he goes to it freely: "No one taketh [my life] from me, but I lay it down of myself" (John 10:18). John does not separate death and exaltation in his account but sees them as inextricably intertwined. The lifting of Jesus upon the cross is also the beginning of his ascension into the glory of God, from whence he will send the Spirit upon the world (John 19:30). "I, if I be lifted up from the earth, will draw all men unto me," Jesus declares (John 12:32).

To draw all men to himself is the essence of Jesus' mission, according to John's writings. He anticipates and accepts death not simply as the consequence of his prophetic calling but as his last service of love. The Passion of Christ is the climax of his ministry, which offers salvation by every action.

John's story of Jesus' Passion includes the farewell to his disciples: the foot-washing at the meal, designation of the betrayer, the commandment of love, the allusion to Peter's denial, consolation for his own, the metaphor of Jesus as the true vine, a discussion of the hatred of the world, and the intercessory prayer (John 13–17).

John's story continues at a special garden place where he and his disciples "ofttimes resorted" (John 18:1–2). John began his Gospel by discussing the Creation narrative alluding to the first garden where the conflict between Adam and Lucifer was played out. Now in a second garden, another conflict between the Savior and the Serpent is played out: "When Jesus had spoken these words, he went forth with his disciples over the brook Cedron, where was a garden, into the which he entered, and his disciples. And Judas also, which betrayed him, knew the place: for Jesus ofttimes resorted thither with his disciples" (John 18:1–2).

For John, Judas is the tool of Satan. Earlier that evening Judas had gone off into the night, the evil night of which Jesus had warned in John 9:10 and 12:35, the night in which men stumble because they have no light. Perhaps that is why the Jews with Judas come out with the lanterns and torches: they have rejected the light of the world, and so they must rely on the artificial light they carry with them.

Now Jesus, totally in control of his fate, leaves the garden to confront the malevolent host before him: "Jesus therefore, knowing all things that should come upon him, went forth, and said unto them, Whom seek ye? They answered him, Jesus of Nazareth. Jesus saith unto them, I am he" (John 18:4–5).

Jesus' simple answer causes this large armed group of Roman soldiers and Jewish temple police to step backwards and fall to the ground (John 18:6). The adversaries of Jesus are prostrate before his divine majesty, leaving us little doubt that John intends "I AM" as a divine name (Greek *ego eimi*).[24] John emphasizes that Jesus, as God, has power over the forces of darkness. This statement reinforces our impression that Jesus could not have been arrested unless he permitted it. That belief is further substantiated by Jesus' statement before Pilate, "Thou couldest have no power at all against me, except it were given thee from above" (John 19:11).

After relating Jesus' trial before Annas and Caiaphas, John tells of Jesus' being brought to the "hall of judgment" to stand before the Roman governor. As Pilate examines Jesus, he asks the question "What is truth?" (John 18:38). John seems intent on warning the reader that no one can avoid judgment when he stands before Jesus. The scene ends with an apotheosis: Pilate makes Jesus sit at his tribunal so he can proclaim Jesus king (John 19:13). "Sit down" may mean that Pilate "made him [Jesus] sit down."[25] For John, Christ is the legitimate judge of men; in condemning him, the Jewish leaders are judging themselves.

John records the place of these events explicitly, even noting the time: "it was the preparation of the passover, and about the sixth hour" (John 19:14). Passover eve, he says — or, since *paraskeue* acquired in Jewish Greek the special sense of "sabbath eve," that is, Friday, the phrase could be rendered, "It was Friday of Passover Week at about 12 o'clock noon."[26]

John sees a deeper meaning in Pilate's words, just as he had seen a prophecy in Caiaphas' words (John 11:49–51). The Roman governor exclaims, "Behold your King!" (John 19:14). Pilate implies that Jesus is the true king of the true Israel, of all the people of God who obey the voice of God. Spoken at midday on Passover Eve, we can infer that Jesus is the true Paschal Lamb about to be sacrificed at the appropriate hour of the appropriate day for the life of his people.

For John, the Jewish trial is a mockery of a prophet and the Roman trial a mockery of a king. Judas, a disciple, hands Jesus over to the Jewish leaders, the chief priests hand Jesus over to a Roman leader, and Pilate hands Jesus over to the soldiers to be crucified. While no one is completely responsible, each person or group hands Jesus over to another individual or group. Therefore, all collectively are responsible. John's Passion narrative ends with the scourging, crowning with thorns, crucifixion, the piercing of Jesus' side, and finally the removal of his body from the cross (John 19:31–42).

CONCLUSION

Because the accounts of Matthew, Mark, Luke, and John of the Passion describe the same series of incidents, it is easy to blend all the narratives in our heads and produce for ourselves our own harmony, so that our version of the Passion story includes Matthew's earthquakes and his story of Pilate's wife and her dream; Luke's scene of agony; and John's memorable quote from Pilate, "What is truth?" In reality, the New Testament writers have actually preserved not one story but four separate versions of the same scenario. For each writer, the Passion narrative is the culmination of his entire Gospel story. Each testifies that Jesus' Passion fulfills the multiple prophecies and testimonies of the Lord.

Although we have a tendency to want one picture of Jesus' life — a single Gospel, as it were — the Gospel narratives do not make a single picture of Jesus, but four beautiful mosaics. They are the words and actions of Jesus as interpreted by authentic witnesses. We do not need to cut and paste them together to form a single picture. "[The first harmonies'] declared purpose," New Testament scholar Heinrich Greeven argues, was "to fuse parallel texts into one single text" and to do so, the compilers had to harmonize and diminish the differences or supposed contradictions between the stories.[27]

If we had four mosaics giving different representations of the same scene, it would not occur to us to say, "These mosaics are so beautiful that I do not want to lose any of them; I shall demolish them and use the enormous pile of stones to make a single mosaic that combines all four of them." Trying to combine the pieces would be an outrageous affront to the artists. Because the four Gospels are different from each other, we must study each one for itself, without demolishing it and using the debris to reconstruct a life of Jesus by making the four Gospels into one Gospel. Even though it is useful to study the Gospels with the aid of such tools as a harmony, we must remember that historical and exegetical methodology and scholarly tools can, in fact, divert our attention from the real drama and the essential issues raised by each of the Gospels. Any tool of study that prevents us from asking the eternally important questions "Whom seekest thou?" and "Lovest thou me?" (John 20:15; 21:15–17) is playing false to the very faith and mission of the Gospels themselves and the early Christians who read and heard these personal and authentic testimonies.

NOTES

1. Greek *synoptos*, "that can be seen at a glance, in full view." H. G. Liddell and Scott, *An Intermediate Greek-English Lexicon* (Oxford: Clarendon Press, 1975), p. 779.

2. An excellent and accessible harmony is found in the LDS Bible Dictionary under the subheading, "Gospel," published in *The Holy Bible* (Salt Lake City: The Church of Jesus Christ of Latter-day Saints, 1979), pp. 684–96. Two harmonies with scholarly apparatus, noncanonical material, and variant manuscript readings are Burton H. Throckmorton, Jr., *Gospel Parallels: A Synopsis of the First Three Gospels* (Nashville, Tenn.: Thomas Nelson Publishers, 1979) and Robert W. Funk, *New Gospel Parallels*, 2 vols. (Philadelphia: Fortress Press, 1985). A recent technical synopsis that also included the so-called Q Document in parallel columns is John S. Kloppenborg, *Q Parallels: Synopsis, Critical Notes, and Concordance* (Sonoma: Polebridge Press, 1988). For a discussion concerning the process of making a harmony, see David Dugan, "Theory of Synopsis Construction," *Biblica* 61 (1980): 305–29.

3. Thomas M. Mumford, *Horizontal Harmony of the Four Gospels in Parallel Columns* (Salt Lake City, Utah: Deseret Book Co., 1976), p. v.

4. Walter W. Skeat, *A Concise Etymological Dictionary of the English Language* (Oxford: Clarendon Press, 1976), p. 218.

5. The Greek *euangelion* (good news) was known to secular authors and was used to announce a victory or great events in the life of the emperor. For a fuller discussion of its usage, see William F. Arndt and Wilbur F. Gingrich, *A Greek-English Lexicon of the New Testament and Other Early Christian Literature* (Chicago: University of Chicago Press, 1957), p. 318.

6. For a recent discussion on the relationship of the Gospels to each other, see Kloppenborg, *Q Parallels*, xxi-xxxiv.

7. An overview of the authorship, dating, audience, and purpose of the individual Gospel accounts may be found in the LDS Bible Dictionary under the subheading "Gospels," pp. 682–83. This overview provides a sound historical context for any serious study of the Gospels.

8. For a discussion of this event, see W. F. Albright and C. S. Mann, *Matthew: A New Translation with Introduction and Commentary* (Garden City, N.Y.: Doubleday, 1986), pp. 314–15.

9. Bruce Metzger explains, "A majority of the Committee [Editorial Committee of the United Bible Societies' Greek New Testament] was of the opinion that the original text of Matthew had the double name in both verses (27:16–17) and that *Iesous* was deliberately suppressed in most witnesses for reverential consideration." See Bruce M. Metzger, *A Textual Commentary on the Greek New Testament* (London: United Bible Societies, 1975), pp. 67–68.

10. Josephus, *De Bello Judaico* (Darmstadt, W. Germany: Wissenschaftliche Buchgesellfchaft, 1959) 7:202ff (the quotation comes from 203). For an English translation, see *The Jewish War*, trans. G. A. Williamson (New York: Penguin Books, 1969), pp. 389–90.

11. For a survey of this subject, see Martin Hengel, *Crucifixion in the Ancient World and the Folly of the Message of the Cross* (Philadelphia: Fortress Press, 1977).

12. The Greek place name is the transliteration of the Aramaic *gulgulta*, which means "skull." The traditional name for the place is "Calvary," which is taken from the Latin *calvaria*. It means the same as Golgotha, but is, strictly speaking, not a biblical name. See Raymond E. Brown, Joseph A. Fitzmyer, and Roland E. Murphy, *The New Jerome Biblical Commentary* (Englewood Cliffs, N.J.: Prentice Hall, 1990), p. 628.

13. *The Septuagint Version of the Old Testament and Apocrypha* (Grand Rapids, Mich.: Zondervan, 1976), p. 47.

14. There are several other Old Testament allusions in Matthew including the darkness from noon to 3:00 p.m. (Matthew 27:45), which may refer to the darkness over Egypt before the first Passover, or perhaps it is a reference to Amos 8:9. Whichever it is, they both are God's act. In both cases "the day" belongs to God and not to the forces of evil.

15. For a complete list of Old Testament quotations in Matthew see Robert G. Bratcher, *Old Testament Quotations in the New Testament* (New York: United Bible Societies, 1984), p. 11.

16. Mark is generally credited with inventing the new literary genre of "the Gospel." See discussion of this point in Frank Kermode, "Introduction to the New Testament," *Literary Guide to the Bible*, ed. Robert Alter and Frank Kermode (Cambridge, Mass.: Harvard University Press, 1987), pp. 375–86.

17. J. B. Phillips, *The New Testament in Modern English* (New York: Macmillan, 1972), pp. 100–101.

18. Joel Marcus, "Mark 14:61: 'Are You the Messiah-Son-of-God?' " *Novum Testamentum* 31 (April 1989): 127.

19. Marcus, "Mark 14:61," p. 140.

20. Arndt and Gingrich, *A Greek-English Lexicon of the New Testament*, p. 854.

21. See Max Zerwick and Mary Grosvenor, *A Grammatical Analysis of the Greek New Testament* (Rome: Biblical Institute Press, 1981), p. 237.

22. G. B. Caird argues, "Its omission is best explained as the work of a scribe who felt that this picture of Jesus overwhelmed with human weakness was incompatible with his own belief in the Divine Son who shared the omnipotence of his Father." G. B. Caird, *The Gospel of Saint Luke* (New York: Penguin Books, 1985), p. 243.

23. The synoptic Gospels agree on this event, but Matthew and Mark place it after Jesus' death (see Matthew 27:51 and Mark 15:38).

24. For a discussion of the use of *ego eimi* in John, see Gerhard Kittel's *Theological Dictionary of the New Testament* (Grand Rapids, Mich.: William B. Eerdmans Publishing Co., 1964), 2:352–54.

25. Robert G. Bratcher, *Marginal Notes for the New Testament* (New York: United Bible Societies, 1988), p. 66. For a fuller discussion of this possible reading, see Barclay M. Newman and Eugene A. Nida, *A Translator's Handbook on the Gospel of John* (New York: United Bible Societies, 1980), p. 581, and Zerwick and Grosvenor, *A Grammatical Analysis*, p. 341.

26. Arndt and Gingrich argue that for the "Jewish usage it was Friday, on which day everything had to be prepared for the Sabbath, when no work was permitted." Arndt and Gingrich, *A Greek-English Lexicon of the New Testament*, p. 637.

27. Heinrich Greeven in Albert Huck, *Synopse der drei ersten Evangelien/ Synopsis of the First Three Gospels with the Addition of the Johannine Parallels* (Tubingen, W. Germany: J.C.B. Mohr [Paul Siebeck], 1981), xxxvi.

CHAPTER SEVEN

Mark and Luke:
Two Facets of a Diamond

Roger R. Keller
Brigham Young University

Elder Bruce R. McConkie makes the following statement concerning the four Gospels: "It is apparent, however, that each inspired author had especial and intimate knowledge of certain circumstances not so well known to others, and that each felt impressed to emphasize different matters because of the particular people to whom he was addressing his personal gospel testimony."[1] In reality each gospel is like a facet of a diamond. It brightens and highlights the picture of Jesus that we receive, and just as a diamond would be terribly uninteresting without its facets, so also would the picture of Jesus be flat and one-dimensional without the composite picture of him that is presented when the four Gospels are brought together. All bear witness of Jesus Christ and teach the plan of salvation but each with a slightly different clarity, cut, and color. In this light, it would have been a great loss to all generations of the Church had we not had both Mark and Luke — two facets of the gospel diamond.

JESUS

In his three years of ministry, Jesus walked and talked with numerous people in a wide range of situations. He gave many public sermons as well as considerable private instruction to his disciples. He met in highly charged situations with the religious leaders of his day. He spoke to prince and pauper, priest and peasant, saint and sinner. No one was so exalted that Jesus was intimidated by him, nor was anyone so insignificant that Jesus did not have time for him or her. Women and children had a special place in his heart and ministry, something that was not always common in the Judaism of his day.[2]

Jesus taught about an immense range of subjects. He dealt with the nature and purposes of God, the plan of salvation, the nature of human destiny, the morality of the kingdom, and many other issues. Much of his teaching among the crowds was done in parables, not merely to put the message in an understandable form but also to hide the message from those who were not yet spiritually prepared to comprehend it (Matthew 13:10–15; Mark 4:10–12; Luke 8:9–10). Later, in private, he also told his disciples in clear language what the parables meant (Matthew 13:18; Mark 4:13; Luke 8:11). Thus, he chose what he would say to whom and how he would say it, depending upon that person's ability to perceive and understand.[3]

John tells us that in the scriptures we have far from all that Jesus said or did (John 21:25). Yet, we have that which the Lord, through the Holy Ghost, guided the Gospel writers to preserve in preparation for the fulness of times in the latter days. No one Gospel portrait of the Lord is complete in itself, but as we encounter Christ and his teachings in all the Gospels, we will come to know him better.

MARK AND LUKE: THE AUTHORS

Neither Mark nor Luke was one of the original Twelve. Their precise relationship with Jesus is not known, although Mark may have been among the larger circle of Jesus' early followers. Tradition says that Mark was a missionary companion of Peter and that the Gospel of Mark represents in large measure Mark's account of Peter's recollections of the Lord and his ministry. That seems probable.[4]

Luke is usually identified as the beloved physician and companion of Paul and was thus a bit more distant from the historical Jesus than was Mark. He is, however, considered by many to have been a very careful, very deliberate historian who gathered all the information he could from "eyewitnesses, and ministers of the word" (Luke 1:2)[5] as he wrote his two-part work, Luke and Acts, which he dedicated to Theophilus, a person otherwise unknown to us.

Mark is traditionally said to have written his gospel in Rome during the time of Nero's persecution of the Church. Many of the slums of Rome had been burned, an act that is probably attributable to Nero, who wanted to make room for public buildings. Nero needed a scapegoat, however, and the Christians, who were not popular anyway because of their rather "narrow" religious views, were a group that could be easily blamed. Thus, the members of the Church among whom Mark worked and served were undergoing tremendous persecution, and suffering greatly. Apparently Mark longed to bring a message of hope to these people in the midst of their sufferings, as well as to explain through Jesus' own words and actions why people suffer in this world when they are doing what the Lord requires of them. Thus, the persecution that Peter and Mark faced in the Roman church determined to a large degree Mark's focus on the suffering in Jesus' life and the lives of his followers.[6]

Luke was in an entirely different situation. He probably lived where there was a large gentile community,[7] where many wanted to know whether the gospel was for them or only for the Jews. Luke himself was a gentile (Colossians 4:10–14).[8] He was a companion of Paul,[9] the apostle to the Gentiles. He knew full well that the gospel was for persons of all races and for all persons — male and female, rich and poor, slave and free. Thus, Jesus' message about the universality of the gospel becomes the focal point of Luke's portrait of the Lord.

Both Mark and Luke accurately portray Jesus' words and deeds, but each sees different aspects of Jesus' ministry. The Lord's words are for all generations and all times, but no one gospel could possibly contain all that Jesus said and did. Each contains a piece of the whole.

THE GOSPEL OF MARK

"And he took the blind man by the hand, and led him out of the town; and when he had spit on his eyes, and put his hands upon him, he asked him if he saw ought. And he looked up, and said, I see men as trees, walking. After that he put his hands again upon his eyes, and made him look up: and he was restored, and saw every man clearly" (Mark 8:23–26).

This passage represents the central point in the Gospel according to Mark. As we come to an understanding of Jesus' true role, we then come to clarity about our own role as his disciples.

This story is unique in the Gospels. At no other time did Jesus make two attempts to heal a person. This healing occurred shortly before Jesus asked his disciples, "Whom do men say that I am?" and "Whom say ye that I am?" Peter, of course, gave his classic answer: Jesus is the Christ (Mark 8:27–30). Jesus then told him that the Son of Man (Jesus) must suffer and die, and Peter immediately reacted by saying that could not happen (Mark 8:31–32). One of Jesus' harshest replies was then immediately directed at Peter. "Get thee behind me, Satan: for thou savourest not the things that be of God, but the things that be of men" (Mark 8:33).

Clearly, Peter — and perhaps we as observers — missed something. What was wrong with Peter's desire that Jesus not suffer? Everything — for Jesus came precisely *to* suffer and die![10]

"Behold, we go up to Jerusalem; and the Son of man shall be delivered unto the chief priests, and unto the scribes; and they shall condemn him to death, and shall deliver him to the Gentiles: And they shall mock him, and shall scourge him, and shall spit upon him, and shall kill him: and the third day he shall rise again. . . . For even the Son of man came not to be ministered unto, but to minister, and to give his life a ransom for many" (Mark 10:33–34, 45).

Anyone who stood in opposition to that purpose did not understand the nature and purpose of Jesus' messiahship. Such a person was like the blind man who, after Jesus' initial attempt to heal him, saw partially but unclearly. By contrast, only those who understood unequivocally that Jesus must die understood the nature of his messiahship as well as the possible consequences of their own discipleship. They would be comparable to the blind man who saw clearly after Jesus' second act of healing.

Peter, however, understood only in part what the actual role of the Messiah would be and thus perceived Christ's mission only dimly. He did not yet understand that the Messiah must suffer and die. Only after Jesus' death and resurrection would he and others finally see more clearly.

Confrontation

Peter knew and declared that Jesus was the Messiah, even though his conception of the Messiah was not predicated on the same understanding that Jesus possessed. What led Peter to this unequivocal testimony of Christ but only a partial understanding of his mission? Perhaps the answer lies in Jesus' ministry to that point.

Mark shows us clearly that Jesus' ministry was characterized by conflict and confrontation from the beginning. The Spirit led Jesus out into the wilderness to be tempted by Satan (Mark 1:12). That cosmic confrontation then became an earthly conflict as Jesus confronted demons, disease, religious leaders, and ultimately even his own disciples who did not understand the nature of his ministry.[11]

Such confusion among his disciples, however, often resulted from Jesus' own actions. He could not turn away persons in need. Thus, immediately after coming out of the wilderness, he was confronted by a man with an unclean spirit in the synagogue at Capernaum. He drove out that spirit, amazing all that were present (Mark 1:21–27). He then went to Peter's home, where he found Peter's mother-in-law ill, and he healed her (Mark 1:29–31). Then people brought the sick and those possessed with devils from the surrounding countryside, and Jesus healed them of their infirmities and cast out the devils (Mark 1:32–34). The next morning, however, the disciples looked for Jesus and could not find him. Ultimately they located him in an isolated spot where he had gone to pray. The disciples were impressed with Jesus' healing ability and indicated to him that many were already waiting to receive such blessings at his hand. Jesus' response to their well-intentioned request is enlightening, for he said, "Let us go into the next towns, that I may preach there also: for therefore came I forth. And he preached in their synagogues throughout all Galilee, and cast out devils" (Mark 1:38–39). Thus, Jesus indicated that his healing ministry, with which all were so impressed, was really not his foremost purpose on earth. He had something more important to do, that is, to proclaim the nearness of the kingdom of God (Mark 1:14; 2:2).[12]

Even so, Jesus continued to heal and to drive out demons (Mark 1:24, 39; 2:10; 5:2–8; 6:56; 7:26–30; 9:23–24), leading to confrontations with religious authorities, who sought ways to get rid of him. Like vultures, they watched to see if he would heal on the Sabbath, so that they might accuse him of breaking the law (Mark 2:24–28; 3:2–6). Later, he even sent his disciples out to accomplish the same things he had, giving them authority to heal the sick and cast out demons (Mark 3:14; 6:7, 13). Both the cosmic order and religious order were being shaken by him. No wonder Peter believed him to be the Messiah! Only the Messiah could do what Jesus did.

Don't Tell Anyone

Jesus forbade the demons to proclaim who he was (Mark 1:25, 34; 3:12), but that is understandable. He did not want demonic testimony to his messiahship. Yet, the knowledge of the demons points up an interesting dichotomy. The minions of Satan recognized and knew who Jesus was, but the religious authorities did not. The scribes, Pharisees, and Sadducees only wanted to rid themselves of him. Mark is appalled at how utterly blind they were.

A more difficult question is why Jesus commanded those whom he healed not to tell what he had done for them (Mark 1:43; 7:36). Shouldn't people have known that the Messiah had come with "compassion and healing in his wings"? Yet, when people ignored his admonition, Jesus found himself having to go into the wilderness to get away from the crowds who wanted him to heal their sick (Mark 1:38, 45). None of the people, including Jesus' disciples, completely understood who he was. They assumed that he was the Messiah, which was correct; but their conception of the Messiah was of one who worked miracles, healed the sick, fed the hungry, and ultimately would cast the Romans out of Judea.[13] They were like the blind man who understood only in part. So also with Peter. Despite revelation from the Father (Matthew 16:16–17), Peter based his intellectual understanding of Jesus as the Messiah on his miracle working and confrontational ministry. That was not the character of Jesus' messiahship, and Jesus knew that Peter did not fully understand his own declaration, "Thou art the Christ, the Son of the living God." Thus, He told Peter not to tell anyone (Mark 8:30).

Suffering

Jesus told Peter plainly that His messiahship required that He suffer and die (Mark 8:31).[14] But that was not Peter's understanding of messiahship. He liked the image of the miracle-working, powerful Messiah who was afraid to confront no one.[15] Thus, he objected (Mark 8:32), and Jesus forcefully chastized Peter for failing to let God readjust his preconceived notions about what the Messiah would be like.[16] From this point in Mark's gospel, Jesus moved inexorably toward the cross, pointing out several times that his destiny was to suffer and die for men (Mark 9:12, 31; 10:33–34, 45; 12:7–8; 14:7–8, 22, 24, 27). Yet, it was a gentile centurion, as he watched Jesus breathe his last, who first comprehended that Jesus in the midst of his suffering was truly "the Son of God" (Mark 15:38–39).

But if Jesus' role was to suffer, then it is highly probable that those who followed him might have to share the same fate (Mark 8:34–35; 10:39–40; 13:9, 12–13). Such was and is the case. Those of the early Church faced torture and death. According to tradition, Peter was crucified upside down.[17] Paul was beheaded.[18] Stephen was stoned (Acts 7:59). James was beheaded (Acts 12:2). Once empowered by the Holy Ghost, however, men who had run and hidden in locked rooms became giants for the faith, unafraid of death itself. What more powerful message could Mark have conveyed to the suffering Church in Rome than this? He told those frightened people that even the Son of God was destined to suffer because the world could not tolerate his presence, his goodness, and his message. So also the world could not tolerate those who followed him, and his disciples would have to suffer, as Jesus had warned them during his lifetime. Evil can not tolerate good. It will do all it can to stamp it out. But good will be conquered only momentarily, for the righteous powers of heaven, which raise men from the very depths of the grave, can never be overcome.

That, therefore, was Mark's message to Rome as he viewed Jesus' life and ministry. So also is his message to us of the latter-day Church who are comfortable and all too often conforming to the model of the world rather than receiving in our lives the impress of heaven. If the world is comfortable with us and we are comfortable with it, we see the mission of the Messiah only as well as the partially healed blind man saw. Like the disciples at Pentecost, who did not see clearly until they received their "second" healing through the bestowal of the Holy Ghost, we, too, must receive the understanding that we will suffer as we faithfully follow the Lord—suffer because we do not agree with the values of the world. And like the disciples who went on to endure grievous persecution, we will be fortified by this clearer vision, knowing that our suffering is linked to His. Then we will more fully comprehend what it means to know that Jesus is "the Christ, the Son of the living God" (Matthew 16:16).

THE GOSPEL OF LUKE

Like Mark, Luke saw certain aspects of Jesus' ministry as being particularly applicable to his day and situation. Of great importance to him was that the gospel be relevant for persons such as himself who were not Israelites. Luke also had a concern for those who seemed to be on the fringes of society. Was the gospel for them, too, or was it a gospel for the privileged classes? He further felt, like Mark, that it was important to explain what it meant to be a disiciple. In Luke, also, one sees an emphasis on the spiritual dimension of Jesus' life, a dimension that could and should be part of the lives of all who follow Christ.

The principal Lucan concerns are initially expressed in the birth narratives in chapters 1 and 2. We can trace them through the Gospel and into Acts, for Luke and Acts are really one whole. Many of the Lucan emphases find their fulfilment in the apostolic ministry.

Witness

Luke expressed at the beginning of his gospel that his narrative should be viewed as an authoritative witness of Jesus Christ, because it had its roots in the accounts of eyewitnesses and ministers of the word (Luke 1:2). Luke demonstrated that his account was accurate, because it could be traced to original witnesses who met, walked, and talked with the Lord, or who were divinely informed about him.[19] Thus, Jesus' birth was heralded by appearances of Gabriel to the witnesses Zacharias (Luke 1:11–20) and Mary (Luke 1:26–38), while the baby in Elisabeth's womb leaped in witnessing recognition of the baby in Mary's womb (Luke 1:41). Both Simeon (Luke 2:25–35) and Anna (Luke 2:36–38) received divine confirmation of Jesus' messiahship and bore testimony of him.[20] Throughout Jesus' ministry in Galilee, people were always with him, hearing every word he spoke and seeing every act he did (Luke 5:1; 6:17; 7:1, 11; 8:1–4, 19, 40, 42). The same thing was true on the long trip to Jerusalem (Luke 10:23–24; 11:29; 12:1; 14:25; 19:37).[21] Witnesses were constantly present. Finally, in choosing an apostle to replace Judas, the remaining apostles determined that he had to be an *eyewitness* of Jesus' entire ministry, so that he could bear authoritative *witness*, or testimony, of the historical ministry of Jesus as well as to Jesus' resurrection:[22] "Wherefore of these men which have companied with us all the time that the Lord Jesus went in and out among us, Beginning from the baptism of John, unto that same day that he was taken up from us, must one be ordained to be a witness with us of his resurrection" (Acts 1:21–22).

Eyewitnesses were the foundation upon which the testimony of the life, ministry, atonement, and resurrection of the Lord were to be proclaimed. One *witnessed* first by seeing, and then one *bore witness* by telling the gospel message to all who would listen. The Gospel according to Luke reflects the eyewitness accounts of the companions of Jesus, and Acts reflects the witnessing proclamation of the disciples from Jerusalem to the center of the known world — Rome: "But ye shall receive power, after that the Holy Ghost is come upon you: and ye shall be *witnesses* unto me both in Jerusalem, and in Judea, and in Samaria, and unto the uttermost part of the earth" (Acts 1:8).

A Universal Gospel

Luke was a Gentile. Thus, the question of whether the gospel was limited to Israel or was for all people was important to him personally.

The gospel was for everyone—rich and poor, men and women, Jew and gentile—although some persons might have more trouble hearing and responding to it than others.

From the very beginning of the Gospel of Luke, the reader is made aware of the Lord's concern for women. In the birth narratives, women are clearly the dominant figures. Elisabeth (Luke 1:5–7, 24), Mary (Luke 1:26–56), and Anna (Luke 2:36–38) play prominent roles. Zacharias and Joseph are essentially silent; Simeon is the only male, apart from Jesus himself, who plays any active role—that being to affirm Jesus' identity and mission. It is Mary, not Joseph, who receives Simeon's witness (Luke 2:34). Luke alone among the synoptic[23] writers included the account of the raising to life of the son of the widow of Nain (Luke 7:12–13), the sinful woman's anointing of Jesus (Luke 7:37–50), the identification of some of the women who followed Jesus (Luke 8:1–3), the account of Mary and Martha (Luke 10:38–42),[24] the woman with a spirit of infirmity (Luke 13:11–17), the woman searching for the lost coin (Luke 15:8), the woman and the unjust judge (Luke 18:2–8), Jesus' words to the women on the way to his crucifixion (Luke 23:27–28), and the account of the disciples that the women amazed them with their story of being unable to find Jesus' body (Luke 24:22–24). Clearly, Jesus violated so many Jewish sanctions against association with women that other writers, like Mark and Matthew, may have been hesitant to include all such accounts. But Luke understood that Jesus had opened the heavens to all persons, regardless of sex, and thus he included Jesus' association with persons who were considered inferior to devout Jewish males.

While Matthew focused on Joseph's response to Mary's pregnancy, Joseph's visionary experiences, and the coming of the Magi, Luke chose to stress another element. He knew that people with little or no status in society were the first to hear the message of the Messiah's birth. Thus, we have from his hand the account of the shepherds to whom the heavens were opened (Luke 2:8–20) and who received the glad tidings—men to whom no self-respecting Jewish religious leader would probably have spoken.[25]

Once again, only Luke among the synoptic writers recorded Jesus' announcement in Nazareth that he was appointed to preach good news to the poor, the captives, the blind, and the oppressed (Luke 4:18). Similarly, he gave us the accounts of the centurion who had the sick servant (Luke 7:2–9), the response to John the Baptist's disciples which stressed the healing of the downtrodden and simple folk (Luke 7:22), the parable of the good Samaritan (Luke 10:30–37), the parable of the wedding feast (Luke 14:12–24), the accounts of the lost coin and the prodigal son (Luke 15:8–32), the story of the rich man and Lazarus (Luke 16:29–31), the account of the ten lepers — the only one who returned to thank Jesus being a Samaritan (Luke 17:11–16), the tax collector's prayer in the temple (Luke 18:13–14), the story of Jesus eating with Zacchaeus the tax collector (Luke 19:2–10), and Jesus' words of forgiveness to the thief on the cross (Luke 23:41–43).

Luke knew that Jesus had thrown the door open wide to all, if they would but come to him. None was to be excluded[26] except those who excluded themselves. Often, these were the rich.[27] Jesus warned against treasures on earth, for wealth had a way of corrupting even the best of intentions. Consequently, Luke recorded Jesus' warning against covetousness (Luke 12:15) and against planning without considering God's purposes (Luke 12:20–21). Similarly, Jesus charged the Pharisees with being lovers of money (Luke 16:14–15) and pronounced the parable of the rich man and Lazarus (Luke 16:19–31).

Each of the Gospel writers recognized that Jesus intended the message of the kingdom of God for all persons, not merely for the Jews. Luke, however, emphasized that fact more clearly than the others, because it was central to his presence in the Church. He was a Gentile.

In his account Luke shows that the gospel is not to be limited to Israel: "his mercy is on them that fear him" (Luke 1:50). It is for "those who sit in darkness and in the shadow of death" (Luke 1:79), and it is to bring peace on earth and "good will toward men" (Luke 2:14). More specifically it is for "all people" (Luke 2:10).[28] Simeon actually surprised Mary and Joseph, who already knew that Jesus was the Son of God, when he said, "Lord, now lettest thou thy servant depart in peace, according to thy word: For mine eyes have seen thy salvation, Which thou hast prepared before the face of all people; A light to lighten the *Gentiles*, and the glory of thy people Israel" (Luke 2:29–32). Even Mary and Joseph did not comprehend the scope of Jesus' work or the full graciousness of God, and thus, Luke recorded, "Joseph and his mother marvelled at those things which were spoken of him" (Luke 2:33).

Luke recorded the whole of the Isaiah passage (Isaiah 40:3–5) which John the Baptist quoted including the words, "and *all flesh* shall see the salvation of God" (Luke 3:6). In addition the genealogy in Luke is more universal, for it traces Jesus' lineage not merely to Abraham but to Adam and ultimately to God (Luke 3:38).[29] Jesus created opposition in Nazareth, not merely by claiming that salvation might be present in him but by further implying that the saving gospel would go to the Gentiles because the unrighteous Jews would not receive it. He made this same point by reminding them of Elijah's being sent only to the woman of Sidon and of Elisha's cleansing only Naaman the Syrian (Luke 4:16–30).[30] We also have solely in Luke the account of Jesus healing the centurion's slave (Luke 7:1–10) and the note "that repentance and remission of sins should be preached in his name *among all nations,* beginning at Jerusalem" (Luke 24:47). The universality of the gospel and its special application to the Gentiles is further delineated by the entirety of Acts. There we see the gospel proceed forth to the ends of the earth.

Israel and the Gospel

Where were the roots of the gospel? Luke knew that they were in Israel and the Old Testament, particularly in the words of the prophets. But knowing it was one thing; communicating it to persons who had no knowledge of the Old Testament was another. Explaining the relationship was a fairly simple matter for Matthew, because he was writing to a Jewish-Christian audience which was thoroughly familiar with the Old Testament. All he had to say was, "Now all this was done, that it might be fulfilled which was spoken of the Lord by the prophet, saying . . . " (Matthew 1:22; see also 2:5, 15, 17, 23, etc.). His readers knew exactly what he meant.

But Gentiles, to whom Luke's account is addressed, would not have that scriptural background. Luke's concern was tying the house of Israel and the Church together and showing their congruence and continuity. He does that by drawing attention to a very clear element in Jesus' ministry. To Jesus, Jerusalem and the temple were sacred places. They were also the central places of Judaism. Even Gentiles would know that. They might not know about the Jewish scriptures, but they almost certainly knew about the Jews' sacred city and their sacred temple. Thus, Luke augments his and the Lord's references to the scriptures[31] by stressing the importance that the Father and Jesus placed on Jerusalem and the temple. Luke's Gospel begins in Jerusalem in the temple with Gabriel's appearance to Zacharias (Luke 1:5–20). Jesus is brought to Jerusalem and the temple at the time of Mary's purification (Luke 2:22). Jesus taught in the temple at age twelve (Luke 2:46–49). He cleansed the temple (Luke 19:45–46). He taught in the temple during his last days (Luke 19:47; 20:1; 21:37–38), and his disciples worshiped in the temple (Luke 24:53) even after Pentecost (Acts 2:46–47; 3:1–8; 5:20; 21:26).

Could even gentile readers miss the implication that the Church is rooted in Israel? Could they doubt that Jesus was heralded by Jewish scriptures when it was so clear that the sacred places of Judaism were also sacred to him and his disciples? Luke hoped that this emphasis on Jerusalem and the temple would help the gentile converts appreciate the importance of Israel and the Old Testament in preparing the way for Christ.

Prayer and the Holy Spirit

Luke also provided deep insights into Jesus' spriritual life. We see Jesus constantly at prayer in those moments when major events were about to occur.[32] In those instances where Luke parallels Mark's account, Luke alone added the observation in several instances that Jesus prayed. At Jesus' baptism, the Holy Ghost descended while Jesus *was praying* (Luke 3:21–22). Jesus went to the wilderness to pray (Luke 5:16). The night before he called the Twelve, he withdrew into the hills and prayed the whole night through (Luke 6:12–13). Before he asked the disciples, "Whom say the people that I am?" he prayed (Luke 9:18). He went up the Mount of Transfiguration to pray and while he was praying he was transfigured (Luke 9:28–29). It was the result of Jesus' praying that led the disciples to ask him to teach them to pray (Luke 11:1). He told Peter that he had prayed for him, so that Satan might not have Peter (Luke 22:31–32). And, of course, prayer was central to the experience in Gethsemane. Jesus commanded the disciples to pray, and he prayed in his agony (Luke 22:40–46). It is in Luke alone that we find Jesus' parables about prayer—the parables of borrowing bread at midnight (Luke 11:5–8) and of the widow and the unjust judge (Luke 18:1–8). Thus, prayer was the very lifeline between the Father and the Son. If Christ needed to pray, how much more do we need prayer.

In addition to teaching the power of prayer, Luke also highlighted the role of the Holy Ghost in the life of Jesus. Throughout the birth narrative in Luke we see the constant work of the Holy Ghost. John was filled with the Holy Ghost, even in his mother's womb (Luke 1:15).

The Holy Ghost would "come upon" Mary (Luke 1:35). Elisabeth was filled with the Holy Ghost when Mary came to her (Luke 1:41). Zacharias, John the Baptist's father, was filled with the Holy Ghost and prophesied of Christ (Luke 1:67). Simeon was guided and spoke by the Holy Ghost as he likewise testified of the arrival of the Lord's salvation (Luke 2:25–27, 30). As with the use of prayer in Jesus' life, Luke makes it clearer than does Mark that it was the *Holy* Ghost which descended on Jesus at the baptism (Luke 3:22). By the power of the Spirit Jesus was led into the wilderness for forty days and in the power of the Spirit he returned to Galilee (Luke 4:1,14). Only in Luke is the passage from Isaiah 61:1 quoted: "The Spirit of the Lord is upon me, because he has anointed me to preach the gospel to the poor" (Luke 4:18). The Holy Ghost would teach and comfort him in times of need and give additional power to his divine ministry (see Luke 12:12; also JST John 3:34). The Prophet Joseph Smith confirmed this unique contribution of Luke when he taught that Jesus had greater power than any man because he was the Son of God and had "the fullness of the Spirit."[33] Jesus rejoiced in the power of the Holy Ghost (Luke 10:21). Luke also records that Christ taught that it was the Holy Ghost who would teach in time of need (Luke 4:14) and that the Father will give the Holy Ghost to those who seek him (Luke 11:13).[34]

Thus the Gospel of Luke not only testifies of the role of the Holy Ghost in helping the Savior fulfill his mission but also points to the role of the Holy Ghost in leading and strengthening the Church. This significant theme begun in his Gospel received even greater emphasis by Luke in the book of Acts, where we read of the great new mission fields of the Church being blessed by the coming of the Holy Ghost (Acts 2:4; 8:17; 10:44; 19:6).[35]

CONCLUSIONS

Through the eyes of Mark and Luke, we see the man Jesus, but we see aspects of his life and ministry that would have been lost to us without both Gospels. From Mark we learn that the disciples did not always understand the significance of Jesus and his work. They were initially attracted by the miracles and compassion of Jesus, but only after his atonement and resurrection did they fully understand that Jesus' messiahship involved suffering and that his disciples might well be called to walk in his footsteps, as many did. It was a poignant and timely message which the disciples in Rome, in their days of persecution, needed to hear.

Mark reminds us that the Christian will never be completely at ease in the world today either. Like the blind man, only when people receive the healing clarity of vision will they understand that Jesus' suffering messiahship is inextricably bound to their own suffering discipleship.

From Luke's Gospel we learn that the gospel is for every person, be they Jew, Gentile, slave, free, man, woman, shepherd, or king. Nobody is left out. Israel continues to be special in its relationship to God, but the Church reaches beyond Israel to the Gentiles and others who had for a time been outside the pale of God's chosen, or elect, people. We also learn that the gospel is built upon the eyewitness reports of people who saw all that Jesus did and heard all that he said. Thus, they could become true witnesses for him—people who could tell what they have experienced and know. And finally, Luke teaches us through Jesus' example about the essential nature of prayer and the critical role of the Holy Ghost.

What beauty would have been lost, had either Mark or Luke been left out of the canon! They, in conjunction with Matthew and John, enable us to have a more complete picture of our Lord and of his mission than would have been available had their Gospels been omitted. A diamond truly sparkles when all its facets can be seen, and thus it is with Jesus Christ, the Lord of the Gospels.

NOTES

1. Bruce R. McConkie, *Doctrinal New Testament Commentary* (Salt Lake City, Utah: Bookcraft, 1987), 1:69.

2. For a general treatment of the place of women in Jesus' day see Joachim Jeremias, *Jerusalem in the Time of Jesus* (Philadelphia: Fortress Press, 1969), pp. 359–76. More specifically, women were essentially to be invisible in public (M. Ab. i.5) and exempt from study of the Torah (Jeremias, p. 373). According to R. Eliezer (c. 90 A.D.) women were not to be given a knowledge of the Torah, stating "If any man gives his daughter a knowledge of the Law it is as though he taught her lechery" (M. Sot. iii.4). Jeremias makes the summary statement, "We have therefore the impression that Judaism in Jesus' time also had a very low opinion of women, which is usual in the Orient where she is chiefly valued for her fecundity, kept as far as possible shut away from the outer world, submissive to the power of her father or her husband, and where she is inferior to men from a religious

point of view" (p. 375). Citations of the Mishnah are from Herbert Danby, *The Mishnah* (London: Oxford University Press, 1967).

3. Latter-day Saints should understand this discussion well. Four accounts of Joseph Smith's first vision are in existence, but they differ in their content, in the main because Joseph related different aspects of the vision to differing people dependent upon their ability to perceive and understand.

4. Vincent Taylor, *The Gospel According to St. Mark*, 2d ed. (New York: St. Martin's Press, 1966), pp. 1–2. Taylor here recounts the tradition received from Papias, Bishop of Hierapolis (c. 140 A.D.) that Mark recorded what he had learned from Peter, although not completely in order.

5. Joseph A. Fitzmyer, *The Gospel According to Luke (I-IX)* (Garden City, N.Y.: Doubleday, 1983), pp. 14–18. *The Gospel of Luke*, ed. E. Earle Ellis (London: Thomas Nelson & Sons Ltd., 1966), pp. 4–9. McConkie, *Doctrinal New Testament Commentary*, 1:69–70.

6. G. B. Caird, *Saint Luke* (Philadelphia: The Westminster Press, 1963), pp. 13–14.

7. As Fitzmyer points out (*Gospel According to Luke*, pp. 53–57) the exact place of composition cannot be determined.

8. In Colossians 4:10–11 Paul lists Aristarchus, Mark, and Jesus called Justus as sending greetings to the Colossians. He then says, "These are the only men *of the circumcision* among my fellow workers for the kingdom of God, and they have been a comfort to me" (RSV). Next, he lists those *not of the circumcision* who also send greetings, i.e., Epaphras, *Luke*, and Demas. Clearly, Luke must be a gentile, if in fact this Luke is the author of the Gospel of Luke.

9. Fitzmyer, *Gospel According to Luke*, pp. 47–51.

10. Robert A. Spivey and D. Moody Smith, Jr., *Anatomy of the New Testament: A Guide to Its Structure and Meaning*, 2d ed. (New York: Macmillan, 1974), p. 99.

11. Ibid., p. 88.

12. Ibid., pp. 91–92.

13. Taylor, *Gospel According to St. Mark*, p. 123. See also Spivey and Smith, *Anatomy of the New Testament*, p. 101.

14. Taylor, *Gospel According to St. Mark*, pp. 124–25. See also Edward J. Mally, "The Gospel According to Mark," *Jerome Biblical Commentary* (Englewood Cliffs, N.J.: Prentice-Hall, 1968), 2:22.

15. Spivey and Smith, *Anatomy of the New Testament*, p. 98.

16. McConkie, *Doctrinal New Testament Commentary*, 1:391.

17. F. V. Filson, "Peter," *The Interpreter's Dictionary of the Bible* (Nashville, Tenn.: Abingdon Press, 1962), 3:755. Eusebius quotes Origen on this point (Euseb. Hist. III.1.2).

18. Richard Lloyd Anderson, *Understanding Paul* (Salt Lake City, Utah: Deseret Book Co., 1983), p. 362. The tradition is recorded in Tertullian, *Scorpiace* 15 (Ante-Nicene Fathers).

19. McConkie, *Doctrinal New Testament Commentary*, 1:69–70. It should be noted here that Luke could not have interviewed all persons who were eyewit-

nesses. He had to depend for some of his information on persons who conveyed accurately the earlier traditions, i.e., "the ministers of the word."

20. Spivey and Smith, *Anatomy of the New Testament,* p. 155.

21. Ibid., p. 167.

22. Ibid., p. 175.

23. The word *synoptic* basically means to see from a similar viewpoint. As one reads Matthew, Mark, and Luke the portrait of Jesus has many similarities. Hence the name "synoptic."

24. Spivey and Smith, *Anatomy of the New Testament,* p. 167.

25. Carroll Stuhlmueller, "The Gospel According to Luke," *Jerome Biblical Commentary* (Englewood Cliffs, N.J.: Prentice-Hall, 1968), 2:117.

26. G. W. H. Lampe, "Luke," *Peake's Commentary on the Bible* (London: Thomas Nelson Ltd., 1962), p. 820.

27. Stuhlmueller, "The Gospel According to Luke," 2:117.

28. McConkie, *Doctrinal New Testament Commentary,* 1:97; Ellis, *The Gospel of Luke,* p. 19.

29. Stuhlmueller, "The Gospel According to Luke," 2:117.

30. Spivey and Smith, *Anatomy of the New Testament,* p. 163.

31. Caird, *Saint Luke,* p. 134. John Martin Creed, *The Gospel According to St. Luke* (New York: St. Martin's Press, 1969), lxxiii.

32. Caird, *Saint Luke,* p. 36.

33. Joseph Smith, *Teachings of the Prophet Joseph Smith,* sel. Joseph Fielding Smith (Salt Lake City: Deseret Book Co, 1976), p. 188.

34. Fitzmyer, *Gospel According to Luke,* pp. 228–30.

35. Fitzmyer, *Gospel According to Luke,* p. 231. To Latter-day Saints, Fitzmyer's comment on the relation between the Holy Ghost and the Twelve is of interest. Fitzmyer is Catholic. "Moreover, it becomes plain in Acts that the Spirit is given only when the Twelve are present or a member of delegate of the Twelve is on community. The reconstitution of the Twelve (1:15–26) is the necessary preparation for the outpouring of the Spirit (2:1–4). This also explains why, though Philip (not one of the Twelve, but one of the Seven appointed to serve tables [6:2–6]) evangelizes Samaria and baptizes there (8:5–13), Peter and John have to be sent before the people in Samaria receive the Spirit (8:17). Similarly, it is only when Paul, indirectly a delegate of the Twelve (see 11:22, 25–26; 13:2–4), arrives in Ephesus that 'some disciple' (i.e. neophyte Christians) are baptized in the name of the Lord Jesus and receive the Spirit through the laying on of Paul's hands (19:1–6)."

CHAPTER EIGHT

Truly All Things Testify of Him

Robert England Lee
CES Curriculum Writer

Three days after his crucifixion, the resurrected Savior walked along the road to Emmaus with two disciples. The Lord listened to these disciples who, not recognizing the Master, described the events surrounding his crucifixion and burial. He heard the hopelessness in their words when they declared, "We trusted that it had been he which should have redeemed Israel" (Luke 24:21). The immortal Messiah listened as the disciples recited details about the empty tomb and angels and witnesses. Yet, because those they trusted most had not seen him, their hearts were slow to believe (see vv. 22–25). The Lord rebuked those disciples; he called them fools. Then, "beginning at Moses and all the prophets, he expounded unto them in all the scriptures the things concerning himself" (v. 27).

Luke's account does not say the Lord changed the scripture text. It says he "expounded" on that which was already there. Moreover, his disciples witnessed to each other that their hearts burned "while he talked with [them] . . . and while he opened to [them] the scriptures" (v. 32). Later, Jesus appeared to these same disciples in the presence of the eleven apostles. He showed them his hands and his feet and invited them to handle his body, that they might witness that he had risen from the dead. He ate a piece of broiled fish and some honey. Then he opened "their understanding, that they might understand the scriptures" (v. 45).

The Lord taught his disciples to look upon the contents of the scriptures and see things "concerning himself." In the standard works, the Lord has provided us with examples that help us see a pattern in the way he reveals himself. First we will look briefly at how the Lord was revealed in the Old Testament. We will see him revealed through obvious, intended symbolism, and we will also see him revealed in unusual ways. Then we will apply what we learn to our reading of the New Testament.

In Joseph Smith's translation of Genesis 4, we read that after Adam was driven out of the Garden of Eden, an angel appeared to him and explained that sacrificing animals, as prescribed by the Lord, was symbolic. The angel said such sacrifices were "a similitude of the sacrifice of the Only Begotten of the Father, which is full of grace and truth" (JST Genesis 4:7; Moses 5:7). Later, the Holy Ghost "fell upon Adam" and explained that God would offer his Only Begotten Son as a sacrifice for the sins of the world, including Adam's transgression, and that all who believed in the Son and repented of their sins would be redeemed by that sacrifice (see Moses 5:9, 14–15; JST Genesis 4:9; 5:1–2).

Similar symbolic sacrifices abound in the law of Moses. Book of Mormon people, living in the first century before Christ, viewed the law of Moses as a "type of [Christ's] coming" and believed that the outward performances of the law should be kept "until the time that [Christ] should be revealed unto them" (Alma 25:15). They did not believe salvation came through obedience to the law of Moses, "but the law . . . did serve to strengthen their faith in Christ; and thus they did retain a hope through faith, unto eternal salvation" (v. 16). Amulek boldly declared that "every whit" of the law of Moses pointed in the direction of "that great and last sacrifice" (Alma 34:14).

Literal events described in the scriptures are also similitudes of Christ. For example, in Numbers, the fourth book of Moses, we read that the children of Israel were bitten by flying serpents whose venom was deadly. The Lord commanded Moses to make a serpent of brass and place it on a pole so that the Israelites might look to it and live (see Numbers 21:4–9). Alma explained that this event contained a type, or a symbolic message, about Christ (Alma 33:19). He taught us about the brass serpent event by drawing from the testimonies of Zenos and Zenock, two Old Testament prophets whose writings are not in our present Bible. Alma tells us that the declaration of Zenos that God's judgment was taken away because of Christ is typified by Moses' raising a brass serpent on a pole "that whosoever would look upon it might live" (v. 19), or be healed from the deadly bites they had received. Alma further teaches us that Zenock's pronouncement that people would have no desire to understand the mercies God had given them through Christ, is typified by those who "would not look" at the brass serpent "because they did not believe that it would heal them" (v. 20). During his mortal ministry the Savior made figurative use of this same literal event to explain the necessity of the Atonement: "As Moses lifted up the serpent in the wilderness, even so must the Son of man be lifted up: That whosoever believeth in him should not perish, but have eternal life" (John 3:14–15).

Another example of a literal event as a similitude of Christ is Abraham's sacrifice of Isaac. The Apostle Paul wrote that Abraham, as a sign of faith, offered "his only begotten son" (Hebrews 11:17). Paul thereby helped us see that the literal sacrifice offered by Abraham could be understood figuratively as a type of Christ, God's Only Begotten Son. Jacob, the brother of Nephi, straightforwardly declared that Abraham's "offering up his son Isaac . . . [was] a similitude of God and his Only Begotten Son" (Jacob 4:5).

People from Book of Mormon days to the present have understood Abraham's sacrifice of Isaac and Moses' brass serpent on a pole to be great foreshadowings of the Atonement. Consider how our attitude toward these events might change if we did not understand them as similitudes pointing to Christ. How would we view these events? What would we think of a God who dealt with his people in this manner? Yet, because our eyes have been opened, our faith in Christ is strengthened as we read these events. Furthermore, with opened eyes, we may in some measure feel the same burning of the heart felt by the disciples along the road to Emmaus as Christ "expounded unto them in all the scriptures the things concerning himself" (Luke 24:27).

Moses descended Mount Sinai twice with the law of the Lord in his hands. The first descent ended with Moses destroying the tablets of stone upon which the law was written (see Exodus 32:19). On the second descent Moses came "with the two tables of testimony in [his] hand," but he did not realize "that the skin of his face shone while [the Lord] talked with him" (Exodus 34:29). The rulers of Israel were afraid to approach Moses because of his appearance. He therefore "put a vail on his face" until he had finished speaking with them (v. 33). When Moses entered the tabernacle to speak with the Lord, "he took the vail off" (v. 34).

Fifteen hundred years later the Apostle Paul lamented that the Israelites of his day could not see the glory of the gospel of Christ because a "vail [was] upon their heart" when they read the books of Moses (2 Corinthians 3:15). He said that the veil that blinded their minds in the days of Moses "until this day remaineth . . . untaken away in the reading of the old testament" (v. 14). Nevertheless, he gave the children of Israel a solution to that problem: "When [their heart] shall turn to the Lord," he said, "the vail shall be taken away" (v. 16).

With the veil taken away, we see that every whit of Moses' writings contains a witness of the Savior. For example, Paul explained that the very creation of the world, recorded by Moses, was in similitude of the Son of God. Referring to the first day of the Creation, he said, "God, who commanded the light to shine out of darkness, hath shined in our hearts, to give the light of the knowledge of the glory of God in the face of Jesus Christ" (2 Corinthians 4:6).

As we have seen in the Old Testament, both events that are symbolic and events that are literal point us to Christ when our understanding is opened and the veil is removed from off our hearts and minds. Thus prepared, we can also see events recorded in the New Testament as being in similitude of Christ.

When Jesus ate the Passover meal with his disciples, "he took bread, and gave thanks, and brake it, and gave [it] unto them, saying, This is my body which is given for you: this do in remembrance of me" (Luke 22:19). Then "he took the cup, and when he had given thanks, he gave it to them: and they all drank of it. And he said unto them, This is my blood of the new testament, which is shed for many" (Mark 14:23–24). When Christ thus instituted the sacrament of the Lord's Supper, he established the symbolic manner by which his followers would remember him, just as he had established that burnt offerings and sacrifices would be the symbol by which his followers would look forward to him. By this action he also established that symbolism would continue to be part of the worship experience of the true believer.

JESUS CASTS OUT A LEGION OF DEVILS

Another literal event recorded in the New Testament that was in similitude of Christ is the miracle of casting out a legion of devils, which occurred either in Gadara (see Mark 51–13; Luke 8:26–33) or Gergesa (see Matthew 8:28–32). Jesus and his disciples arrived by ship, having endured a near-fatal trip on the sea. In the midst of a great tempest, they were saved by the Master, who rebuked the wind and commanded the sea, "Peace, be still" (Mark 4:39; Luke 8:24; Matthew 8:26), and all was calm.

All was not calm at the place where they landed. A man was terrorizing the community. He lived among the tombs and was so fierce that none dared to go near him. He had no real home and no clothing. Men from the community tried to bind him, using fetters and chains, but he could not be bound. He was controlled by devils, many of them, who drove him from place to place (see Mark 5:1–10; Luke 8:26–29; Matthew 8:28–29).

When Jesus arrived in the town, the possessed man ran to meet the Savior and worshiped him. The devils who possessed the man pleaded with Christ that he not torment them by casting them into the deep. Jesus sent them into a herd of swine, which then plunged into the deep, taking the devils with them. When the townspeople saw the fierce man again, he was calm and clothed and "in his right mind" (Mark 5:15; Luke 8:35).

How may we discover a similitude of Christ in this scriptural event? One way is to ask ourselves questions about the parts of each event, compare them with other scriptural events, and draw parallels between them. In this case we may ask, for example, who dwells among the tombs, is "exceeding fierce" (Matthew 8:28), cries, cuts himself with stones (see Mark 5:5), and wears no clothing (see Luke 8:27) but who, through Christ, becomes "clothed, and in his right mind"? (Mark 5:15).

Jacob, the brother of Nephi, explained that each of us is in the grasp of the "awful monster; yea, that monster, death and hell" (2 Nephi 9:10). The possessed man in the New Testament story thus personifies us as we would be if there had been no atonement. Jacob said that without the Atonement we would be subject to the devil (see 2 Nephi 9:8), just as the possessed man was "driven of the devil" (Luke 8:29). Jacob taught that we would be in eternal misery like unto the devil (see 2 Nephi 9:9), just as the possessed man was "always . . . crying, and cutting himself with stones" (Mark 5:5). Lehi declared that only through the "merits, and mercy, and grace of the Holy Messiah" can we dwell in the presence of God (2 Nephi 2:8). The power of man cannot overcome the awful monster death and hell. Of the possessed man Mark said, "No *man* could bind him. . . . neither could any *man* tame him" (Mark 5:3– 4; emphasis added).

Mark said that when the possessed man "saw Jesus afar off, he ran and worshipped him" (v. 6). It is as if the devils who possessed the man had brought him to stand before Christ. Jacob said, "Death and hell must deliver up . . . its captive spirits, and the grave must deliver up its captive bodies, and the bodies and the spirits of men will be restored one to the other" (2 Nephi 9:12); then "they must appear before the judgment seat of the Holy One of Israel" (v. 15).

Remember that Luke said the possessed man wore no clothes (see Luke 8:27). Jacob states that after we are delivered up, "our knowledge shall be perfect. Wherefore, we shall have a perfect knowledge of all our guilt, and our uncleanness, and our *nakedness*" (2 Nephi 9:13–14; emphasis added).

In the possessed man we see ourselves standing before God without an atoning Savior. We see our eternal torment and our eternal misery; we see ourselves in the eternal grasp of the awful monster death and hell; we have a perfect knowledge of our guilt and our utter nakedness before God. And, if the veil has been taken from our hearts, we understand what our condition would be without the Atonement, and we join with Jacob and say, "O the wisdom of God, his mercy and grace! . . . O how great the goodness of our God, who prepareth a way for our escape from the grasp of this awful monster. . . . O how great the plan of our God" (2 Nephi 9:8, 10, 13).

Near the possessed man was a "herd of many swine feeding on the mountain" (Luke 8:32). The devils who possessed the man requested to be sent into this herd, rather than into the deep (see vv. 31–32). Swine appear in important teaching moments throughout scripture. During his mortal ministry the Lord exhorted his disciples not to cast their pearls before swine (see Matthew 7:6). He repeated this same injunction to the righteous Nephites (see 3 Nephi 14:6) and again to the elders of the Church in 1831 (see D&C 41:6). Mormon likened the wicked Nephites to swine when he said, "The more part of the people had turned from their righteousness, . . . like the sow to her wallowing in the mire" (3 Nephi 7:8). In the law of Moses, swine were among those animals labeled "unclean" (see Leviticus 11:7).

It was to the swine, which typify unrighteousness, that the devils asked to be sent. In so doing they appear to have believed that they could escape the inevitable consequence that awaited them. What was that consequence? It was that they would be tormented and cast "into the deep" (Luke 8:31); or, in other words, into the nearby Sea of Galilee.

Jaocb taught that the wicked, those made unclean or filthy by sin, "shall be filthy still" when they stand before God to be judged. "Wherefore, they who are filthy are the devil and his angels; and they shall go away into everlasting fire, prepared for them; and their torment is as a *lake* of fire and brimstone, whose flame ascendeth up forever and ever and has no end" (2 Nephi 9:16; emphasis added).

After the devils were cast out of the possessed man, we see him "sitting at the feet of Jesus, *clothed*, and in his right mind" (Luke 8:35; emphasis added). With the devils removed from him, he is no longer the personification of those in the grasp of the awful monster death and hell. He has become the personification of those who are made clean through the atonement of Christ. This man might be said to personify those who have believed in the Holy One of Israel, endured the crosses of the world, repented, and were baptized in his name, having perfect faith in the Holy One of Israel. He is the personification of those who are restored to that God who gave them breath (see 2 Nephi 9:18, 23, 26). These, Jacob said, "have a perfect knowledge of their enjoyment, and their righteousness, being *clothed* with purity, yea, even with the *robe* of righteousness" (v. 14; emphasis added).

As we come to understand that only through the Atonement may we wear the robes of righteousness spoken of, we may feel impressed to join with Jacob in saying, "O the greatness of the mercy of our God, the Holy One of Israel! For he delivereth his saints from that awful monster the devil, and death, and hell, and that lake of fire and brimstone, which is endless torment. O how great the holiness of our God" (vv. 19–20).

JESUS WALKS ON THE WATER

Before he walked on the Sea of Galilee, the Savior fed bread and fish to a large multitude. After his miraculous walk, he delivered what has come to be called the Bread of Life Sermon. We will look at the bread miracle and the bread sermon in an effort to establish the context for Christ's walking on the water, which was a type of his atonement.

A great multitude (five thousand men, plus women and children) gathered about Jesus and his disciples in "a desert place belonging to the city called Bethsaida" (Luke 9:10). Mark described these people as "sheep not having a shepherd" (Mark 6:34). Jesus had compassion on this shepherdless flock. He spoke to them about the kingdom of God, and he healed their sick (see Luke 9:11).

When evening came the apostles wanted to send the people away so that they might buy food, but Jesus told them to feed the multitude. The Twelve protested that it would require "two hundred pennyworth of bread" (Mark 6:37), and they had only five loaves of bread and two fish. In other words, they could not do what he had requested of them. Jesus said, "Bring them hither to me" (Matthew 14:18).

Jesus commanded the apostles to "make all sit down by companies upon the green grass. And they sat down in ranks, by hundreds, and by fifties" (Mark 6:39–40). Then Jesus blessed and broke the bread and fish and gave the morsels to the Twelve, instructing them to give the food to the multitude. "And they did all eat, and were filled" (Matthew 14:20). Then the Lord commanded the apostles to "gather up the fragments that remain, that nothing be lost. Therefore they gathered them together, and filled twelve baskets with the fragments" (John 6:12–13).

The next day Jesus explained the significance of this event. He acknowledged that people were still following him because he had fed them and filled them the day before. Then he compared himself to the bread which came from heaven in the time of Moses. Said he, "The bread of God is he which cometh down from heaven, and giveth life unto the world" (v. 33); "I am that bread of life" (v. 48); "the bread that I will give is my flesh, which I will give for the life of the world" (v. 51).

With these words Christ helps us see the bread given to the multitude as a type of his atoning sacrifice. That sacrifice could not be provided by any of the Twelve Apostles or any other person. Only Christ could offer an infinite sacrifice for the sins of the world. Yet, the apostles could organize the people to receive the blessings of the Atonement and make those blessings available to mankind, even as they organized the multitude to receive the bread and fish from the Lord.

Only a few days before the miracle of the loaves and fishes, the Lord had called the Twelve together and given them power to cast out unclean spirits and heal all types of sickness and disease. Furthermore, he commanded that they should go to the lost sheep of the house of Israel and preach. They went out as they had been assigned, "preaching the gospel, and healing every where" (Luke 9:6). As the morsels of bread and fish had come from Christ, so too had the power to preach and heal come from him. And, as the Galilean sheep without a shepherd had been filled with bread and fish, so too were the lost sheep of the house of Israel filled with the gospel. In this manner Christ fulfilled his promise that "all they that do hunger and thirst after righteousness, . . . shall be filled with the Holy Ghost" (JST Matt. 5:8), even as all who partook of the bread and fish had been filled.

When Christ visited the "great world of the spirits of the dead" (D&C 138:57), he organized the righteous spirits and "appointed messengers, clothed with power and authority, and commissioned them to go forth and carry the light of the gospel to them that were in darkness, even to all the spirits of men" (v. 30). These messengers carried the light, but they were not its source. They carried the light, as the apostles carried the bread and fish to the multitude.

Speaking to the Twelve in this generation, the Lord said, "You are they who are ordained of me to ordain priests and teachers; to declare my gospel, according to the power of the Holy Ghost which is in you" (D&C 18:32). The Lord also revealed that the Twelve were called to be special witnesses of Christ in all the world (see D&C 107:23), "to officiate in the name of the Lord" (v. 33), to build up and regulate the affairs of the Church in all nations (see v. 33), and to "ordain and set in order all the . . . officers of the church" (v. 58).

Later, the Lord, through Brigham Young, said, "Let all the people of the Church of Jesus Christ of Latter-day Saints, and those who journey with them, be organized into companies, with a covenant and promise to keep all the commandments and statutes of the Lord our God. Let the companies be organized with captains of hundreds, captains of fifties, and captains of tens, with a president and his two counselors at their head, under the direction of the Twelve Apostles. And this shall be our covenant—that we will walk in all the ordinances of the Lord" (D&C 136:2–4).

In these examples the Lord gave his appointed messengers authority to organize his people and take the Master's power, ordinances, commandments, and statutes to those they had organized. That which the Twelve did in feeding the five thousand was a type of the mission of the apostles in former times, and that same mission continues in these latter days.

After feeding the five thousand, the Lord commanded that all the fragments be gathered "that nothing be lost" (John 6:12). In the Bread of Life Sermon he spoke of things that should not be lost. The Lord said it was the will of the Father that Christ should "lose nothing" that the Father had given him (v. 39). Who are those given by the Father to the Son? The Lord explained that they are those who hear the voice of the Father and are taught by him (see v. 45). They are drawn by the Father to the Son and come unto Christ (see vv. 44– 45). They eat the flesh and drink the blood of Christ (see v. 54). Therefore, they will be lifted up "in the resurrection of the just at the last day" (JST, John 6:40). They are as Peter the Apostle, who knew that Jesus was the Christ, the Son of the living God, not because flesh and blood had revealed it to him but because it had been revealed to him by the Father (see Matthew 16:16–17).

Those who shall be saved are typified by the fragments of bread and fish the apostles carried in baskets back to the Lord. These fragments may represent the children of Israel, the twelve tribes of Israel, the covenant people of the Lord, those who inherit the blessings of the house of Jacob. They are those, whether Gentile or Jew, who repent and believe in the Son of God (see 2 Nephi 30:2). And they are brought to Christ by the Twelve Apostles. In the beginning of this dispensation, the Lord said to the Twelve, "By *your hands* I will work a marvelous work among the children of men, unto the convincing of many of their sins, that they may come unto repentance, and that they may come unto the kingdom of my Father" (D&C 18:44; emphasis added).

After the multitude was filled and the fragments gathered, the Lord urged the Twelve to "get into a ship, and to go before him unto the other side, while he sent the multitudes away" (Matthew 14:22). Then Jesus went to a mountain to pray. In the evening he was alone on the land and "the ship was in the midst of the sea" (Mark 6:47). As the sky darkened the Twelve were tossed about upon the waves of the sea (see Matthew 14:24). The wind was blowing against them as they toiled to row the ship. They continued in this toil all during the night.

What would it be like to row all night, being tossed by the waves and the wind, making no progress? Can we feel the pain in our hands, stomach, thighs, shoulders, and back? Can we feel the beating of the waves against our bodies? Can we see the blackness of the night? If we sense these things, we may have a deeper appreciation for what Alma called the "endless night of darkness" (Alma 41:7). In those words Alma described the condition of souls who had not repented, which would be the condition of all souls if there had been no atonement and repentance were not possible. The ship on the sea may be seen as a type of the endless condition of all mankind if there were no Redeemer. Furthermore, it is a type of the long night of apostasy. It is the time, seen by Nephi, when the multitudes of the earth "were gathered together to fight against the apostles of the Lamb. . . . yea, behold the house of Israel hath gathered together to fight against the twelve apostles of the Lamb" (1 Nephi 11:34–35).

In 4 Nephi we read what happened to the Nephite apostles during an equivalent period of apostasy in the New World. They were cast into prison (see 4 Nephi 1:30); people sought to kill them (see v. 31). They were cast into "furnaces of fire" (v. 32) and into "dens of wild beasts" (v. 33). The general wickedness of the people increased until "there were none that were righteous save it were the disciples of Jesus" (v. 46). Mormon said that the wicked Nephites were "without Christ and God in the world" (Mormon 5:16). They were "led about by Satan, even as chaff is driven before the wind, or as a vessel is tossed about upon the waves, without sail or anchor, or without anything wherewith to steer her" (v. 18). They were as the people described by Paul, who were "tossed to and fro, and carried about by every wind of doctrine, by the sleight of men, and [by] cunning craftiness" (Ephesians 4:14).

Both situations typified by the ship on the sea — the endless night of darkness if there were no Redeemer, and the persecution of Christ's disciples and the general wickedness of the covenant people during the long night of apostasy — were dramatically altered through the direct intervention of the Lord Jesus.

Alma explained that all will not be consigned to an endless night of darkness, for "mercy claimeth the penitent, and mercy cometh because of the atonement; and the atonement bringeth to pass the resurrection of the dead; and the resurrection of the dead bringeth back men into the presence of God" (Alma 42:23).

Ammon said: "We have reason to praise him forever, for he is the Most High God, and has loosed our brethren from the chains of hell. Yea, they were encircled about with everlasting darkness and destruction [as the men in the ship were surrounded by darkness and raging water]; but behold, he has brought them into his everlasting light, yea, into everlasting salvation [which happened when Christ, the light and the life of the world, entered the ship]; and they are encircled about by the matchless bounty of his love [which is typified by the calm which came upon the sea when he entered the boat]; . . . Therefore," said Ammon, "let us glory" (Alma 26:14–16).

When Christ appeared near the ship, Peter wanted to go to the Savior by walking on the water. Christ invited him to do so. "And when Peter was come down out of the ship, he walked on the water, to go to Jesus" (Matthew 14:29). During that brief moment Peter became the type of all who are striving to come to Christ. Said Christ of these people, "No man can come to me, except the Father which hath sent me draw him: and I will raise him up at the last day" (John 6:44). "Every one which seeth the Son, and believeth on him, may have everlasting life: and I will raise him up at the last day" (v. 40).

Yet, when Peter walked toward the Son of God, he began to sink. Had he not seen the Savior and believed in him? Was he not coming to Christ? Why then did he sink? Matthew explains it this way: "When he saw the wind boisterous, he was afraid" (Matthew 14:30). Peter became distracted by the boisterous wind. His eyes were no longer single to (or focused on) the glory of God, and he wavered.

The Apostle James said, "He that wavereth is like a wave of the sea driven with the wind and tossed" (James 1:6). And, like all those who waver, Peter began to sink into the tempestuous sea. As we hear Peter cry out, "Lord, save me" (Matthew 14:30), we simultaneously hear Alma the Younger crying out, "O Jesus, thou Son of God, have mercy on me, who am in the gall of bitterness, and am encircled about by the everlasting chains of death" (Alma 36:18). That is the cry of all those who awaken to the realization that they are "without God in the world" (Alma 41:11).

Nephi found himself in a position similar to Peter's. Because of the afflictions he had suffered, he lingered in the valley of sorrow, his strength was slackened, and his heart wept (see 2 Nephi 4:26). Nevertheless, he began to awaken to his condition and asked,

"Why should I yield to sin, because of my flesh? Yea, why should I give way to temptations, that the evil one have place in my heart to destroy my peace and afflict my soul? . . . Awake, my soul! No longer droop in sin. Rejoice, O my heart, and give place no more for the enemy of my soul. . . . O Lord, wilt thou redeem my soul? Wilt thou deliver me out of the hands of mine enemies? Wilt thou make me that I may shake at the appearance of sin? May the gates of hell be shut continually before me, because that my heart is broken and my spirit is contrite! . . . O Lord, I have trusted in thee, and I will trust in thee forever. I will not put my trust in the arm of flesh. . . . I will cry unto thee, my God, the rock of my righteousness. Behold, my voice shall forever ascend up unto thee, my rock and mine everlasting God" (vv. 27–28, 31–32, 34–35).

The Lord heard Nephi's prayer and the prayer of Alma the Younger, just as he heard Peter's cry and immediately "stretched forth his hand, and caught him" (Matthew 14:31). What would it have been like to be Peter at that moment? What would it be like to know that we were powerless to deliver ourselves from the sea? Can we feel our hearts breaking and the contrition of our spirits as our arm stretches up in hope and our voice cries out, "Save me, Lord"? Can we feel the power in the outstretched hand of the Son of God as he grasps our own feeble arm and pulls us from the deep? If we can feel these things, we can begin to appreciate the meaning of the atonement of Christ in our lives, for without him we too are powerless to be delivered from the night of endless darkness. The difference between being without Christ in the world and having him as our companion is illustrated by Mark when he said, "And he went up unto them into the ship; and the wind ceased" (Mark 6:51).

The ship contained the apostles, those who had been commissioned to administer the affairs of the Church. Christ was now at the helm. In this scene we see a type of the Restoration, that event which began through the miraculous intervention of God himself when he and his Beloved Son appeared to the boy Joseph Smith. The Lord, through the prophet Isaiah, described what that restoration would be like: "O thou afflicted, tossed with tempest, and not comforted, behold. . . . all thy children shall be taught of the Lord; and great shall be the peace of thy children" (Isaiah 54:11, 13).

With the waters calm, the ship was able to proceed on its course. As the sun rose, the ship landed at Gennesaret (see Mark 6:53). The people recognized Christ and "ran through that whole region round about" and brought their sick to him (v. 55). "And whithersoever he entered, into villages, or cities, or country, they laid the sick in the streets, and [the sick] besought him that they might touch if it were but the border of his garment: and as many as touched him were made whole" (v. 56).

We see in this event the dawning of a brighter day, the day of restoration. And all who knew of Christ's power brought their family and friends into his path to be healed, even as we in this generation seek to do all in our power to bring souls to Christ.

These stories from the New Testament represent a small fraction of the similitudes waiting to be discovered and pondered. To search for and discover types of Christ in the New Testament is to open a wellspring of new thoughts and emotions relative to the Atonement.

As we read the Gospels, may we see the events of the life of Christ as a type of his atonement and his glorious second coming, that thereby we may retain a hope of eternal salvation through faith in Jesus Christ (see Alma 25:16). For, as Nephi said, "All things which have been given of God from the beginning of the world . . . are the typifying of him" (2 Nephi 11:4).

CHAPTER NINE

"Wilt Thou Be Made Whole?" Medicine and Healing in the Time of Jesus

Ann N. Madsen

Brigham Young University

"Now there is at Jerusalem by the sheep market a pool, which is called in the Hebrew tongue Bethesda, having five porches. In these lay a great multitude of impotent folk, of blind, halt, withered, waiting for the moving of the water. . . . whosoever then first after the troubling of the water stepped in was made whole of whatsoever disease he had. And a certain man was there, which had an infirmity thirty and eight years. When Jesus saw him lie, and knew that he had been now a long time in that case, he saith unto him, Wilt thou be made whole? . . . [he answered that he couldn't get to the water.] Jesus saith unto him, Rise, take up thy bed and walk. And immediately the man was made whole, and took up his bed and walked" (John 5:2–9).

Sick people had flocked to the pool of Bethesda[1] for centuries to be healed; it was known as a place for healing. Richard M. Mackowski, a scholar who has lived and taught extensively in Jerusalem, suggests that this pool may have been a sanctuary for the believers in Asklepios, the preeminent Greek god of medicine and healing since the days of Antiochus IV (Epiphanes), ca. 175 to 164 B.C., who had, by royal decree, turned Jerusalem into a city of pagan altars and shrines.[2] Augustus Caesar (27 B.C. to A.D. 14) was the first in a long line of Roman emperors to show a renewed interest in Asklepios.[3] If the pool at Bethesda were, indeed, an Asklepieion, or a sanctuary to Asklepios, there would have been a statue of the god enshrined in a central area with adjacent porches open on all sides. The walls would have been lined with inscribed testimonials of past healings, and there would have been votive objects brought back to display, fulfilling vows made after healings had occurred.

In 1866, a broken marble foot was found in the debris near the pools while Bethesda was being excavated. The Greek inscription on the foot tells of a Roman lady who had visited the place and left a token of her visit to recall the healing of her own foot. Other such objects have also been unearthed there. Most have been dated to Hadrian's reign, A.D. 117 to 138, about eighty-five years after Jesus would have been in Jerusalem.

Jesus visited Bethesda pool with the five porches or porticos. "Walking alongside one of these porticoes Jesus saw the paralytic and cured him, for he had come there to teach by example that he alone was the true source of life and the healer of the sick."[4] There were others who healed in this era. Who were the physicians in Jesus' time? What was the environment into which the Great Physician came? What were the beliefs of the people about their health? What were their concepts of disease and its causes?

As I embarked on this study, I became aware that the layman's understanding of his own body has changed amazingly little from 3000 B.C. Egypt to our own time. Scientifically, we know more about the mechanism of the body. The microscope and, more recently, the computer have enhanced our ability to see and compile data. Technology has made dramatic gains in diagnostic machines. X-rays, sonograms, and CAT scans allow physicians today to peer inside the human body without cutting it open. Giant pharmaceutical companies continue to discover new and more potent drugs that allay pain and kill the microorganisms that attack our bodies. Still, there is precious little that medical intervention can accomplish except to buy time to allow the miraculous human body to heal itself.[5] I once heard heart surgeon Elder Russell M. Nelson exclaim over the paradox that our bodies have the power to heal themselves while at the same time they slowly wind down and die. The human body is indeed a miraculous machine.

President J. Reuben Clark described his own awe of the body in the following words: "The wonders of our majestic material universe, stretching out through space across billions of light years, with its billions of galaxies, seem to my own mind ... no more wonderful, ... [than] the cellular (all but infinitely small) universes that build this body of ours — each organ and gland and circulatory system and bone and muscle and sinew and tendon a galaxy — all bound together in a most intimate relation that baffles the human mind to comprehend. To my own mind the majesty of the physical world is far overmatched by the yet *unsolved miracles* involved in the body and its operations."[6]

Throughout the world's history, people have shared this awe of their own bodies. They have sought to maintain health, but failing that, they have looked for ways to heal themselves of the illnesses to which all people fall prey. "Sicknesses emerge, proliferate, gain hold and then die out. There are both old and young diseases. Antiquity didn't know all the diseases of modern times and similarly, not all diseases of antiquity—particularly epidemics—are extant today."[7] AIDS is an example of a new disease. This study will examine some of the medical practices inherited by those living at the time of Jesus, thus contributing to our understanding of the environment in which Jesus lived and ministered.

EGYPTIAN MEDICINE

The earliest medical records known were written four thousand years ago in Egypt, before the time of Abraham. The physicians of Egypt were famous throughout the ancient world. Babylonian and Persian kings employed Egyptian physicians in their courts.[8] But Egyptians had many misconceptions about the way the body functions.[9] They believed that the main systems of the body all passed through the heart. Egyptian physicians attempted to cure both scientifically and through magic.[10] Many extant medical papyri attempt to categorize diseases.[11] The famous Ebers Papyrus is the longest and lists 877 prescriptions for combatting 250 illnesses.[12] Another papyri contains a thorough manual of gynecology.[13] The Egyptians learned the use of many herbs and fruits for drugs and "realized the importance of rest and care of the patient, as well as basic hygiene."[14] Alongside these scientific records is a large corpus of magical papyri that includes potions and spells.[15]

Beginning with these early Egyptian physicians and continuing to our own time I found that distinctions among the terms *medicine*, *magic*, *miracles*, and *healing* were blurred; often these words are used interchangeably. In this paper the following definitions will be used:

Healing: to restore or return to health or wholeness or "Well-being in every aspect of life." Today we speak of healing as causing a physical body to be sound. Originally, health included the concept of well-being in *every* aspect of life. Perhaps there is a distinction between "cure" and "healing." Michael Wilson suggests that *cure* means "a restoration to function in society" while healing involves "a restoration to purposeful living in society"—what we now call of "quality of life."[16]

The three major modes of healing are as follows:

Medicine: man's own efforts to restore health using the means at his disposal, including diet, rest, medicants and herbs, surgery, etc.

Miracle: God's or gods' intervention in restoring health

Magic: man's efforts to harness supernatural powers involving soothsayers, astrologers, shaman—medicine men. Magic usually includes the use of amulets to prevent or heal illness or magic potions whose ingredients are chosen for superstitious rather than practical reasons.

Because we are considering Jesus as healer, our list must also include the delegated power of God, or priesthood, vouchsafed to chosen men to use God's power to effect the wholeness of healing. Anciently, Jesus gave the Twelve and the Seventy the priesthood, as he has again in our own time.

OLD TESTAMENT MEDICINE

The medical legacy that the Israelites of the Old Testament period bequeathed to their posterity living in Jesus' time was largely composed of dietary laws and a tradition of healing. There are very few references to "physician" in the Old Testament (see Genesis 50:2; Job 13:4; Jeremiah 8:22). The Israelites looked to God as the great healer. The Law of Moses gave priests medical prerogatives to diagnose and pronounce a person healed. God also gave dietary laws, which we might call preventive medicine (cf. D&C 89). Diet has always been seen as a key to good health or the restoration of health. Old Testament diet recommendations and restrictions compare to those of Christ's time, because the Jews still lived the Law of Moses, although perhaps the Jews had even stricter rabbinical prohibitions. "Like their neighbours, [the Hebrews'] staple diet was grain, vegetables and fruit and there was no restriction on these (Gen 1:29–30; 2:16). Meat was consumed rarely and restricted to that killed for the purpose with the life blood drained from it. Nutrition was generally adequate through a rich variety of easily obtainable foods: [specifically] barley and wheat, vegetables, fruits . . . , dairy products, figs, dates, and some meat, fish and fowl. The essential nutriments and energy intake calculated from the ancient documents compare well with modern records and the vitamin intake recommended by UNFAO today."[17] But since the people depended on local agriculture, drought, flood, or pestilence could cause famines, which were inevitably accompanied by sickness.

Although many diseases of today were unknown anciently, a few of today's diseases have been identified from biblical accounts. "Scurvy [a disease caused by Vitamin C deficiency that results in bleeding and weakness] was known in Egypt and Babylonia and Kinnier-Wilson identifies it with the 'evil-smelling disease' . . . described in the account of the siege of Jerusalem in 588/7 B.C. He also finds evidence for blindness following vitamin A deficiency."[18]

Various herbs with healing properties are mentioned in the Old Testament. The best known is the "balm of Gilead" (Jeremiah 8:22; see also Genesis 37:25; 43:11; Jeremiah 46:11; 51:8; Ezekiel 27:17; 47:12). In Isaiah 38:21 a "lump of figs" is laid upon Hezekiah's boil, which heals him. The prescription comes from Isaiah (see also Revelation 22:2; Alma 46:40 for references to healing leaves, whose therapeutic effects were ascribed to God). The Israelites likely lived everyday life just as we do today, using what we would call folk remedies. "In matters of therapy the Hebrews did not differ substantially from their neighbours with whom, through local traditions, many common remedies were known."[19] "The therapeutic effect of music and of prayer were known [viz., Saul and David]. Moses' prayer for Miriam's recovery—'O God, heal her, please'—is the shortest recorded prayer in the Bible (Num. 12:13). Later Jews considered prayer for healing 'to be efficacious if offered by the proper person at the proper time with proper intent under the proper circumstances'!"[20]

Thus we see that the healing legacy of the Old Testament Israelites centered on the concept of God as the great healer and provider of foods to nourish and herbs to soothe and heal. Any physician mentioned in the Old Testament is subordinate to God. As in every age, including our own, folk medicine was practiced, using whatever herbs or balms were available, much as today's Jewish mothers prescribe and provide chicken soup!

GREEK MEDICINE

During the last few centuries of the Old Testament period, Greek medicine revolutionized the world and set the stage for the New Testament era. Its influence is still felt today. The Greek Hippocrates (ca. 460–377 B.C.) is usually referred to as the father of medicine. Hippocrates founded a school of medicine that stressed the need for observation and experimentation.[21] The collection of writings (much of which is available to us today) by Hippocrates and his fellow physicians contains detailed case reports of various diseases. [22] Hippocrates and his followers originated a theory that was to persist in European medical circles until the eighteenth century—more than two thousand years. The human body, they taught, contained four humors, or fluids: blood, phlegm, black bile, and yellow bile. In a healthy body these were in perfect balance; too much or too little of any particular humor caused sickness.

One of Hippocrates' prescriptions was bloodletting, performed with leeches or the process of cupping, whereby blood was extracted from a person to restore the sought-for balance. Leeches are used today in medicine but for a far different purpose They enhance blood flow after plastic surgery.[23]

Hippocrates declared medicine to be a separate craft, whereas before it had been grouped with the common manual trades. His name is associated with the famous Hippocratic oath, which sets forth high principles of medical ethics. The Oath absolutely precludes abortion and any kind of euthanasia. Amazingly, nearly twenty-five hundred years later the debate over these issues continues. The Hippocratic school was limited because the physicians sought knowledge of the natural world philosophically—through logic and speculation—while lacking empirical data on which to base their hypotheses.

EARLY MEDICAL THEORIES AND PRACTITIONERS

Seven items summarize the ancient theories held by the common people to explain sickness, suffering, and pain. They will sound familiar. Sickness is caused by:

1. A whim of God or the gods (Mesopotamians and early Egyptians 3000 B.C.).

2. An imbalance in the body's elements or "humors" (Greeks).

3. The result of sin: evil caused illness—sin caused sickness (see the book of Job).

4. Possession by demons.

5. A curse, for which counter magic must be employed.

6. A functional disorder of the body, which required careful diagnosis and a prescribed remedy.

7. A poison, which had invaded the system and needed removal.

Several important historical figures practiced medicine. The following great physicians and medical writers lived before, during, or shortly after New Testament times. Noting them will give us the historical context in which to examine the window of time when Jesus healed.

Imhotep, the Egyptian, ca. 2650 B.C., vizier, architect of Step Pyramid

Hippocrates, the Greek, ca. 460 B.C.

Celsus, the Roman, ca. 25 B.C. in Rome—died A.D. 37.

Galen, the Greek, who came to Rome, born ca. A.D. 130—died ca. A.D. 200.

In addition to these men, there have been gods to whom the people appealed for healing. Besides Jehovah, most pagan gods were approached to help heal, but a few emerged as "specialists" who were believed to have unique healing powers. Around these gods and goddesses cults arose and temples were built. Medical schools were established in connection with such temples in Cos (Hippocrates), Epidaurus, Pergamum (Galen), Corinth, and Alexandria. Some of these gods and goddesses in ancient Egypt were Imhotep and Isis (Isis was also borrowed later by the Greeks and Romans). The Greeks adopted Apollo, Hygieia, and Asklepios from Hippocrates' time (460 B.C.) and thereafter. The farflung cult of Asklepios may well have included the shrine at Bethesda where Jesus healed the paralytic. The serpent symbol of Asklepios remains as the symbol used by physicians today. And, notably, it was a serpent that Moses lifted up on a pole eight centuries earlier. The Book of Mormon explains that the Israelites were not healed because they refused to look to that serpent.

MEDICINE PRACTICED IN CHRIST'S LIFETIME

Greek medicinal arts were the standard for professional practice at the time of Jesus. Greek medicine was introduced to the Romans in 293 B.C.[24] There had been a terrible pestilence, and Roman envoys were sent to the Greek god, Asklepios, at his temple in Epidaurus. The priests of the temple directed the envoys to build a similar temple at Rome. To alleviate their plague, the priests even gave the Romans a sacred serpent to transfer sanctity to the new edifice built on an island in the Tiber River. Because the pestilence abated, the popularity of the new sanctuary was assured.

The prevailing view of medical practice at the time of Christ is described by Celsus, Pliny, and Galen—contemporaries, or near contemporaries, of Jesus.

Celsus, who was born about twenty years before Jesus and died three or four years after the Crucifixion, was an encyclopedist and collector of medical information, not a physician himself. His work, *Di Medicina*, was the second part of a six-part encyclopedia. (The other five subjects covered are agriculture, military art, rhetoric, philosophy, and jurisprudence.) *Di Medicina* follows three themes: How the healthy should act to maintain good health, description of diseases, and curing diseases. It is generally agreed that Celsus wrote during the reign of Tiberias — exactly during Jesus' lifetime. Celsus describes the symptoms of many diseases of his time, including tuberculosis, dropsy, kidney stone disease, and bladder disorders. He also describes problems from pregnancy. His cures include bloodletting, purging, baths, heating, cooling, rubbing, rocking, vomiting, and sweating.[25]

Celsus often quotes an important Greek physician who came to Rome from Bithynia around 100 B.C. named Asclepiades. Pliny and Galen also wrote of him. He rejected the Hippocratic theory of the humors and with it the purgings and vomitings that were prescribed to dispose of offending materials. His cures were effected principally by diet, exercise, massage, and a bracing cold water cure. (This may explain why there were cold-water baths in Herod's palaces.) He used few drugs with the exception of wine, which he considered the "aspirin" of his day, the universal remedy. Pliny reports that he was very popular (Pliny, xxvi 13).

Celsus agrees with Asclepiades about drugs. He categorizes diseases into those which can be helped through diet and those which require drugs. He presents a long list of drugs classified according to their uses. He describes many surgical procedures, but critics question how he obtained such knowledge, because he was not a physician himself. Nevertheless, surgeons give him high praise for his descriptions of the mechanical aspects of surgery.

Both Celsus and Pliny were wealthy landowners in Rome and near contemporaries in the first century after Christ. They came from the upper class and were well educated.[26] Such men learned about medicine in order to treat their own slaves and families — likely in that order. Pliny's counterpart to Celsus' *Di Medicina* is his thirty-seven volume *Natural History*. Books twenty through twenty-seven are especially concerned with the uses of trees, plants, and flowers in medicine, but medical ideas are scattered throughout his entire work. His writings are as diffuse as Celsus' work is precise. He quotes more than a hundred other authorities to buttress his ideas. Absurd theories and practices are found alongside sensible notions. For example:

"The proper season to prepare elaterium [a powdered drug derived from cucumber seeds] is the autumn, and no drug keeps for a longer period. It begins to be potent when three years old. . . . The older it is the better, and it has been known to keep, so Theophrastus tells us, for two hundred years, and its power to put out the flame of a lamp it retains right up to the fiftieth year. Indeed, the test of genuine elaterium is whether its application makes a flame flicker up and down before putting it out. . . . The regular dose as purge or emetic is from half to one obolus [.66 grams], according to the idiosyncrasy of the patient, a larger dose being fatal. . . . Mixed with honey or old olive oil it is used to cure quinsy and tracheal affections. . . . A decoction of it in vinegar applied externally gives immediate relief to gout and to diseases of the joints. . . . It is good for asthma and also for jaundice when injected into the nostrils. Smeared in the sunshine on the face, it removes therefrom freckles and spots."[27]

In addition to the humor theory, which persisted almost to our own time, some believed that too little or too much of one of the four elements (fire, water, air, and earth) caused disease. In Roman times, there were those who worked their medicine by reasoned theory as had been done earlier, but that approach was more often combined with knowledge based on observation obtained through dissection. Repulsive as it is to us, vivisection (cutting open a living person or animal) was also allowed with a dual purpose: early physicians learned more about the human body while torturing criminals or prisoners of war.

Galen the Greek (130–200 A.D.) was born at Pergamum and lived in Rome a hundred years after Jesus. He was probably the most famous physician of antiquity. He claimed to return to the original truths of Hippocrates. His dogmatic attention to the "humor" theory has influenced and hindered the practice of medicine almost to the present day. Only within the past two hundred years have medical researchers dared to move away from the "humor" theory and discover more precisely how the body really works. In spite of that, though, he is recognized as one of the most accomplished and prolific scientific writers ever. It is estimated that his writings number five hundred volumes or more. "His great aim in medicine was to unite the conflicting sects and divergent streams of doctrine, and to frame a synthesis which should

combine his own results with those of his predecessors. He succeeded
so far that Greek medicine in Galen reached its highest point."[28]

A person who lived in the time of Jesus and became sick had at
least five options in seeking a cure.

1. He would probably have begun with current folk medicine.
Through the ages man has discovered and passed along remedies which
work—hot lemonade, hot bath, bed rest. We still say, "Feed a fever,
starve a cold." Most families have their favorite home remedies.

2. If he had the means, he could go to a physician. There would
have been two varieties—what we would call the family practioner, and
the surgeon. "The physician was often considered a manual worker.
The word for manual work is 'ummanut which can mean manual work,
a profession or a skill. An 'umman(a) indicates a labourer, an artist, a
leech, a surgeon, a bath attendant, a circumciser. So the medical profession [was] considered along with trades. According to the Talmud there
were doctors in every city and in every large place. . . . Josephus received medical care after a fall from his horse in Capernaum."[29]

Roman generals took Greek physicians on their campaigns. Troops
stationed in Rome had four physicians to each cohort. The legions also
had physicians assigned to them, but the number is uncertain. This
would mean that in Palestine, the Roman troops likely had physicians
in their organization. "All military medical officers were Roman citizens
and had the rank of *principales* with immunity from civic duties.
. . . [Eye] surgery was an important part of military medicine, since the
seals of Roman oculists, attached to boxes of ointment . . . have often
been found . . . in connexion with military camps."[30]

There was also the temple doctor. His specific duty was to minister
to the priests when they hurt themselves in performing their duties
or when they fell ill. The priests were required to go barefoot on the
stones in the temple complex both summer and winter and so were
often ill. "Even more injurious to their health was their diet, which
had a high meat content with only water to drink, as wine was forbidden
to them."[31] The high meat content of their diet, of course, came from
parts of the sacrificial animals they were given to eat. There are records
of prescriptions for "the beneficial effect of the waters of the Gihon
which the priests drank to counteract their rich meat diet."[32]

3. He could go to a cultic healing place—temples of such healing
gods as Asklepios or Isis—and seek a miraculous healing. He might
resort to going there after the physician had failed to help. It might

even be on his recommendation. In an Asklepieion, incubation, the temple sleep, was a primary treatment. There were places to lie down, because sleeping in these environs was thought to be therapeutic. Often the cure came to the person himself in a dream. Many votive offerings (representing healed parts) would be displayed as well as inscriptions thanking the god and the priests for various healings. Abundant water seemed to be a requirement. Again, the Pool of Bethesda may fit this category.

4. He might secretly go to a magician. There he would be treated with incantations, secret words, and secret herbs or other items to counteract the demons causing his illness. He might be given an amulet to ward off further disease or combat the present malady.

5. He might seek out a miracle-worker, who worked publicly to alleviate sickness. Miracle-workers gathered followers around them. They founded movements or "schools." The much-cited Apollonius of Tyana is a typical example. We learn of Apollonius, a contemporary of Jesus, from Philastratus' biography, written a century later. He is presented as a man of great wisdom, presumably a result of the presence of [the god] Apollo within him. According to Philastratus, he was always careful to explain that his cures were the result of natural therapy, although many stories of his healing skills sound like magic. Since magicians charged a fee for their services, Philastratus is quick to point out that Apollonius performed without a fee. His success "is the direct result of his special knowledge of the natural world and of his closeness to the gods. It is this divine wisdom which enables him to expel demons and effect cures."[33]

If our afflicted person living in the time of Jesus were a Jew, he would be torn between the options. Because the Israelite faith believed that sickness and healing were the work of God, Jehovah had a healing monopoly.[34] Of course, prayer and medicine could be combined effectively, just as in our day.

JESUS AS HEALER

Now let us look to the Savior and how he dealt with the common event of sickness. In teaching the New Testament for the past few years, I have been struck over and over again with the image of Jesus Christ as the healer or Great Physician. Of the thirty-six miracles mentioned in the gospels, twenty-seven are classified as healings. People flocked to him "to be healed." That could not have been unplanned. He came to reveal his Father in both word and action. The Old Testament God was the great Healer, and Jesus was the God of the Old Testament.

The record doesn't tell us how much Jesus knew of medical practices and physicians of his day. But we do know that he used the term "physician" twice, once when he said, "Physician, heal thyself" (Luke 4:23), and again, "They that be whole need not a physician" (Matthew 9:12). The woman with the issue of blood who touched the hem of his garment is described as having "spent all her living upon physicians, neither could be healed of any" (Luke 8:43). The only other reference to a physician is Paul's reference to "Luke, the beloved physician" (Colossians 4:14). Some scholars have studied Luke, trying to isolate medical references to validate the assertion that he was a physician.

We have no record of Christ's having been sick, but Alma tells us: "He shall go forth, suffering pains and afflictions and temptations of every kind; and this that the word might be fulfilled which saith he will take upon him the pains and the sicknesses of his people . . . that he may know according to the flesh how to succor his people according to their infirmities" (Alma 7:11–12).

Healing was itself one of the greatest lessons Jesus sought to teach. His parable of the good Samaritan describes a gentle man who gave first aid – a healer. No one was ever more long-suffering than Jesus nor more patient beyond every frustration. He healed men, women, and children, bond and free, Roman and Samaritan, as well as Israelites, "the chosen people." He was, truly, no respecter of persons.

His healings suggest that there is a connection between sickness and sin. Sin always brings suffering eventually, but suffering is not always the result of sin. That is the lesson of Job as well as of the man born blind. One is certainly an apt metaphor for the other.

Jesus used a variety of methods in healing. He healed:

1. By touch – taking the hand, touching the eyes or injured area sometimes with a medicant (saliva was considered a medicant in his time).

2. By word – without touch, sometimes over great distances.

3. By sending others to whom he gave the power to heal and bless.

On occasion he simply said, "Thy sins are forgiven thee." Forgiveness works as a cure in our lives because guilt may cause or perpetuate illness.[35] Repentance is a healing process. Wholeness is the goal. Un-wholeness, un-health, or dis-ease requires healing. As Jesus said, "They that be whole need not a physician" (Matthew 9:12).

After Jesus had healed a leper, he sent him to the priest to complete the requirements for ritual cleanliness in the Law of Moses. Anyone touching a leper would be defiled, for lepers were considered unclean. In order for the leper to be readmitted to the congregation, he must be pronounced clean. That was not considered a cure for the disease but a problem of ritual impurity. The priest's final cleansing word (see Leviticus 14:2–9) was required to allow the already-healed to return to society, no longer in a position to defile those around him.[36]

Today leprosy refers to a particular disease, but in Christ's time the term likely applied to many skin disorders. True leprosy "is a chronic disease characterized by widespread defined skin swellings, ulcerated destruction of the extremities, and facial disfigurement. It is incurable in its later stages and contagious. Leprosy in the New Testament was an obvious and physical blemish in the skin of human beings; its disappearance was to be noted by patient, priest and ordinary people. It does not affect cloth or leather or the walls of houses."[37]

Another disease known to us which Jesus healed was epilepsy. Long before Jesus' time, "the Egyptians and Babylonians certainly knew of epilepsy, the latter described the symptoms as 'falls with eyes wide open, head turned to the right (or left), clenched fist, averted eyes, an epileptic cry, foaming at the mouth.' "[38] Although epilepsy is never named in the New Testament, scholars agree that the boy whose symptoms are described in Mark 9:14–29 may have been suffering from this disease for which modern medicine still has no cure. Jesus' instant and final cure of the boy is thus particularly striking in medical terms.

The Savior also succored in patience and love while those around him overcame their sins and sicknesses (see Mosiah 18:8–9). Like the Lord, we must be willing to contribute patiently to the overcoming of infirmities in ourselves and others. That is the true healing process. We can save each other. We can be "Savior/healers on Mount Zion" in this way as well as kneeling in temples on behalf of our dead.

Jesus healed as the response of a loving God. His mission required it. He delegated priesthood power to exemplify the way (D&C 121:41–46), but he fulfilled his own admonition to "lift up the hands that hang down and strengthen the feeble knees" (D&C 81:5; see also Isaiah 35:3; Hebrews 12:12). And we must as well.

As Dennis Rasmussen has written: "To hallow my life he taught me to endure sorrow rather than cause it, to restrain anger rather than heed it, to bear injustice rather than inflict it. 'Resist not evil' he said in the Sermon on the Mount (Matthew 5:39.) Evil multiplies by the response it seeks to provoke, and when I return evil for evil, I engender corruption myself. The chain of evil is broken for good when a pure and loving heart absorbs a hurt and forbears to hurt in return. The forgiveness of Christ bears no grudge. The love of Christ allows no offense to endure. The compassion of Christ embraces all things and draws them toward himself. Deep within every child of God the Light of Christ resides, guiding, comforting, purifying the heart that turns to him."[39]

Even as we seek to heal others we, ourselves need the ultimate healing of the Master. His atonement can remedy our entire fallen state.

People have sought to heal themselves through medicine since the ancient Egyptians and Greeks. They have met with mixed success because of their lack of knowledge of the physical body. Yet Jesus, through his power and their faith, was able to miraculously heal those he met.

Jesus asked the lame man at the pool of Bethesda, "Wilt thou be made whole?" and then challenged, "Rise and walk!" We, with the lame man, would rise. We and all mankind declare in honesty, "We are not whole, but we wish to be," just as the leper who pleaded with Jesus, "If thou wilt, thou canst make me clean," we long for that gracious reply, "I will; Be thou clean" (Matthew 8:2–3).

NOTES

1. May mean "House of mercy."

2. Richard M. Mackowski, *Jerusalem: City of Jesus* (Grand Rapids, Mich.: William B. Eerdmans Publishing Co., 1980), p. 82.

3. Ralph Jackson, *Doctors and Diseases in the Roman Empire* (Norman, Okla.: University of Oklahoma Press, 1988), p. 149.

4. Mackowski, *Jerusalem: City of Jesus*, p. 83.

5. See Russell M. Nelson, "The Magnificence of Man" BYU Fireside, 29 Mar. 1987, and J. Reuben Clark, Jr., "Man, God's Greatest Miracle," *J. Reuben Clark: Selected Papers*, vol. 3, ed. David H. Yarn, Jr. (Provo, Utah: Brigham Young University Press, 1984), p. 115.

6. Clark, "Man, God's Greatest Miracle," *Selected Papers*, vol. 3, p. 115.

7. Klaus Seybold and Ulrich B. Mueller, *Sickness and Healing* (Nashville, Tenn.: Abingdon, 1978), p. 10.

8. One of the earliest and most revered among them was the vizier, Imhotep who was also the famous architect who supervised the building of the first pyramid at Sakkara, the Step Pyramid, which he built for Zoser in about 2700 B.C.

9. Miriam Stead, *Egyptian Life* (London: British Museum Publications, 1986), p. 70.

10. J. E. Manchip White, *Ancient Egypt: Its Culture and History* (New York: Dover Publications, 1970), p. 105. "If the trouble was external the patient stood a fair chance of recovery. Breaks and fractures were cleverly set. The practice of amputation and the use of splints, bandages and compresses were well developed. Internal disorders were an entirely different matter. Here the physician was reduced to reciting spells and prescribing such potions as woman's milk with oil and salt or goat's milk with honey. It was thought that life depended on a series of vessels which started from the heart. In these vessels ran air, water, blood, semen, urine and feces."

11. Ibid., pp. 104–6. They compare to many modern procedures, examinations, treatments, and prognoses. Most of these date to the Middle Kingdom (ca. 1900 B.C. near Abraham's time) but claim to be copies of works written in the Old Kingdom (ca. 2700 B.C.) often credited to Imhotep.

12. Seybold and Mueller, *Sickness and Healing,* p. 33. It describes the illnesses and the amount and method of administration of the drugs to treat each one. Freely interspersed among the prescriptions are magical spells and formulae. Another papyrus details treatment of wounds and fractures.

13. White, *Ancient Egypt,* p. 106. "This branch of medicine was particularly well advanced, for there was ample scope for study in a country where a woman bore her first child at the age of twelve and seldom produced less than six or seven all told."

14. Stead, *Egyptian Life,* pp. 69–70.

15. *The Greek Magical Papyri in Translation, Including the Demotic Spells,* ed. Hans Dieter Betz (Chicago: University of Chicago Press, 1989), p. xli.

16. Michael Wilson, *The Church Is Healing* (London: SCM Press, 1966), p. 18.

17. *Medicine and the Bible,* ed. Bernard Palmer (Exeter: Paternoster Press, 1986), pp. 37–38. See also Fred Rosner, M.D., *Medicine in the Bible and the Talmud* (New York: KTAV Publishing House, 1977).

18. Palmer, *Medicine and the Bible,* p. 38.

19. Ibid. "These included washings, ointments and herbal remedies. The Egyptians listed more than five hundred, mostly made from vegetable products, compounded from mineral drugs or from the products of thirty different animals. There, as in Palestine and Babylonia, some remedies were prepared by perfumers working either in a temple or a private establishment."

20. Ibid.

21. Howard Clark Kee, *Medicine, Miracle, and Magic in New Testament Times* (Cambridge: Cambridge University Press, 1988), p. 29. "The aim was to discern

through practical experience how the various parts of the body functioned, in order to assist the natural curative forces of the body itself."

22. An illness was diagnosed according to its symptoms. Diagnoses combined philisophical theories with practical observation. Treatment often consisted in changes in the patient's diet, environment, or hygienic habits. Hippocrates rejected religion and magic in the treatment of disease, teaching instead that natural means could be employed to fight disease.

23. Richard E. Hayden, John G. Phillips, and Patrick W. McLear, "Leeches: Objective Monitoring of Altered Perfusion in Congested Flaps," *Arch Otolaryngol Head Neck Surg,* vol. 114, Dec. 1988.

24. *A Companion to Latin Studies,* ed. Sir John Edwin Sandys (New York: Hafner Publishing Co., 1968), p. 716.

25. Kee, *Medicine, Miracle and Magic,* pp. 36–37.

26. Jackson, *Doctors and Diseases in the Roman Empire,* pp. 9–10.

27. Pliny, *Natural History in Ten Volumes, Volume VI Libri XX–XXIII,* trans. W. H. S. Jones (Cambridge, Mass.: Harvard University Press, 1969), pp. 5–9.

28. Sandys, *A Companion to Latin Studies,* p. 723. See also Rudolph S. Siegel, *Galen's System of Physiology and Medicine* (Basel: S. Karger, 1968).

29. Joachim Jeremias, *Jerusalem in the Time of Jesus,* trans. F. H. and C. H. Cave (Philadelphia: Fortress Press, 1969), pp. 17–18; see footnote.

30. Sandys, *A Companion to Latin Studies,* p. 727.

31. Jeremias, *Jerusalem in the Time of Jesus,* p. 26. See also F. F. Bruce, *New Testament History* (Garden City, N. Y.: Doubleday, 1969).

32. Ibid, p. 106.

33. Kee, *Medicine, Miracle and Magic,* p. 86.

34. Asklepios and Isis were not thought to be the exclusive purveyors of healing.

35. N. Lee Smith, "Healing As the Master Healed," *The Journal of Collegium Aesculapium,* Winter, 1988, pp. 17–27

36. Kee, *Medicine, Miracle and Magic,* pp. 10–11.

37. Palmer, *Medicine and the Bible,* pp. 116 – 18.

38. Ibid., pp. 27, 71, 168. Old Testament examples: "The Midianite, Balaam who describes himself as 'one who fell down with his eyes open' (Numbers 24:4) and Saul, who 'fell down every day and every night' (1 Samuel 19:24)."

39. Dennis Rasmussen, *The Lord's Question* (Provo, Utah: Keter Foundation, 1985), pp. 63–64.

CHAPTER TEN

"Behold, the Lamb of God": The Savior's Use of Animals as Symbols

Byron R. Merrill

Brigham Young University

When was the last time you sat quietly and observed the world around you? Often we become so involved with the stressful pace of modern society that we fail to step back long enough to observe, ponder, and marvel at the grandeur of nature that surrounds us. A sense of wonder about the creations of God pervades the scriptures. Earnest searching and thoughtful contemplation of the scriptures have the therapeutic effect of a soothing balm, bestowing peace and eternal perspective in the midst of a chaotic world. Even in the Church, we sometimes become so involved in meeting schedules and perpetuating programs that we do not pay enough attention to the grand spectacle of creation around us, the very handiwork of God in the panorama of nature. But he who knows all and watches over all does not neglect such things. Did not the Lord tell us to consider the fowls of the air and the lilies of the field that we might be filled with gratitude and reverence and better appreciate the breadth and depth of his providential care?

To more fully understand the Savior's teachings and thereby increase our love for him, we must often look beyond the literal objects about which he spoke to the deeper symbolic meanings and spiritual messages that they convey. Members of the animal kingdom are among the symbols most widely used by Jesus Christ and his prophets to teach spiritual lessons. They teach eternal truths by employing references or allegories in which animals are used symbolically to convey deeper meanings. Understanding the messages intended from the animal imagery requires more than mere superficial reading of the scriptures. True understanding demands prayerful searching—examining which animals are chosen, how they are used, and the underlying cultural significance of that choice. These questions must be asked to answer the larger question, "What would the Lord have us understand by the use of such a symbol?" We can know the scriptures better by understanding the role of animals in general, their place as symbols in particular, and the specific symbolic use of certain animals by the Savior and his prophets.

That the Lord would deem it appropriate to employ animals symbolically so often, as well as the way in which he uses them, should convey to us a sense of reverence and appreciation for animal life in general. That attitude should in turn encourage our considerate treatment and concern for them. As President Joseph F. Smith said, "The unnecessary destruction of life begets a spirit of destruction which grows within the soul. . . . It hardens the heart of man. . . . The unnecessary destruction of life is a distinct spiritual loss to the human family. Men cannot worship the Creator and look with careless indifference upon his creations."[1] As President George Q. Cannon stated: "God, our Father, has made the beasts, the birds and the fish, and he has placed them on the earth for man's use. He has made us lords over them, and he is a coward and a tyrant who would abuse or inflict pain upon them."[2]

THE PLACE OF ANIMALS

In all scriptural accounts of the Creation, animals stand next to man in the order of their appearance on earth. Man was then given dominion over them (Moses 2:28, 5:1; Genesis 1:26), and President Kimball indicated that animals were created "for man's respectful use."[3] St. Francis of Assisi taught that all creation was brought into being "to praise the Creator; every species in existence praises God in its own special way."[4]

Joseph Fielding Smith said that Latter-day Saints "do not take the view that animals have no reason, and cannot think. We have divine knowledge that each possesses a spirit in the likeness of its body, and that each was created spiritually before it was naturally."[5] He explained that while there is some measure of intelligence in members of the animal kingdom, the limited bounds beyond which they cannot pass are set by divine decree. These limits are not set on man, who is the offspring of God and has received commandments to become perfect like his Father. President Smith concluded that God "placed each [animal] in its sphere, gave it commandments commensurate with its position. They have been commanded to multiply, not to pray."[6] Latter-day scripture states that animal-kind will have part in the resurrection (D&C 29:24–25). Brigham Young indicated that animals abide the law of their Creator, unlike men and women who are the only creations of God that are disobedient.[7] Some refer to wicked acts as resulting from our "animal nature," but sins are really human failings, the result of evil choices, and not bestial at all.

WHY ANIMALS AS SYMBOLS?

Because of the close relationship between animals and man throughout history, animals have been used in all cultures to reflect the nature of humanity, symbolizing societal and individual characteristics. The traits of individual animals are very simple to observe and recognize, whereas human behavior is more intricate and difficult to describe. Animals are familiar creatures, which mutely encourage projection of people's emotions and attitudes onto them. Animals can be used to convey deep dimensions of human feelings and ideas. For instance, in blessings pronounced on seven of the twelve sons of Jacob as recorded in Genesis 49 and Deuteronomy 33, the Lord uses animals symbolically to indicate the assignments given those heads of tribes.

The Lord makes use of readily observable animal traits to help us grasp the meaning of his words. A single symbol may be used simultaneously to express and interrelate many different levels of background and comprehension. The Hebraic cultural tradition permeating scripture affects how a symbol is used and how it is to be understood. In an increasingly urban, industrialized world, many people have only the briefest exposure to animals. Thus, quite frequently our understanding of the Savior's beautiful scriptural imagery is lacking. Failure to understand the symbolic meanings may lead us to lack the desire either to embrace or eschew those traits mirrored in the animal symbols the Master has employed to teach us his will. Let us then examine the use of certain specific animals.

Serpent

The very first animal used as a symbol in the Bible is the serpent. Since the Fall of Adam, the serpent has symbolized treachery and subtlety and all that is evil. Hence, Christ said, when expounding the goodness of our Father in Heaven, "Or what man is there of you, whom if his son ask bread, will he give him a stone? Or if he ask a fish, will he give him a serpent? If ye then, being evil, know how to give good gifts unto your children, how much more shall your Father which is in heaven give good things to them that ask him?" (Matthew 7:9–11).

The serpent is an unusual animal. In Hebrew lore, it is one of the only animals that does injury without any gain for itself and therefore epitomizes slander.[8] As a serpent grows stronger with age, so does Satan seem to grow stronger with time, society deteriorating under the sway of his power. It appears that with each successive year he becomes more and more adroit in his evil ploy to "destroy the world" (Moses 4:6). Similarly, his perception of our weaknesses is so keen, like the serpent, that he can "lie in wait to deceive" (Ephesians 4:14).

Certainly the most striking similarity between the serpent, or viper, and Lucifer is its destructive poison. Venom injected into the prey builds in the lymph vessels and then slowly courses through the tissues, destroying cells and rupturing capillaries as it goes until it causes death by massive internal hemorrhage.[9] The venom does not necessarily cause intense pain. The victim may even feel better for some time, while the work of destruction progresses internally. If the snakebite is left untreated, internal disintegration continues until the muscles are paralyzed and functioning becomes impossible. In like manner Satan's venom breaks down our spiritual systems. Victims of this more deadly spiritual venom may actually enjoy the initial spiritual decay. Eventually, unless the victim seeks help, the spiritual disintegration culminates in spiritual dysfunction, paralysis, and death. The Savior used this symbol to make a stinging rebuke: "Woe unto you, scribes and Pharisees, hypocrites! . . . Ye serpents, ye generation of vipers, how can ye escape the damnation of hell?" (Matthew 23:29, 33).

Camel

The camel is used as a symbol on only two occasions in the New Testament. Other references to the camel are literal, but even these references help us understand the Lord's use of the camel as a symbol. Since Abrahamic times, the camel has been a symbol of wealth. The scriptural narrative describing Abram's wealth says that "he had sheep, and oxen, and he asses, and menservants, and maidservants, and she asses, and camels" (Genesis 12:16). The camel is the livelihood of the merchant and the nomad, for it is the basic transportation for these desert wanderers who carry all they have with them. A man with more camels can carry more merchandise. During our Savior's sojourn on earth, the trade routes were well established, and Jerusalem was a hub of commerce from Egypt to India.

The Lord's use of the camel as a symbol is most instructive: "And again I say unto you, It is easier for a camel to go through the eye of a needle, than for a rich man to enter into the kingdom of God" (Matthew 19:24). Jesus could have been even more hyperbolic and used an elephant rather than a camel. But the camel represents the merchant, the trains of merchandise, and the love of lucre, and thus the camel makes a more fitting symbol for the Lord's warning: "a rich man shall hardly enter into the kingdom of heaven" (Matthew 19:23). It is so hard, in fact, that the Lord says it is easier for the camel to pass through the eye of a needle. "With men this is impossible; but if they will forsake all things for my sake, with God whatsoever things I speak are possible" (JST Matthew 19:26). In order for man to do that which is ordinarily impossible, he must no longer trust in man's ways (in this case, the ways of the camel and the caravan), but trust in God instead. The Savior used camels to illustrate a similar contrast between the large and truly significant and the minute and petty. He warned the Pharisees — accustomed to literally straining gnats out of their beverages — against figuratively straining gnats and swallowing camels (Matthew 23:24).

Dog

The Lord always uses the dog as a derogatory symbol. To us a dog is a pet or a mascot, although few would consider "dog" to be a term of endearment. To the Hebrew mind in Jesus' day, a dog had a negative connotation. The Jews in Jesus' time probably viewed the dog more like we view its cousins, the wolf and jackal, sleeping much in the day and roaming in packs to howl and scavenge at night.[10] Perhaps the dog's scavenging habits added to its negative image. In any case, the Lord and his servants employ the dog as a symbol of that which is vile. "Give not that which is holy unto the dogs," the Lord commanded his disciples (Matthew 7:6).

When the Syrophoenician woman besought the Lord to cast the devil out of her daughter, he responded, "Let the children first be filled: for it is not meet to take the children's bread, and to cast it unto the dogs" (Mark 7:27). Here the Greek word used for dog is *kunarion*, meaning "puppy," which is the diminutive form of the word normally used for dog, *kuon*. The softened word may suggest a certain affection and care on Jesus' part, but the distinction between the children of the covenant and those who are not of Israel remains. Perhaps the woman was acknowledging that she was a sinner and expressing her desire for help and willingness to change when she said, "Yes, Lord: yet the dogs under the table eat of the children's crumbs" (Mark 7:28). In John's apocalyptic vision, he saw outside the celestial city "dogs, and sorcerers, and whoremongers, and murderers, and idolaters, and whosoever loveth and maketh a lie" (Revelation 22:15). Once again the children of God are within, and the dogs, those who reject the covenant, are without.

Horse and Ass

Although there are many references to horses in the Bible, very few are in the New Testament. Except for a passing reference to horsemen in Acts 23 (vv. 23, 32) and an analogy James makes between bridling one's passions and putting a bit in a horse's mouth (James 3:2–3), the book of Revelation is the only book in the New Testament that refers to horses. In Hebraic tradition the horse is the animal of war. It was the armored tank of the ancient world and thus the very symbol of warfare (see Job 39:19–25; 2 Samuel 8:4).

Even with its warlike image, the horse was not seen as an intrinsically evil animal. Job gives one of the most beautiful poetic portrayals in scripture of a horse in battle. Divine intervention by horses and chariots of fire occurs in the experiences of both Elijah (2 Kings 2:11) and Elisha (2 Kings 6:17). The apostle John wrote of the Savior's second coming, "And I saw heaven opened, and behold a white horse; and he that sat upon him was called Faithful and True, and in righteousness he doth judge and make war" (Revelation 19:11). The color white symbolizes purity, holiness, and triumph,[11] but even in this positive portrayal, the horse is always associated with power and might.

How different from the majestic appearance of the Lord astride a white horse as he comes to usher in his millennial reign is that of his entry into Jerusalem "sitting upon an ass, and a colt the foal of an ass" (Matthew 21:5). The ass is mentioned more than 130 times in the Bible. The Hebrew language — not noted for its extensive vocabulary — has a number of words to designate asses, depending on color, age, sex, and so on.[12] The domestic ass appears throughout scripture as a symbol of humble servitude and peace.

The entry of Jesus into Jerusalem on an animal of peace and meekness posed no threat to the Romans, who would have expected any claimant to power to have arrived on a horse, the symbol of war and power. But Jesus' mount proclaimed kingship to the Jews, in part because of two particular Old Testament prophecies. The first is a portion of Jacob's blessing upon Judah: "The sceptre shall not depart from Judah, nor a lawgiver from between his feet, until Shiloh come; and unto him shall the gathering of the people be. Binding his foal unto the vine, and his ass's colt unto the choice vine" (Genesis 49:10–11). In John 15:1, the Savior declared: "I am the true vine." The references to sceptre and Shiloh and the choice vine being bound to an ass's colt all come together as the Savior made his triumphal entry into Jerusalem astride an ass's colt, days before his being crowned with thorns as "The King of the Jews." That supernal moment, as he entered the city in glory, also fulfilled in perfect detail the prophecy of Zechariah: "Rejoice greatly, O daughter of Zion; shout, O daughter of Jerusalem: behold, thy King cometh unto thee: he is just, and having salvation; lowly, and riding upon an ass, and upon a colt the foal of an ass" (Zechariah 9:9). The ass symbolizes some of the characteristics of the true King: humility, submissiveness, and peace.

Dove

Joseph Smith said: "The sign of the dove was instituted before the creation of the world, a witness for the Holy Ghost, and the devil cannot come in the sign of a dove. The Holy Ghost is a personage, and is in the form of a personage. It does not confine itself to the form of the dove, but in sign of the dove. The Holy Ghost cannot be transformed into a dove; but the sign of a dove was given to John to signify the truth of the deed, as the dove is an emblem or token of truth and innocence."[13]

The dove was the emblem chosen from the beginning to represent truth, innocence, and the Spirit itself. The second facsimile in the Book of Abraham confirms this by showing "the sign of the Holy Ghost unto Abraham, in the form of a dove" (Abraham, Facsimile 2, Figure 7).

The most well-known instance of the sign of the dove is at the baptism of our Lord. By it John knew for a certainty that he had baptized the Son of God (John 1:32–33). By this same sign it was manifest unto Noah that the Lord had made peace with the earth (Genesis 8:8–12). The dove was given as a sign in connection with the two most important baptisms of history, the Lord's and the earth's. It is the symbol of peace, purity, truth, and the power of the Holy Ghost, all of which can come in their full measure only after the sacred baptismal ordinance.

The Hebrew word for dove is *yonah,* which means moaning sound, presumably from the cooing which doves and pigeons make. In Mosaic ritual, the dove was used as the poor man's sacrifice. Possibly, the dove simultaneously represents the Spirit, purity, and also the moaning or remorse of conscience for our sins?

The dove has no means of defense except swift flight. If its young are attacked, rather than being furious and revengeful like other animals, it will flutter anxiously about, grieving and moaning. In like manner the Spirit of the Lord, if offended, will not retaliate but will simply retire (D&C 121:36–37). Rather than being furious, it will grieve for the victim.

Hen

During Jesus' last days on the earth, he taught at the temple. After pronouncing woes on the scribes and Pharisees and before departing with his disciples to the Mount of Olives, the Lord uttered the famous words, "O Jerusalem, Jerusalem, thou that killest the prophets, and stonest them which are sent unto thee, how often would I have gathered thy children together, even as a hen gathereth her chickens under her wings, and ye would not! Behold, your house is left unto you desolate" (Matthew 23:37–38).

The Lord made this same comparison to the Nephites and Lamanites in 3 Nephi 10 and on three occasions to the Latter-day Saints in the Doctrine and Covenants (see D&C 10:65; 29:2; 43:24). During the period of darkness that covered the new world after the Savior's crucifixion, the Lord spoke to all those who had survived, identifying himself and calling the people to repentance. Silence followed for the space of many hours and then his voice came again: "O ye people of these great cities . . . how oft have I gathered you as a hen gathereth her chickens under her wings, and have nourished you. And again, how oft would I have gathered you as a hen gathereth her chickens under her wings, . . . and ye would not. O ye house of Israel whom I have spared, how oft will I gather you as a hen gathereth her chickens under her wings, if ye will repent and return unto me with full purpose of heart" (3 Nephi 10:4–6).

Understanding why a hen gathers her chicks and how she does so deepens our appreciation of the Lord's symbolism. A mother hen nurtures, cares for, and shows continual concern for her young brood, whereas a male fowl, or cock, is disinterested and uninvolved after breeding. The hen communicates with her young using a variety of sounds. She gathers the chicks for feeding and watering by a low clucking sound known as a brooding call. This exemplifies the teaching, nurturing aspect of the Savior's care (see 3 Nephi 10:4). The hen also "serves as a sentry, a defense force . . . her sentry duties are nearly continuous. She is forever alert."[14] When danger approaches she gives an alarm call in a different frequency from her brooding sounds.[15] The chicks then run to their mother. With her chicks gathered under her wings, she will fluff her feathers to look as large and impressive as possible in hopes of frightening an intruder. If danger persists or draws too close, she may attack. Many a farmer has experienced sufficient beaks or claws to learn the defensive power of a protective mother hen. Hence, the symbol of the Lord's protecting care over his own.

The mother hen uses an assembly call to gather her chicks when they are spread out in a large area. On tests done with a wild hen, the hen would call, and even though her chicks had strayed over about forty acres, by the following day they would all be together again with their mother. The assembly call, when recognized, draws the errant young from great distances.[16] Therein lies perhaps the most significant element of the analogy of the hen and her chicks. "For verily the voice of the Lord is unto all men, and there is none to escape; and there is no eye that shall not see, neither ear that shall not hear, neither heart that shall not be penetrated" (D&C 1:2). The voice of the Lord is unto all, but those who are too self-assured or too preoccupied with the things of the world to respond to his voice and gather when called are as vulnerable as young chicks alone before a predator. As Jacob warned, "Wo unto the deaf that *will not* hear; for they shall perish" (2 Nephi 9:31). The Lord does not condemn those who cannot hear, only those who willingly refuse to hear.

In Doctrine and Covenants 29, the Lord sets forth some of the signs of destruction that will accompany his coming "to take vengeance upon the wicked" (v. 17). It begins with these words of comfort to those that follow him: "Listen to the voice of Jesus Christ . . . Who will gather his people even as a hen gathereth her chickens under her wings, even as many as will hearken to my voice and humble themselves before me, and call upon me in mighty prayer" (vv. 1–2). In the dark days ahead when the righteous will be gathered to Christ as they have been instructed, the Lord will symbolically raise the wings of his power to cover and protect his own. Then, in the fearful majesty of his might, he will destroy those who threaten his brood.

Wolf

Whereas the wolf is frequently mentioned literally in the Old Testament, all references in the New Testament are symbolic. Each New Testament reference represents apostate members or false teachers who come to destroy. Individually, wolves are wary and sneak up on their prey to take it unaware. In packs, however, wolves are more dangerous, attacking from all sides. Wolves, like certain other carnivores, sometimes kill well beyond what they need for food, as if they had an insatiable desire not to let anything innocent remain living.[17]

Christ warned against the dangers of the wolves among the flock: "Beware of false prophets, which come to you in sheep's clothing, but inwardly they are ravening wolves" (Matthew 7:15). A Church member or any false teacher may appear innocent but when hiding a private agenda and seeking for power or personal gain, he is as a wolf among lambs. The Savior and the apostles foresaw and foretold this danger. "Go your ways," said the Lord to the seventy, "Behold, I send you forth as lambs among wolves" (Luke 10:3). Paul made similar reference to the Church as it would be without the apostles: "For I know this, that after my departing shall grievous wolves enter in among you, not sparing the flock" (Acts 20:29). Foreshadowing the void left after his own and the apostles' death, the Lord declared: "He that is an hireling, and not the shepherd, whose own the sheep are not, seeth the wolf coming, and leaveth the sheep, and fleeth: and the wolf catcheth them, and scattereth the sheep" (John 10:12). Once the true shepherds were gone, those who were merely hirelings fled, for they cared not for the sheep. Even some who had been sheep, or at least had worn sheep's clothing, became ravenous wolves.[18]

Yet after the night of universal and individual apostasy, there is a future day of hope. When that millennial day comes, the returned Savior "with righteousness shall . . . judge the poor, and reprove with equity for the meek of the earth. . . . The wolf also shall dwell with the lamb, and the leopard shall lie down with the kid" (Isaiah 11:4, 6). This imagery could have both literal and symbolic fulfillment in the millennial day. The enmity between beasts will cease, and many of the people who scattered the sheep, now repentant, will become as lambs, resting and rejoicing with their former prey.

Goat

Symbolic references to goats in the Bible are fairly infrequent except as sacrifices, obviously symbolic in itself. The use of goats as symbols largely concerns their relationship with sheep. Young goats or kids are so much like lambs that in many instances they could be used interchangeably with a lamb for sacrifice (see Exodus 12:5; Leviticus 1:10). With maturity, however, the hair of goats is not as useful and hence is less valuable than wool from sheep. A male goat, or buck, is typically more impetuous and wild than a ram; and a goat's native, insatiable curiosity, is very different from the general docility and tractability of sheep. When we consider goats, we are reminded of scriptures like "looking beyond the mark" (Jacob 4:14) and "ever learning but never coming to a knowledge of the truth" (2 Timothy 3:7). In biblical days, goats and sheep were frequently herded together. Because they often have similar shape and color, they are difficult to distinguish from a distance. But they are easily identified upon close inspection, and proper division provides no problem for the owner. Goats and sheep herded together continue to follow their specific bell-laden leader, recognizing the sound of the specific bell they have been trained to follow. People, though living together and appearing similar, also follow their chosen leader and symbolically reveal their true character as sheep and goats. Hence the Savior's famous parable that compares all mankind to a large mixed flock: "When the Son of man shall come in his glory, and all the holy angels with him, then shall he sit upon the throne of his glory: And before him shall be gathered all nations: and he shall separate them one from another, as a shepherd divideth his sheep from the goats: And he shall set the sheep on his right hand, but the goats on the left" (Matthew 25:31–33).

Sheep

Sheep carry more detailed and deeper symbolic meaning than any other animals in the Bible. In the early books of the Old Testament, there are many literal references to sheep enumerating wealth or sacrifice. They were the source of meat, milk, leather, and wool, the staples of life. From the book of Psalms onward, most references are figurative, and of the seventy times sheep are mentioned in the New Testament, only five are wholly literal.

An interesting verse in the apocryphal book of 4 Ezra reads, "You, Lord, out of all the woods of trees chose for yourself the vine, out of all flowers – the lily, out of all birds – the dove, out of all quadrupeds – the sheep."[19] The nature of sheep makes them the most apt of symbols. They are generally docile, quiet, and patient. Some people see them as stupid creatures, but that is less a reflection of sheep's innate intelligence than their very timid, peaceful nature and their ready willingness to be followers. A peculiarity of sheep is that they are easily led when trained. Perhaps that trait is one of the foremost reasons they stand as a type of those who follow the Savior, whose disciples follow by choice, not by force.

Sheep demonstrate great affection for one another. They are extremely gregarious, feeding with their heads close together, and crying or bleating when separated. Ewes, while preferring not to be caught or handled by people, will often stand still before, during, and shortly after giving birth as though sensing their need for help. The quiet nuzzling of a ewe to her lambs expresses great tenderness. Rams can be large and powerful, but because of a strong sense of bonding usually remain with the flock. In general, rams are not as aggressive as other adult male animals.

Sheep are virtually defenseless against predators. They may struggle initially, but once firmly caught they become completely submissive. This submissiveness and helplessness necessitates almost constant care by a shepherd. Without a shepherd, they are easily scattered and destroyed. These characteristics of sheep make them a powerful symbol of human frailty, humility, patience, and long-suffering. They willingly follow a shepherd wherever he leads, be it to food and drink, to shearing, or to slaughter. They thus exemplify faith and trust. Their close bonding or flocking instinct speaks of care for one another. Newborn lambs are much weaker and more dependent than calves or foals. As they grow, lambs are active, the epitome of innocence. They acknowledge their need for help and are willing followers. In all these attributes, they mirror the natural characteristics of children, those traits which we are commmanded to recover.

The Good Shepherd

A sheep is the ideal symbol for mankind – sociable, caring, helpless, easily led, prone to get lost and be unable to find the way back. The

Lord uses the shepherd as an ideal symbol for his role as our leader and protector. Indeed, we could argue that sheep are used as symbols precisely because of their relationship to the shepherd. Hence, we have an incomplete understanding of how sheep are used as symbols unless we also understand the symbol of the shepherd.

Psalms 95:7 reads, "For he is our God; and we are the people of his pasture, and the sheep of his hand." The famous Psalm 23 states, "The Lord is my shepherd; I shall not want. He maketh me to lie down in green pastures: he leadeth me beside the still waters. He restoreth my soul" (vv. 1–3). Not only does the psalmist employ this beautiful analogy, but the Lord applies it to himself: "I am the good shepherd, and know my sheep, and am known of mine" (John 10:14). He compares coming into his kingdom to entering a sheepfold: "Verily, verily, I say unto you, He that entereth not by the door into the sheepfold, but climbeth up some other way, the same is a thief and a robber. But he that entereth in by the door is the shepherd of the sheep" (John 10:1–2). He then indicates that his followers know him: "To him the porter openeth; and the sheep hear his voice: and he calleth his own sheep by name, and leadeth them out. And when he putteth forth his own sheep, he goeth before them, and the sheep follow him: for they know his voice. And a stranger will they not follow, but will flee from him: for they know not the voice of strangers" (John 10:3–5).

In the old world, shepherds are known to their sheep. Several flocks will often mingle at watering troughs at certain times of the day. When the sheep are filled, the shepherds leave in different directions, calling their respective flocks. The sheep follow, each his own shepherd. Thus, the Savior scolded the unbelieving Jews: "Ye believe not, because ye are not of my sheep, as I said unto you. My sheep hear my voice, and I know them, and they follow me" (John 10:26–27).

Referring to his followers elsewhere, Jesus said, "And other sheep I have, which are not of this fold: them also I must bring, and they shall hear my voice; and there shall be one fold, and one shepherd" (John 10:16; see also 3 Nephi 15:16–24; 16:1). The risen Lord said to some of those other sheep: "Ye have both heard my voice, and seen me; and ye are my sheep" (3 Nephi 15:24), referring to two methods of recognition common to both sheep and people. This order, first hearing and then seeing, fits the known behavior of sheep and is also the order of receiving a spiritual witness in mankind as well. One first hears the voice of the Lord through his servants and his Spirit and then, knowing him, is ultimately able to see him.

Among the professions, no better example of care and nurturing exists than the shepherd. According to Jewish tradition, Moses and David were chosen as leaders of Israel because God had noted their gentle and understanding treatment of their flocks.[20] A shepherd lives a life of solitude. The Lord, also, knew loneliness. There is pathos in these words: "The foxes have holes, and the birds of the air have nests; but the Son of man hath not where to lay his head" (Matthew 8:20).

Jesus gives the parable of the lost sheep in response to criticism by the Pharisees and scribes that the Savior ate with "sinners" (Luke 15:2). In conclusion he says, "Likewise joy shall be in heaven over one sinner that repenteth, more than over ninety and nine just persons, which need no repentance" (Luke 15:7). But where does one find ninety-nine just persons who need no repentance? Joseph Smith commented on this parable and self-righteousness in these words:

"The hundred sheep represent one hundred Sadducees and Pharisees, as though Jesus had said, 'If you Sadducees and Pharisees are in the sheepfold, I have no mission for you; I am sent to look up sheep that are lost; and when I have found them, I will back them up and make joy in heaven.' This represents hunting after a few individuals, or one poor publican, which the Pharisees and Sadducees despised . . . I say unto you, there is joy in the presence of the angels of God over one sinner that repenteth, more than over ninety-and-nine just persons that are so righteous; they will be damned anyhow; you cannot save them."[21]

We all truly are lost sheep. Each of us should feel, in the words of Harry Rowe Shelley:

> The King of love my Shepherd is,
> Whose goodness faileth never;
> I nothing lack if I am His,
> And He is mine forever.
>
> . . . .
>
> Perverse and foolish oft I stray'd,
> But yet in love He sought me,
> And on His shoulder gently laid,
> And home rejoicing brought me.[22]

After the resurrection, Christ asked Peter, "Lovest thou me more than these?" Whether Jesus meant to ask if Peter loved Him more than the other apostles loved Him, or whether Peter loved Jesus more than he loved the other apostles, or whether Peter loved Jesus more than he loved the fish (meaning his occupation and mortal desires) is a matter of debate. The Savior's injunction nonetheless is the same: "Feed my lambs, feed my sheep. Care for those who hear my voice, who are mine" (see John 21:15–17). The Lord's words of comfort to us today are as reassuring as those he spoke to the early Saints: "Fear not, little flock" (D&C 6:34; Luke 12:32).

Among the most comprehensive chapters of scripture utilizing the meanings of sheep and shepherd is Ezekiel 34, where the inspired prophet castigates the hypocritical, self-indulgent leaders of Israel. While these verses can be read in the historical context of the Babylonian captivity, they also stand as a dire warning to leaders in the Lord's Church today who might exercise priesthood authority unrighteously:

"Son of man, prophesy against the shepherds of Israel, prophesy, and say unto them, Thus saith the Lord God unto the shepherds; Woe be to the shepherds of Israel that do feed themselves! should not the shepherds feed the flocks? . . . But with force and with cruelty have ye ruled them. And they were scattered, because there is no shepherd . . . Thus saith the Lord God; Behold, I am against the shepherds; and I will require my flock at their hand, and cause them to cease from feeding the flock; neither shall the shepherds feed themselves any more" (Ezekiel 34:2, 4–5, 10).

For us to avoid the same punishment Ezekiel pronounced against the ecclesiastical leaders of his day, we who are leaders in the Lord's kingdom should learn from a clue given in one of our modern hymns. Our prayer should be:

Make us thy true undershepherds;
Give us a love that is deep.
Send us out into the desert,
Seeking thy wandering sheep.
(*Hymns,* 1985, no. 221)

In Ezekiel 34, the Lord also promised to gather his flock again:

"For thus saith the Lord God; Behold, I, even I, will both search my sheep, and seek them out. As a shepherd seeketh out his flock in the day that he is among his sheep that are scattered; so will I seek out my sheep, and will deliver them out of all places where they have been scattered in the cloudy and dark day. And I will bring them out from the people, and gather them from the countries, and will bring them to their own land, and feed them upon the mountains of Israel by the rivers, and in all the inhabited places of the country" (Ezekiel 34:11–13).

The powerful analogy closes with this beautiful promise:

"And I will make with them a covenant of peace, and will cause the evil beasts to cease out of the land: and they shall dwell safely in the wilderness, and sleep in the woods. And I will make them and the places round about my hill a blessing; and I will cause the shower to come down in his season; there shall be showers of blessing . . . Thus shall they know that I the Lord their God am with them, and that they, even the house of Israel, are my people, saith the Lord God. And ye my flock, the flock of my pasture, are men, and I am your God, saith the Lord God" (Ezekiel 34:25–26, 30–31).

In concert with this promise of gathering and protection, the Savior describes his ultimate act of love: "I am the good shepherd: the good shepherd giveth his life for the sheep. . . . As the Father knoweth me, even so know I the Father: and I lay down my life for the sheep. . . . Therefore doth my Father love me, because I lay down my life, that I might take it again" (John 10:11, 15, 17).

The Lamb of God

In this supreme act of sacrifice, he who is the one and only Good Shepherd, fulfilling his unique role as the Only Begotten of the Father in the flesh, joins the throngs of his spirit brothers and sisters in a tabernacle of clay and symbolically becomes one of the sheep. But because he is the only one of the whole flock who is spotless and without blemish (see 1 Peter 1:18–20), he willingly offers himself as "the Lamb of God, which taketh away the sin of the world" (John 1:29). Indeed, the timeless sacrifice is made by and through the offering of the "Lamb slain from the foundation of the world" (Revelation 13:8; see also Moses 7:47). The imagery of purity, innocence, and submissiveness is all contained in one phrase, "the Lamb of God." He is both Shepherd and Lamb, the majestic leader and the humble sacrifice. It is symbolic as well as literal that shepherds in the fields near Bethlehem were the first to be invited to witness the birth of the Lamb who would become the Good Shepherd.

From the days of Moses the passover lamb, unblemished and without broken bones, foreshadowed the "great and last sacrifice" (Alma 34:14). The symbol of the deliverance of Israel from slavery becomes the symbol of the deliverance of mankind from sin and death. Isaiah beautifully foretold the vicarious sacrifice of the Savior:

"But he was wounded for our transgressions, he was bruised for our iniquities: the chastisement of our peace was upon him; and with his stripes we are healed. All we like sheep have gone astray; we have turned every one to his own way; and the Lord hath laid on him the iniquity of us all. He was oppressed, and he was afflicted, yet he opened not his mouth: he is brought as a lamb to the slaughter, and as a sheep before her shearers is dumb, so he openeth not his mouth. He was taken from prison and from judgment: and who shall declare his generation? for he was cut off out of the land of the living: for the transgression of my people was he stricken" (Isaiah 53:5–8).

We can feel the Lord's suffering in the shadows in Gethsemane in this verse from Elizabeth Clephane's poem about the parable of the lost sheep:

> But none of the ransomed ever knew
> How deep were the waters crossed;
> Nor how dark was the night that the Lord passed through,
> Ere he found His sheep that was lost.[23]

The makeup of our current Bible reveals an interesting pattern. The first specific animal named in Genesis is the serpent. This symbol of evil whose subtlety and lies would result in death and sin entering into the world appears in the Garden of Eden. The next animal named is the sheep. In Genesis 4 we read, "Abel was a keeper of sheep" (Genesis 4:2). The symbol of darkness and death is immediately followed by the animal that symbolizes the Lord of light and life. A juxtaposition of the same symbols occurs at the end of the book of Revelation. The last use of the word *serpent* is this: "And he laid hold on the dragon, that old serpent, which is the Devil, and Satan, and bound him a thousand years" (Revelation 20:2). In the three following chapters, which finish the book, the word *Lamb* is employed exactly seven times (Revelation 21:9–27; 22:1–3). The triumph of the Lamb over the serpent is complete.

The first use of the singular word *lamb* in the Bible occurred in the deeply symbolic setting of the journey of Abraham and his son Isaac to Mount Moriah. Isaac, beholding fire and wood for a sacrifice, innocently asked, "Where is the lamb?" On a symbolic level, that is the question of eternity. Abraham responded, "My son, God will provide himself a lamb" (Genesis 22:8). The fulfillment of that answer is the focal point of all scripture. Truly, the Almighty would provide a lamb, the Lamb of God.

CONCLUSION

We can develop a spirit of reverence and gratitude through contemplating the Savior's use of such elemental symbols as the beasts of the field and the fowls of the air. To prayerfully search and ponder the Lord's words is to marvel at their depth, breadth, and beautiful imagery, to deepen our appreciation for the symbols he chose and, more especially, to increase our love for him as the ultimate source of life, light, and truth. Isaiah wrote: "Come now, and let us reason together, saith the Lord: though your sins be as scarlet, they shall be as white as snow; though they be red like crimson, they shall be as wool" (Isaiah 1:18). Lambs' wool is a symbol of whiteness and purity. The innocent lamb is slaughtered so that through his scarlet blood the sins of the sheep may be washed as clean as wool. Each time we hear the words "the Lamb" we may remember not only who he is but what he did. That simple phrase may evoke within us sorrow for his suffering and especially godly sorrow for our personal sins, which he bore. Through complete acceptance of and obedience to Him, each of us may be numbered with those seen by John the Revelator who "came out of great tribulation, and have washed their robes, and made them white in the blood of the Lamb" (Revelation 7:14).

NOTES

1. "Humane Day," in *Juvenile Instructor*, ed. Joseph F. Smith, Apr. 1918, pp. 182–83.

2. "Editorial Thoughts," in *Juvenile Instructor*, ed. George Q. Cannon, 13 May 1871, p. 76.

3. *The Teachings of Spencer W. Kimball*, ed. Edward L. Kimball (Salt Lake City, Utah: Bookcraft, 1982), p. 190.

4. *The Encyclopedia of Religion*, 16 vols., ed. Mircea Eliade (New York: Macmillan, 1987), 4:326.

5. Joseph Fielding Smith, *Man: His Origin and Destiny* (Salt Lake City, Utah: Deseret Book Co., 1954), p. 194.

6. Ibid., p. 195.

7. Brigham Young, in *Journal of Discourses*, 26 vols. (London: Latter-day Saints' Book Depot, 1855–86), 9:246–47.

8. Simon Cohen, "Animals," in *The Universal Jewish Encyclopedia*, 10 vols., ed. Isaac Landman (New York: Universal Jewish Encyclopedia, 1939), 1:328.

9. Arthur Carl Stimson, *The Snake's Advocate* (Houston, Tex.: Eakin Press, 1982), p. 20.

10. Roy Pinney, *The Animals in the Bible* (Philadelphia: Chilton Books, 1968), pp. 118–19.

11. Joseph Fielding McConkie, *Gospel Symbolism* (Salt Lake City, Utah: Bookcraft, 1985), pp. 256–57.

12. Pinney, *Animals in the Bible*, p. 94.

13. *Teachings of the Prophet Joseph Smith,*, sel. Joseph Fielding Smith (Salt Lake City, Utah: Deseret Book Co., 1977), p. 276.

14. William L. Robinson, *Fool Hen: The Spruce Grouse on the Yellow Dog Plains* (Madison, Wis.: University of Wisconsin Press, 1980), p. 100.

15. Mark Ridley, *Animal Behaviour: A Concise Introduction* (Oxford: Blackwell Scientific Publications, 1986), pp. 126–27.

16. Robinson, *Fool Hen*, pp. 100–101.

17. Juliet Clutton-Brock, *Domesticated Animals from Early Times* (Austin, Texas: University of Texas Press, 1981), pp. 173–74.

18. *Didache*, 16:3, in *Ancient Christian Writers: The Works of the Fathers in Translation*, ed. Johannes Quasten and Joseph C. Plumpe, trans. James A. Kleist, (New York: Newman Press, 1948), 6:24.

19. *The Armenian Version of IV Ezra*, trans. Michael E. Stone (Ann Arbor, Mich.: Scholars Press, 1978), p. 73.

20. Louis Ginsburg, *The Legends of the Jews*, 7 vols., trans. Henrietta Szold (Philadelphia: The Jewish Publication Society of America, 1948), 2:300–301.

21. *Teachings of the Prophet Joseph Smith*, pp. 277–78.

22. Sheet music: Harry Rowe Shelley, "The King of Love My Shepherd Is" (New York: G. Schirmer, 1886).

23. Elizabeth C. Clephane, "There Were Ninety and Nine," *The World's Great Religious Poetry*, ed. Caroline Miles Hill (New York: Macmillan, 1928), p. 548.

CHAPTER ELEVEN

The Lord's Teachings on the Use of This World's Goods

J. Philip Schaelling
Director, Institute of Religion, Austin, Texas

The Lord created a beautiful world for us, complete with everything we would need to learn our earthly lessons and to find our way back to him. He has instructed us to use his gifts wisely lest we set our hearts upon the bounties of this earth and turn away from him. As the ancient children of Israel journeyed toward the promised land, the Lord told them that they were being led into "a land of wheat, and barley, and vines, and fig trees, and pomegranates; a land of oil olive, and honey." He then cautioned them:

"Beware that thou forget not the Lord thy God, in not keeping his commandments, and his judgments, and his statutes, which I command thee this day:

"Lest when thou hast eaten and art full, and hast built goodly houses, and dwelt therein;

"And when thy herds and thy flocks multiply, and thy silver and thy gold is multiplied, and all that thou hast is multiplied;

"Then thine heart be lifted up, and thou forget the Lord thy God, which brought thee forth out of the land of Egypt, from the house of bondage. . . .

"And thou say in thine heart, My power and the might of mine hand hath gotten me this wealth.

"But thou shalt remember the Lord thy God: for it is he that giveth thee power to get wealth, that he may establish his covenant which he sware unto thy fathers, as it is this day" (Deuteronomy 8:8, 11–14, 17–18).

During his mortal ministry, the Lord reemphasized that concern and gave specific instructions about how the goods of this earth were meant to be used. In three of his parables, the Savior illustrated these principles. In the parable of the foolish rich man, Christ identified the problem; in the second parable of the unjust steward, he pointed out how earthly things can be used well; in the parable of the rich man and Lazarus, he taught the eternal ramifications of ignoring this important lesson.

THE FOOLISH RICH MAN

One day while Jesus was teaching a multitude of people, he was approached for help in a family disagreement over material goods. "And one of the company said unto him, Master, speak to my brother, that he divide the inheritance with me. And he said unto him, Man, who made me a judge or a divider over you?" (Luke 12:13–14).

Obviously the man did not comprehend or appreciate the opportunity he had to stand in the presence of the Son of God, to hear him discourse on eternal truths, to have the privilege of asking him questions and learning at his feet, for he attempted to take advantage of the Lord by trying to enlist his support for selfish, temporal gain. It is no wonder that Jesus used the occasion to teach the futility of devoting one's life to the acquisition of temporal things. "And he said unto them, Take heed, and beware of covetousness: for a man's life consisteth not in the abundance of the things which he possesseth." He then illustrated a more eternal perspective with this parable:

"And he spake a parable unto them, saying, The ground of a certain rich man brought forth plentifully:

"And he thought within himself, saying, What shall I do, because I have no room where to bestow my fruits?

"And he said, This will I do: I will pull down my barns, and build greater; and there will I bestow all my fruits and my goods.

"And I will say to my soul, Soul, thou hast much goods laid up for many years; take thine ease, eat, drink, and be merry.

"But God said unto him, Thou fool, this night thy soul shall be required of thee: then whose shall those things be, which thou hast provided?

"So is he that layeth up treasure for himself, and is not rich toward God" (Luke 12:16–21).

Commenting on the foolish rich man, Elder James E. Talmage observed: "His sin was two-fold; first, he regarded his great store chiefly as the means of securing personal ease and sensuous indulgence; secondly, in his material prosperity he failed to acknowledge God, and even counted the years as his own."[1] Elder Bruce R.

McConkie noted that "God himself here says that a man who sets his heart on wealth and the worldly ease that accompanies it is a fool and shall lose his soul."[2]

The Savior affirmed these principles when he taught the Sermon on the Mount: "Lay not up for yourselves treasures upon earth, where moth and rust doth corrupt, and where thieves break through and steal: But lay up for yourselves treasures in heaven, where neither moth nor rust doth corrupt, and where thieves do not break through nor steal: For where your treasure is, there will your heart be also" (Matthew 6:19–21).

In Greek, Christ's admonition "beware of covetousness" could be translated more literally as, "Be on your guard against greediness of every kind." Greediness comes in many forms, but it is always destructive. We are repeatedly warned against the danger of never feeling satisfied, of coveting riches, of wanting more than is necessary to fulfill our purpose in life. The Apostle Paul put it this way: "For we brought nothing into this world, and it is certain we can carry nothing out. And having food and raiment let us be therewith content" (1 Timothy 6:7–8).

Whether rich or poor, we all return to the dust in temporal equality. In Euripides' tragedy *The Trojan Women,* Hecuba, unable to bury her infant grandson in the manner befitting his noble heritage, observes, "I think it makes small difference to the dead, if they are buried in the tokens of luxury. All this is an empty glorification left for those who live."[3]

Paul says: "But they that will be rich fall into temptation and a snare, and into many foolish and hurtful lusts, which drown men in destruction and perdition" (1 Timothy 6:9).

Paul does not talk about *being* rich but about the *wish* to be rich. The word *epithumia,* here translated "lusts," refers to the feeling of craving something. Some people feel certain that if they could only possess that one thing upon which their hearts are set, they could be truly happy. Then, after they acquire it, they enjoy it for a season, but soon they find one more thing, the acquisition of which, they are sure, will bring happiness. Obtaining that "one more thing" can become an obsession as we try to outdo each other in the number and nature of our possessions and thus we may waste and squander our lives by giving in to greed.

Paul observes: "For the love of money [the desire to be rich] is the root of all evil: which while some coveted after, they have erred from the faith, and pierced themselves through with many sorrows" (1 Timothy 6:10).

Our desire to be rich, instead of being content with having sufficient for our needs, causes us to stray from that which is right and can also bring us sorrow. Transient things bring transient pleasure. Eternal joy is produced only by eternal values and relationships. Wealth, in and of itself, will never bring eternal joy. Joseph Smith said, "Happiness is the object and design of our existence; and will be the end thereof, if we pursue the path that leads to it; and this path is virtue, uprightness, faithfulness, holiness, and keeping all the commandments of God."[4] If we could put a happiness barometer on those who are wealthy and those who have only sufficient for their needs, it might be that we would find no positive correlation between money and happiness. Often, those who are convinced that money equals happiness find instead that it brings sorrow.

Paul counsels: "But thou, O man of God, flee these things; and follow after righteousness, godliness, faith, love, patience, meekness" (1 Timothy 6:11). When we pursue the attributes Paul describes, we gain a different perspective. Elder John H. Groberg has observed, "As we begin to comprehend eternity, we gain a whole new catalog of values."[5] The necessity of this eternal value system is reflected in this parable of the foolish rich man.

As members of The Church of Jesus Christ of Latter-day Saints, we should ensure that we give proper priority to those things that have eternal value instead of those that have only temporal value. In 1831, at the meeting where it was decided to print the Book of Commandments, "the conference voted that they prize the revelations to be worth to the Church the riches of the whole earth, speaking temporally."[6]

If members of the Church today were asked which was of more value — money, or the Word of God as found in the holy scriptures — almost without exception they would choose the word of God. In my own experience, however, when I ask members why they do not have a regular reading program, they respond that they simply do not have time. I then ask, "If I gave you $100 per page, how long would it take you to read the Book of Mormon?" Suddenly they have lots of time. I then ask, "If I only gave you $10 per page, how long would it take you to read the Book of Mormon?" I find that they still have considerable time. If I say, "What if I gave you only $1 per page? (That would be $531.)" I find that people are still able to find time to read the scriptures even at $1 per page. How incredible! We say that the scriptures are of more worth than riches, but when it comes down to our behavior and use of time, money takes priority over the word of God.

Life should be defined not by time but by priority. We must understand that no one has time for everything that can be done in life. While it is appropriate that we seek to have sufficient for our needs, the Lord has instructed us, "Seek ye first the kingdom of God, and his righteousness; and all these things shall be added unto you" (Matthew 6:33). The word "first" can refer either to sequence or to rank. The New English Bible translates this same passage: "Set your mind on God's kingdom and his justice before everything else." It comes down to a question of priorities. Our use of time and energy defines that which is to be the most important thing in our life.

In the Doctrine and Covenants, the Lord commanded, "Seek not for riches but for wisdom, and behold, the mysteries of God shall be unfolded unto you, and then shall you be made rich. Behold, he that hath eternal life is rich" (D&C 6:7; 11:7). Note that he did not say, "While you are seeking for riches, make sure that you obtain wisdom." He specifically said, "Seek *not* for riches, but for wisdom." If we are to be blessed with the goods of this world, that is for God to decide, *but it should not be our quest.* If wisdom could be defined as "learning to think as God thinks, and learning to value as God values," then both our course and purpose in life are made clear.

THE UNJUST STEWARD

The Lord has placed upon this earth "enough and to spare" (D&C 104:17), and we must understand the proper use of that abundance with which he has blessed us. Though overheard by the Pharisees, the parable of the unjust steward was addressed specifically to Jesus' disciples. This parable does not preach repentance to the wicked but challenges righteous followers of Christ to greater growth as they are instructed regarding their stewardship in earthly things.

"There was a certain rich man, which had a steward; and the same was accused unto him that he had wasted his goods.

"And he called him, and said unto him, How is it that I hear this of thee? give an account of thy stewardship; for thou mayest be no longer steward.

"Then the steward said within himself, What shall I do? for my lord taketh away from me the stewardship: I cannot dig; to beg I am ashamed.

"I am resolved what to do, that when I am put out of the stewardship, they may receive me into their houses.

"So he called every one of his lord's debtors unto him, and said unto the first, How much owest thou unto my lord?

"And he said, An hundred measures of oil. And he said unto him, Take thy bill, and sit down quickly, and write fifty.

"Then said he to another, And how much owest thou? And he said, An hundred measures of wheat. And he said unto him, Take thy bill, and write fourscore.

"And the lord commended the unjust steward because he had done wisely: for the children of this world are in their generation wiser than the children of light" (Luke 16:1–8).

The term *oikonomos,* or *steward,* literally means "one who manages a household"[7] and was also used to refer to the manager of a large estate or even a public administrator. Elder Talmage explains, "The steward in the story was the duly authorized agent of his employer, holding what we would call the power-of-attorney to act in his master's name."[8]

The steward is not being dismissed because he has been cheating the owner, but because he has been handling his master's goods wastefully. The same word is used in the parable of the prodigal son who "wasted his substance with riotous living" (Luke 15:13).

Because the steward is being dismissed, he must hand over the account, or record, of his stewardship. Now that he will be out of a job, he wonders what he can do in the future. His idea, of course, is to use his stewardship to benefit those who are in debt to his master so that they will be more kindly disposed towards him and more likely to welcome him into their homes when his stewardship has come to an end.

The master of the steward actually commends his cunning. The word translated "wisely" can also mean "shrewdly" or "intelligently." This phrase is problematic. One scholar notes that "no parable in the Gospels has been the subject of so much controversy as this."[9] The debate stems from the praise of the steward's master in light of the steward's charging the creditors less than their full debt in his own selfish interest.

This parable is based on the world's way of doing business. Jesus is not telling us to handle our business affairs this way, but he is using the dealings of the business world to illustrate an eternal principle. The master in this parable is a shrewd businessman, and he recognizes that the steward has made a shrewd business move to protect his personal future. The strategy is *so* shrewd that he cannot help but admire it.

The moral of the story seemingly praises worldliness. The word *generation* means "family" or "clan." "The children of this age are more prudent in relation to their own clan (i.e., people of their own kind) than are the children of light."[10] Here the Savior divides mankind into two groups, the family of the world and the family of light. He points out that the children of the world are more astute in using their temporal stewardship to procure their temporal security than are the children of light in using their temporal stewardship to procure their eternal security. Elder Talmage explains it this way:

"Our Lord's purpose was to show the contrast between the care, thoughtfulness, and devotion of men engaged in the money-making affairs of earth, and the half hearted ways of many who are professedly striving after spiritual riches. Worldly-minded men do not neglect provision for their future years, and often are sinfully eager to amass plenty; while the 'children of light,' or those who believe spiritual wealth to be above all earthly possessions, are less energetic, prudent, or wise."[11]

In our world, many men of affairs will single-mindedly devote their lives to bettering their worldly status. Should not the "children of light" be equally focused on the values of eternity? The Savior goes on to add this ironic admonition: "And I say unto you, Make to yourselves friends of the mammon of unrighteousness; that, when ye fail, they may receive you into everlasting habitations" (Luke 16:9).

Mammon is an Aramaic word meaning riches (see Bible Dictionary). The word translated "fail" means "come to an end." The Savior is telling us that we must learn to use the riches of the world to create eternal friends. Just as the steward used this earth's goods to relieve those in debt to his master, thus gaining temporal friends who would welcome him into their homes when his job ended, the children of light must learn to use this earth's goods to bless those indebted to the Savior (all mankind). Then, when our years have come to an end, they will welcome us into everlasting habitations. Elder McConkie puts it this way: "Ye saints of God, be as wise and prudent in spiritual things as the unjust steward was in worldly things. Use the things of this world—which are God's and with reference to which you are stewards—to feed the hungry, clothe the naked, and heal the sick, always remembering that when ye do any of these things unto the least of one of these my brethren, ye do it unto me. By such a course, when your money is gone and your life is past, your friends in heaven will welcome you into eternal mansions of bliss."[12]

In the Book of Mormon, the prophet Jacob also teaches that the proper use of wealth is not for self but for others. He indicates that we must first love each other enough to share our wealth equally. Then we must seek for the kingdom of God with no thought of seeking for riches. Only after we have done these things and obtained a "hope in Christ," may we be justified in seeking for riches. Even then, we are not to use those riches for ourselves but to bless those who are in need. At no point does God grant us the right to have or even to wish for more than we need or for more than others have (see Jacob 2:17–19).

We must remember that using this world's goods to bless others is not restricted to giving to the poor. As we provide food and shelter in the righteous raising of children, resources for missionary and temple work, education for those who could not have it otherwise, or anything that helps others become better people, brings them back to God, and helps them fulfill their potential, we are fulfilling the intent of this parable.

The Savior then concludes his lesson in stewardship:

"He that is faithful in that which is least is faithful also in much: and he that is unjust in the least is unjust also in much.

"If therefore ye have not been faithful in the unrighteous mammon, who will commit to your trust the true riches?

"And if ye have not been faithful in that which is another man's, who shall give you that which is your own?

"No servant can serve two masters: for either he will hate the one, and love the other; or else he will hold to the one, and despise the other. Ye cannot serve God and mammon" (Luke 16:10–13).

We must learn that riches and the material objects of this world have no intrinsic value unless we learn to use them for eternal purposes. If we are unable to learn to use the riches of the earth in this way, "who will commit to your trust the true riches?" Elder McConkie counsels: "If you earthly stewards are not faithful in handling the wealth of the world which the Lord has entrusted to you, using it for the furtherance of his purposes, why do you think he will commit to you kingdoms and thrones and eternal riches hereafter. For he that is faithful over an earthly stewardship will be faithful over kingdoms and dominions in the world to come, but he that is unjust and does not use his wealth aright here, would be unjust in administering eternal riches."[13]

Moreover, the word translated "servant" actually means "slave." This passage literally reads, "No slave can be a slave to two masters." This distinction is important because it is quite conceivable that a servant could be a servant to two different people, each hiring him for a portion of his time. Being a slave, however, implies total submission to one master. The intended lesson is that one either learns to consecrate the riches of this earth to serve God or he becomes enslaved by those riches. There is no middle ground.

In the Book of Mormon, Nephi specifically forbids the quest for riches as an end in themselves by saying that "the laborer in Zion shall labor for Zion; for if they labor for money they shall perish" (2 Nephi 26:31). A latter-day prophet, President Spencer W. Kimball, confirmed this principle:

"The Lord has blessed us as a people with a prosperity unequaled in times past. The resources that have been placed in our power are good, and necessary to our work here on the earth. But I am afraid that many of us have been surfeited with flocks and herds and acres and barns and wealth and have begun to worship them as false gods, and they have power over us. Do we have more of these good things than our faith can stand? Many people spend most of their time working in the service of a self-image that includes sufficient money, stocks, bonds, investment portfolios, property, credit cards, furnishings, automobiles, and the like to *guarantee* carnal security throughout, it is hoped, a long and happy life. Forgotten is the fact that our assignment is to use these many resources in our families and quorums to build up the kingdom of God—to further the missionary effort and the genealogical and temple work; to raise our children up as fruitful servants unto the Lord; to bless others in every way, that they may also be fruitful. Instead, we expend these blessings on our own desires, and as Moroni said, 'Ye adorn yourselves with that which hath no life, and yet suffer the hungry, and the needy, and the naked, and the sick and the afflicted to pass by you, and notice them not.' (Morm. 8:39.)

"As the Lord himself said in our day, 'They seek not the Lord to establish his righteousness, but every man walketh in his own way, and after the image of his own God, whose image is in the likeness of the world, and *whose substance is that of an idol*, which waxeth old and shall perish in Babylon, even Babylon the great, which shall fall' (D&C 1:16; italics added.). . . .

"To set aside all these great promises in favor of a chest of gold and a sense of carnal security is a mistake in perspective of colossal proportions. To think that he has settled for so little is a saddening and pitiful prospect indeed; the souls of men are far more precious than this."[14]

THE RICH MAN AND LAZARUS

The parable of the rich man and Lazarus immediately follows the parable of the unjust steward. Elder Talmage notes that it is "addressed to the Pharisees as an instructive rebuke for the derision and scorn with which they had received the Lord's warning concerning the dangers attending servitude to mammon."[15] This parable also alludes to the unrighteous refusal of the Pharisees to share the healing richness of God's law with the spiritually ailing people of the Jewish nation. In the Joseph Smith Translation, the Savior emphasizes the direct application to them by saying:

"Verily I say unto you, I will liken you unto the rich man" (JST, Luke 16:3).

The parable then continues:

"There was a certain rich man, which was clothed in purple and fine linen, and fared sumptuously every day:

"And there was a certain beggar named Lazarus, which was laid at his gate, full of sores,

"And desiring to be fed with the crumbs which fell from the rich man's table: moreover the dogs came and licked his sores.

"And it came to pass, that the beggar died, and was carried by the angels into Abraham's bosom: the rich man also died, and was buried;

"And in hell he lift up his eyes, being in torments, and seeth Abraham afar off, and Lazarus in his bosom.

"And he cried and said, Father Abraham, have mercy on me, and send Lazarus, that he may dip the tip of his finger in water, and cool my tongue; for I am tormented in this flame.

"But Abraham said, Son, remember that thou in thy lifetime

receivedst thy good things, and likewise Lazarus evil things: but now he is comforted, and thou art tormented" (Luke 16:19–25).

The lavish description of the rich man's dress and life-style highlight his flagrant and egocentric use of wealth. His outer attire of purple clothing was very expensive.[16] The "fine linen" refers to the fact that even his underclothing is extravagant. To "fare sumptuously" every day could also be translated as "to enjoy oneself splendidly" every day. His entire life was devoted to using his wealth for his own pleasure.

On the other hand, the description of Lazarus is designed to contrast sharply with that of the rich man. Not only is Lazarus a beggar, depending on crumbs for sustenance, but he is further plagued with painful, infected ulcers. He is in such a helpless and pitiful state that even the dogs take advantage of him.

Death, however, brings many changes, including the standard by which wealth is measured. After death, wealth will not be assessed by the way in which one's body is clothed but by the way in which one's soul is clothed. Lazarus, though dressed in rags, was apparently rich in the things of eternity, while the rich man could no longer hide the poverty of his soul. He who was rich now becomes the beggar.

Remember that the parable of the rich man and Lazarus was given in response to Pharisaic covetousness. It was not that the rich man had money that caused him to be sent to hell but his excessive, insatiable desire for wealth and his selfish use of it. Likewise, it was not necessarily Lazarus's poverty that caused him to find refuge in Abraham's bosom. The poor can covet as well as the rich. It was his righteous endurance and the absence of coveting in his heart that earned Lazarus eternal riches. In latter-day revelation, the Lord warns:

"Wo unto you rich men, that will not give your substance to the poor, for your riches will canker your souls; and this shall be your lamentation in the day of visitation, and of judgement, and of indignation: The harvest is past, the summer is ended, and my soul is not saved!

"Wo unto you poor men, whose hearts are not broken, whose spirits are not contrite, and whose bellies are not satisfied, and whose hands are not stayed from laying hold upon other men's goods, whose eyes are full of greediness, and who will not labor with your own hands!

"But blessed are the poor who are pure in heart, whose hearts are broken, and whose spirits are contrite, for they shall see the kingdom of God coming in power and great glory unto their deliverance; for the fatness of the earth shall be theirs" (D&C 56:16–18).

When the rich young man asked Jesus what he needed to do to gain eternal life, Christ admonished him to "sell all that thou hast, and distribute unto the poor, and thou shalt have treasure in heaven." When the young man went away sorrowing, the Savior lamented that "it is easier for a camel to go through a needle's eye, than for a rich man to enter into the kingdom of God" (Luke 18:22, 25). Contrary to common belief, there is no gate in Jerusalem with this name, through which a camel, after shedding its load, might pass.[17] The Savior here refers to the impossibility of a camel passing through the eye of an actual sewing needle.

Why is it impossible for a rich man to enter the kingdom of God? Because his wealth, like the cumbersome load on a camel, stands as condemning evidence that he places the acquiring and hording of riches above helping his fellow men and building the kingdom of God. The prophet Moroni condemned such people: "For behold, ye do love money, and your substance, and your fine apparel, . . . more than ye love the poor and the needy, the sick and the afflicted. . . . Why do ye adorn yourselves with that which hath no life, and yet suffer the hungry, and the needy, and the naked, and the sick and the afflicted to pass by you, and notice them not?" (Mormon 8:37, 39).

Astonished at the Savior's strict pronouncement against the rich, those who heard asked, "Who then can be saved?" In the Joseph Smith Translation, the Savior responds, "It is impossible for them who trust in riches, to enter into the kingdom of God; but he who forsaketh the things of this world, it is possible with God, that he should enter in" (JST Luke 18:27).

There are members of the Church today who have "enough and to spare" and who say, "If the Brethren or the Lord ask me to give everything, I am prepared to do so." What they do not understand is that the Lord *has* asked.

"And it is my purpose to provide for my saints, for all things are mine.

"But it must needs be done in mine own way; and behold this is the way that I, the Lord, have decreed to provide for my saints, that the poor shall be exalted, in that the rich are made low.

"For the earth is full, and there is enough and to spare; yea, I prepared all things, and have given unto the children of men to be agents unto themselves.

"Therefore, if any man shall take of the abundance which I have made, and impart not his portion, according to the law of my gospel, unto the poor and the needy, he shall, with the wicked, lift up his eyes in hell, being in torment" (D&C 104:15–18).

Thus we have been warned again in our day that we will also suffer the fate of the rich man in the parable of the rich man and Lazarus if our material possessions are not employed to meet our spiritual obligations. We may not be asked to give everything at once, but we can begin by asking ourselves whether we serve God or mammon. Next, with the help of the Holy Spirit, we can learn to differentiate between valid needs and excessive desires or wishes. Then we can refine our value system so that it more closely reflects God's value system. In his system, earthly riches can be transformed into eternal treasures as we let the Holy Spirit guide us to become sensitive to those whom we might bless with whatever abundance we have. Finally, we can learn to consecrate our time, talents, and everything of this world with which we have been blessed to bring about God's eternal purposes. God has consecrated all that he creates, all that he comes in contact with, "to the immortality and eternal life of man." He has given us stewardship over the bounties of the earth, that we may learn to do the same.

NOTES

1. James E. Talmage, *Jesus the Christ* (Salt Lake City, Utah: Deseret Book Co., 1978), p. 439.

2. Bruce R. McConkie, *Doctrinal New Testament Commentary,* 3 vols. (Salt Lake City, Utah: Bookcraft, 1966), 1:474.

3. Euripides, *The Trojan Women,* 1248–1250.

4. Joseph Smith, *History of The Church of Jesus Christ of Latter-day Saints,* 7 vols. (Salt Lake City, Utah: Deseret Book Co., 1957), 5:134–35.

5. In Conference Report, Oct. 1978, p. 95.

6. *History of the Church,* 1:235.

7. H. G. Liddell and R. Scott, *A Greek-English Lexicon,* 9th ed., s.v. "steward."

8. Talmage, *Jesus the Christ,* p. 462.

9. Henry Alford, *Alford's Greek Testament,* 4 vols. (Grand Rapids, Mich.: Guardian Press, 1976), 1:596.

10. Walter Bauer, *A Greek-English Lexicon of the New Testament,* trans. W. F. Arndt and F. W. Gingrich (Chicago: University of Chicago Press, 1979), p. 154. s.v. "generation."

11. Talmage, *Jesus the Christ,* p. 463.

12. McConkie, *Doctrinal New Testament Commentary,* 1:515.

13. Ibid.

14. Spencer W. Kimball, "The False Gods We Worship," *Ensign,* June 1976, pp. 4–5.

15. Talmage, *Jesus the Christ,* p. 468.

16. Alfred Edersheim, *The Life and Times of Jesus the Messiah* (Grand Rapids, Mich.: William B. Eerdmans Publishing Co., 1974), 4:278.

17. See J. R. Dummelow, *A Commentary on the Holy Bible* (New York: Macmillan Publishing Co., 1973), p. 690, and Bruce R. McConkie, *The Mortal Messiah,* 4 vols. (Salt Lake City, Utah: Deseret Book Co., 1984), 3:304.

CHAPTER TWELVE

"I Am He":
Jesus' Public Declarations of
His Own Identity

Jonathan H. Stephenson

CES Curriculum Writer

A few years ago a controversy stirred in America surrounding Hollywood's release of a movie about the life of Jesus Christ. One leading news magazine, *Time,* ran a cover feature entitled "Who Was Jesus?" It reported some modern scholars' opinions that Jesus did not actually claim to be the Messiah, that such assertions represent the Church's later belief inserted by Gospel writers into their accounts, and that when Jesus said he was the "Son of God" or the "Lamb," he did not mean to be taken literally, only metaphorically.[1] Present-day scholars, the article continued, emphasize Jesus' human qualities. Five current diverse theories about Jesus emerge: "itinerant sage," "Hellenistic cynic," "apocalyptic prophet," "inspired rabbi," and "classic Jesus."[2]

In the midst of the public controversy surrounding the movie about Christ, Richard P. Lindsay, managing director of the Public Communications Department of the Church, released an official statement: "As our name implies, members of The Church of Jesus Christ of Latter-day Saints revere Jesus Christ as the Son of God, the Savior of the world. Having experienced the uplifting power of His Spirit, we encourage all people to truly seek the Savior and the eternal truths He taught, and to shun those things that detract from the dignity and spirit of His divine mission."[3]

The world may debate "Who was Jesus?" but faithful Latter-day Saints need not get caught up in a web of skepticism and unbelief. Modern revelation confirms the witness of the writers of the Gospels that Jesus Christ is the Son of the living God. Indeed, Jesus in his mortal ministry again and again bore witness of his own divinity. The

Joseph Smith Translation (JST) aids us considerably in our quest to understand the Lord's declarations.

DECLARATIONS OF HIS DIVINE SONSHIP

One way Jesus taught his own identity was to speak of the father-son relationship he had with God, calling himself "the Son" and God "my Father." Repeatedly he emphasized that God was his only Father and that he was God's only begotten Son on earth.

When Jesus entered Jerusalem to begin his public ministry, he made his way to the temple where "changers of money" infested its outer courtyard. He commanded the merchants to leave the temple, saying, "Make not my Father's house an house of merchandise" (John 2:16). The temple at Jerusalem was perhaps the greatest source of inspiration and pride for the Jews. This was holy space where God himself could come and where the Jews went to offer sacrifices and confess their sins before God. When Jesus challenged the authority of the temple rulers, attention throughout Jerusalem fell upon him. Religious leaders treated him with contempt; the masses watched and wondered. Jesus taught his identity to the gathering crowds by calling the temple "my father's house," not "our father's house." Jesus' declaration meant that he was not merely a mortal man but the Son of God himself.

When Jesus returned to Jerusalem to celebrate another Jewish feast, he drew tremendous attention to himself by healing a man on the Sabbath day. Jesus defended the timing of this action by declaring, "My Father worketh hitherto, and I work" (John 5:17). His explanation openly confronted the strict laws and practices of the Jewish Sabbath. His audience protested his words, for they understood him to say that "God was his Father, making himself equal with God" (v. 18). Jesus further taught, "The Son can do nothing of himself, but what he seeth the Father do. . . . For the Father loveth the Son, and sheweth him all things that himself doeth. . . . All men should honour the Son, even as they honour the Father" (vv. 19–20, 23). He concluded his statement by declaring, "I am come in my Father's name" (v. 43). For all who had ears to hear and hearts to understand, Jesus had openly taught that God was his Father and that he was the divine Son of God.

During his Galilean ministry, Jesus fed the five thousand. This action caused many to follow him, seeking more such miracles. They eagerly asked Jesus to repeat Moses' miracle and provide manna from heaven. The Lord explained, "Moses gave you not that bread from heaven; but my Father giveth you the true bread from heaven" (John 6:32). Twice more, the Savior defined his relationship with God, his Father: "All that the Father giveth me shall come to me" (v. 37); "No man can come to me, except the Father which hath sent me draw him" (v. 44). Because Jesus was plain and straightforward in declaring his unique relationship with God, "from that time many of his disciples went back, and walked no more with him" (v. 66).

While visiting Jerusalem for the feast of the Tabernacles, Jesus again declared his relationship with his Father. The Pharisees debated him, questioning him about his right to bear record of himself. Jesus responded, "I am not alone, but I and the Father that sent me. . . . I speak that which I have seen with my Father" (John 8:16, 38). As the debate turned to a discussion of fathers, Jesus said, "If God were your Father, ye would love me: for I proceeded forth and came from God. . . . I honour my Father, and ye do dishonour me. . . . It is my Father that honoureth me; of whom ye say, that he is your God" (vv. 42, 49, 54).

The Lord's bold claims made the Pharisees extremely angry. They felt that Jesus had blasphemed in declaring that God was his Father and that God honored him as his Son. Such blasphemy was punishable by death according to Jewish law. The Pharisees attempted to kill Jesus but failed.

Later that day, Jesus again taught the multitudes in the temple. He compared himself to a good shepherd and said, "As the Father knoweth me, even so know I the Father: and I lay down my life for the sheep. . . . Therefore doth my Father love me. . . . This commandment have I received of my Father" (John 10:15, 17–18). These words immediately caused a division among the Jews. Some rejected him as one having "a devil" (v. 20), while others wondered if he truly might be the Son of God.

When Jesus returned to Jerusalem several months later for the feast of Dedication, the Jews besought him to tell them plainly if he was the Christ. Jesus did not shy away from their request. He declared before all gathered in the temple in Solomon's porch, "My Father . . . is greater than all; and no man is able to pluck them [my sheep] out of my Father's hand. I and my Father are one" (John 10:29–30). Again Jewish leaders attempted to stone Jesus for what they considered to be his blasphemy. He responded by reiterating his Sonship of the Father (see vv. 32, 37–38).

Jesus escaped from Jerusalem, crossed the River Jordan, and began to teach in the province of Perea, which borders Judea on the east. A man from the multitude approached Jesus and asked what he should do to obtain eternal life. Jesus explained how difficult it is for a rich person to enter God's kingdom. When his disciples marveled at his teaching, he said, "How hardly shall they that have riches enter into the kingdom of my Father!" (JST Mark 10:22). Again, Jesus taught plainly that it was God, his Father, who would grant eternal life.

Just before closing his public ministry, Jesus once more emphasized the difference between his relationship with God the Father and the relationship all others have with him. A group of Greek proselytes to Judaism who had traveled to Jerusalem to celebrate the Passover wanted to see Jesus. He met them and promised, "If any man serve me, let him follow me; and where I am, there shall also my servant be: if any man serve me, him will my Father honour" (John 12:26). Those assembled then heard a voice as thunder from heaven as a witness of the truth of his sayings.

DECLARATIONS OF HIS DIVINE MESSIAHSHIP

In addition to teaching his divine Sonship, Jesus identified himself as the fulfillment of the messianic predictions made by the ancient prophets to the children of Israel. No greater prophetic figure existed in Jewish tradition and literature than the Messiah. The Messiah was the focus of Jewish hopes for national deliverance and represented the highest glory of Israel. Frequently Jesus plainly declared that he was the promised Messiah.

Jesus opened his Galilean ministry in Nazareth by declaring his messiahship. Word of Jesus' miracles in Jerusalem had spread rapidly, and many friends and acquaintances stood in the synagogue on the Sabbath to hear him speak. As all eyes focused on him, the Lord took the prophetic books into his hands and read aloud Isaiah 61:1–2. These words were familiar to them, beautiful words of hope concerning the long-awaited Messiah. Jesus closed the book and said, "This day is this scripture fulfilled in your ears" (Luke 4:21). Jesus' declaration was unmistakable: he was the Messiah. His hometown acquaintances were so angered that they "rose up and thrust him out of the city" (v. 29).

At the feast of the Passover in Jerusalem, Jesus responded to accusations of his enemies by invoking the recorded words of the prophets to substantiate his claim of being the Messiah: "Search the scriptures; . . . they are they which testify of me. . . . For had ye believed Moses, ye would have believed me: for he wrote of me. But if ye believe not his writings, how shall ye believe my words?" (John 5:39, 46–47).

Back in Galilee, Jesus amassed a tremendous following after feeding the five thousand. He taught them his messianic identity by saying, "It is written in the prophets, And they shall be all taught of God. Every man therefore that hath heard . . . cometh unto me" (John 6:45). He was thus fulfilling a prophecy of Isaiah (probably 54:13).

When Jesus returned to Jerusalem for the feast of the Tabernacles, he quoted a messianic prophecy (possibly Isaiah 12:3 or 55:1), teaching those in the temple his real identity. "If any man thirst, let him come unto me, and drink. He that believeth on me, as the scripture hath said, out of his belly shall flow rivers of living water" (John 7:37–38). Jesus' candid declaration caused many people to proclaim, "Of a truth this is the Prophet" (v. 40). Others exclaimed, "This is the Christ" (v. 41). A great division arose among the people. Jesus had so powerfully asserted his divine identity that certain officers who had been sent by the chief priests to arrest Jesus returned without him, saying, "Never man spake like this man" (v. 46).

Jesus testified of his messiahship frequently during the final weeks of his mortal ministry. In Perea, just before his final and triumphant entry into Jerusalem, Jesus taught a great multitude about discipleship. Some, seeking to justify themselves, claimed that they were disciples of Moses and the prophets. Jesus responded, "Ye know not Moses, neither the prophets; for if ye had known them, ye would have believed on me; for to this intent they were written. For I am sent that ye might have life" (JST Luke 14:36). Jesus taught that a disciple of Jesus could not give preeminence to ancient prophets, for the Messiah was greater than them all; he was the source of everlasting life.

Still in Perea, Jesus taught many parables to a crowd of disciples, publicans, sinners, and Pharisees. The Pharisees ridiculed him when he finished. "Then said Jesus unto them, The law and the prophets testify of me; yea, and all the prophets who have written, even until John, have foretold of these days. . . . And why teach ye the law, and deny that which is written; and condemn him whom the Father hath sent to fulfil the law, that ye might all be redeemed?" (JST Luke 16:17,

20). The Pharisees had insisted that the Law and the Prophets would save them. But Jesus countered their claim by stating that redemption was in him alone. As the Messiah, he was both the fulfillment of the words of the prophets and the fulfillment of the Law of Moses.

As Jesus taught in the temple during the final week of his mortal ministry, he publicly lamented the fate of Jerusalem's inhabitants who would not believe in him. "Ye shall not see me henceforth, and know that I am he of whom it is written by the prophets" (JST Matthew 23:39). He added that he would fulfill the messianic words of Psalm 118:26 by one day returning to Jerusalem in great glory with his holy angels.

DECLARATIONS OF HIS DIVINE RIGHTS AND POWERS

Jesus spoke of his own identity in a third manner by teaching publicly about his divine rights and power. He claimed to possess powers the Almighty himself had claimed—powers and rights ascribed to God by the writers of the holy scriptures. By asserting himself to be the source of these rights and powers, he claimed to be God.

Shortly after beginning his Galilean ministry, Jesus taught and healed many people in a crowded house. A man with palsy could not enter through the door, so his friends lowered him into the house through an opening in the roof. Knowing that there were Pharisees and doctors of the law sitting nearby, Jesus addressed the afflicted man: "Man, thy sins are forgiven thee. And the scribes and the Pharisees began to reason, saying, Who is this which speaketh blasphemies? Who can forgive sins, but God alone?" (Luke 5:20–21). Jesus responded simply, "That ye may know that the Son of Man hath power upon earth to forgive sins, I said it" (JST Luke 5:24).

After Jesus had called Matthew to be his disciple, Jesus ate supper at Matthew's house with Matthew's fellow tax collectors. The Pharisees saw that as irregular and suspect conduct and began questioning Jesus: "Why will ye not receive us with our baptism, seeing we keep the whole law? But Jesus said unto them, Ye keep not the law. If ye had kept the law, ye would have received me, for I am he who gave the law" (JST Matthew 9:18–19). The Jews revered the Law of Moses almost above all else. Now when Jesus claimed to have given this law to the Israelites, there was no mistaking his meaning. Jesus claimed to be that Jehovah who had spoken to Moses from Mount Sinai. Furthermore, Jesus asserted his right to interpret the meaning of the law and to instruct them on how it should be practiced.

Jesus claimed to be divine by identifying himself as the author of the law of the Sabbath. The Pharisees confronted him after he healed a man in Jerusalem on the Sabbath. As Jesus' disciples were foraging for food in a wheat field, the Pharisees asked, "Why do they on the sabbath day that which is not lawful?" (Mark 2:24). Using again the title "Son of Man" to refer to himself, Jesus answered, "The Son of Man made the Sabbath day, therefore the Son of Man is Lord also of the Sabbath" (JST, Mark 2:27). The Jews had developed sacred traditions regarding the Sabbath. Certain scriptures taught that the Sabbath came from God and was an everlasting sign between Jehovah and Israel (Genesis 2:3; Exodus 16:23–29; 20:11; 31:16–17; Ezekiel 20:12, 21). Jesus claimed that because he had originated the Sabbath, he now had the right to decide how his disciples would keep the Sabbath.

Another divine power claimed by Jesus was that of sustainer of Israel. Beside the Sea of Galilee, Jesus fed five thousand men and their families from five loaves and two fishes. When the multitudes later desired more food, they asked the Lord for bread from heaven. Jesus responded, "The bread of God is he which cometh down from heaven, and giveth life unto the world" (John 6:33). When they clamored, "Give us this bread," Jesus testified, "I am the bread of life" (vv. 34–35). Manna was "angels' food" (Psalm 78:25), and its daily appearance in the wilderness was a long-remembered symbol of God's mercy toward them. But Moses had taught them that manna, or physical bread alone, could not save them (Deuteronomy 8:3). The multitudes already understood that Jesus offered himself as the spiritual source for their sustenance for eternal life, but now he claimed an all-inclusive sustaining power to himself.

Jesus used the messianic symbolism in the Jewish feasts to make two powerful declarations concerning himself.

Elder Bruce R. McConkie writes of the Savior's teachings in Jerusalem at the feast of the Tabernacles:

"Jesus chose one of the most solemn and dramatic moments of Jewish worship. On each of the eight days of the feast of Tabernacles, as most authorities agree, it was custom, for the priest as part of the temple service, to take water in golden vessels from the stream of Siloam, which flowed under the temple-mountain, and pour it upon the altar. Then the words of Isaiah were sung: 'With joy shall ye draw water out of the wells of salvation.' (Isa. 12:3.) And it was at this very moment of religious climax that Jesus stepped forth and offered draughts of living refreshment."[4] Jesus fearlessly proclaimed, "If any man thirst, let him come unto me, and drink" (John 7:37). Like bread, water was precious to the Jews in their desert homeland. Therefore, it too had taken on figurative meaning. Isaiah compared the pouring of water to the pouring of God's spirit upon Israel's seed (see Isaiah 44:3), and God had promised to cleanse his people of their sins: "Then will I sprinkle clean water upon you" (Ezekiel 36:25). Jesus' solemn invitation could not have been mistaken. Jesus openly was laying claim to the power to sustain and cleanse his people.

The feast of Tabernacles also included a ceremonial lighting of the temple's great golden lamps. Jesus once more declared who he was, saying, "I am the light of the world: he that followeth me shall not walk in darkness, but shall have the light of life" (John 8:12). His hearers knew that the Messiah would be a light to the world (see Isaiah 60:1–2) and that King David had said of the Messiah, "The Lord is my light and my salvation" (Psalm 27:1). As Israel's light Jesus claimed to possess the divine source of knowledge and salvation. Angered by his assertion, the leading Jews threatened to kill him for blasphemy. Jesus responded, "When ye have lifted up the Son of man, then shall ye know that I am he . . . but as my Father hath taught me, I speak these things" (John 8:28).

A group of Jews continued to debate with Jesus about his identity. They began to discuss Abraham, the father of the Hebrew race and one of most revered men of all time to the Jews. To his combatants' claims of special parentage from Abraham, Jesus simply said, "Before Abraham was, I am" (v. 58). This claim to be superior to Abraham so inflamed those Jews that immediately "took they up stones to cast at him" (v. 59). Clearly, they understood his allusion: "I am Jehovah, the Great I Am."

Before leaving Jerusalem and the feast of Tabernacles, Jesus used one more symbolic image of his divine powers in his public teaching. Elder McConkie explains further: "Among the pastoral people of Palestine, service as a pastor or shepherd was one of the most honorable and respected vocations. Accordingly, many of the prophets had used the shepherd's vocation as a basis for teaching great spiritual truths and as a means of foretelling the coming of the Messiah who would be the Good Shepherd."[5] Jesus taught the multitudes in the temple, "I

am the door of the sheep" (John 10:7). He continued, saying, "I am
the good shepherd" (John 10:14). He was himself the fulfillment of
David's messianic psalm — Psalm 23 — and of Isaiah's prophetic words,
"He shall feed his flock like a shepherd" (Isaiah 40:11). He had power
to care for and watch over all his "sheep," for how could a man claim
to be King David's "shepherd?" A great debate arose among the people.
Jesus withdrew from them, leaving them to decide for themselves.

In Bethany, the Lord both asserted and demonstrated his divine
power. While Jesus was ministering in Perea, he was told of the death
of his good friend Lazarus. By the time Jesus arrived in Bethany,
Lazarus had been dead for four days. Jesus was met by Lazarus' sisters,
Mary and Martha, and many of the Jews who had come to comfort the
family. To the grieving Martha, Jesus said, "Thy brother shall rise
again. . . . I am the resurrection, and the life: he that believeth in me,
though he were dead, yet shall he live: And whosoever liveth and
believeth in me shall never die" (John 11:23, 25–26).

Jesus stood before the tomb, and in a majestic and dramatic demonstration of his power said, "Lazarus, come forth" (v. 43). Lazarus'
emergence from the tomb confirmed that Jesus truly held power over
life and death.

Following his arrest, Jesus was taken before a council of chief
priests and rulers of the Jews, the Sanhedrin. They had already con-
spired to condemn him to death, but after finding no evidence against
him, "the high priest asked him, . . . Art thou the Christ, the Son of
the Blessed?" (Mark 14:61). Jewish leaders knew that Jesus had openly
declared his divinity over and over again among the people, but they
wanted to have a clear charge against him. One more blasphemous
statement from his lips, they knew, could unanimously condemn him
to death. Jesus then closed his public ministry the same way he began
it, by declaring his identity: "Jesus said, I am: and ye shall see the Son
of man sitting on the right hand of power, and coming in the clouds of
heaven" (v. 62).

In the Book of Mormon, the prophet Jacob prophesied, "It must
needs be expedient that Christ . . . should come among the Jews, among
those who are the more wicked part of the world; and they shall crucify
him — for thus it behooveth our God, and there is none other nation
on earth that would crucify their God" (2 Nephi 10:3). How was it
possible for this nation to kill their God? Perhaps it was because he
said he was "THE KING OF THE JEWS" (Mark 15:26).

CONCLUSIONS

We live in a day when many doubt or do not know who Jesus was. Some believe that Jesus did not know who he was or, if he did, he never clearly told others during his mortal ministry. Some accept the divinity of Christ but say that Jesus left the affirmation of his identity to John the Baptist and his own disciples. Elder Dallin H. Oaks has said:

"When the gospel was first restored, the pulpits of this land were aflame with the testimony of Jesus, the divine Son of God and Savior of the world . . . Today, our missionaries cannot make that assumption. There are still many God-fearing people who testify of the divinity of Jesus Christ. But there are many more—even in the formal ranks of Christianity—who doubt his existence or deny his divinity. As I see the deterioration in religious faith that has happened in my own lifetime, I am convinced that we who are members of his Church need to be increasingly valiant in the testimony of Jesus."[6]

Elder Oaks pleaded for the Saints to bear witness of Jesus Christ:

"Latter-day Saints can become so preoccupied with their own agendas that we can forget to witness and testify of Christ. I quote from a recent letter I received from a member in the United States. He described what he heard in his fast and testimony meeting:

" 'I sat and listened to seventeen testimonies and never heard Jesus mentioned or referred to in any way. I thought I might be in [some other denomination], but I suppose not because there were no references to God either . . .

" 'The following Sunday I again attended church. I sat through Priesthood lesson, a Gospel Doctrine lesson, and seven Sacrament meeting speakers, and never once heard the name of Jesus or any reference to him.' "[7]

The Lord's public declarations not only assure us that Jesus knew who he was but they also set the example for all Christians to likewise testify with great power and conviction concerning his divinity. We testify of Jesus by expressing our beliefs that he is the actual son of the Father in the flesh, thereby being the only person ever to walk this earth qualified to atone for sins and resurrect himself so that all mankind might be saved; and that he has received all power from the Father and represents the Father in all things pertaining to this earth. We testify of Jesus by affirming that we believe that he was God before he came to this earth; that he is the creator of universes and this world,

"the Father of heaven and earth" (Mosiah 3:8); that he is Jehovah, the
god of the Old Testament; that his premortal, mortal, and resurrected
ministries, as seen and prophesied by holy prophets, will all be fulfilled
as he has said; that he is the true messiah; and that he will yet come
a second time with his angels in great glory. Finally, we testify of Jesus
by referring to the symbolic images that Jesus used—that he is the
bread of life, the living water, the door to the sheepfold, the good
shepherd, and the light, life, and law of mankind.

NOTES

1. Richard N. Ostling, in *Time*, 15 Aug. 1988, pp. 37–42.
2. The "sage" theory states that Jesus was a man like Gandhi, Socrates, and
other wandering, charismatic moralists. It rejects the idea that Jesus was concerned
about the end of the world and that he focused on the poor, sick, the handicapped,
and the injustices of the world he saw around him (*Time*, p. 39).
The "cynic" theory is a variation of the sage theme. It says that Jesus was a
product of the cross-cultural factors in Galilee, mixing ancient Greek philosophy,
Roman influences and Jewish thought, and that his message was concerned with
the general unnatural and unjust relationships among people of different social
classes (*Time*, p. 39).
The "prophet" theory views Jesus as a stern prophet who predicted the coming
judgment of God, and that he had a keen sense of mission and knew that his death
would fulfill it. It sees Jesus as clearly influenced by John the Baptist's preaching
of repentance and perhaps by the apocalyptic warnings of the Essenes (*Time*, pp.
39–40).
The "rabbi" theory says that Jesus was a rabbinical genius whose teachings
were in keeping with the liberal Jewish scholarship of his day. It says that Jesus
represents a humanistic trend in Judaism and sought a Judaism purified of hatred
(*Time*, p. 40).
The "classic" theory asserts that no single image of Jesus will do, and that
Jesus must be seen as both apocalyptic prophet, reformist sage, a purifier of
Judaism, and a builder of a new order (*Time*, p. 41).
3. *Church News*, 20 Aug. 1988, p. 4.
4. Bruce R. McConkie, *Doctrinal New Testament Commentary*, 3 vols. (Salt
Lake City: Bookcraft, 1965–73), 1:446.
5. McConkie, *Doctrinal New Testament Commentary*, 1:483.
6. *Ensign*, Nov. 1990, p. 31.
7. Ibid., p. 30.

CHAPTER THIRTEEN

John's Testimony of the Bread of Life

Thomas R. Valletta

CES Area Coordinator, Chicago, Illinois

The sixth chapter of John, which includes the Bread of Life discourse, bears powerful testimony of the divinity of Jesus Christ. This paper suggests five main points for consideration: John's account of events surrounding the sermon are part of his personal testimony; the Beloved Disciple wrote with an abundance of symbolism; events in this chapter are patterned after Exodus typology; the Bread of Life discourse can be more fully understood within the context of the entire chapter John 6; John takes the similitudes of the first Passover, the Exodus, and the miraculous manna in the wilderness and blends them with the emblems of the sacrament of the Lord's Supper in his testimony of Jesus Christ as the living bread.

THE GOSPEL OF JOHN AS PERSONAL TESTIMONY

The closing lines of John's Gospel contain an inspired confirmation "that his testimony is true" (John 21:24). When the Prophet Joseph Smith translated the "Gospel of St. John," he altered the title to the "Testimony of St. John."[1] This change is in concert with the Lord's own reference to "John's testimony concerning me" (D&C 88:141). John's personal witness of the Savior reflects his own distinctive style and emphasis. He does not include everything the Savior taught and accomplished but only that which supports his own purpose in writing (John 21:25; 20:30). His avowed purpose is "that ye might believe that Jesus is the Christ, the Son of God; and that believing ye might have life through his name" (John 20:31). What John includes and how he includes it often vary from the content of the synoptic Gospels. One could credit some of these peculiarities to the time, place, and audience of his writing, but even a cursory reading of his testimony reveals dissimilarities that run deeper than the setting. Reading the sermon of the Bread of Life and its surrounding narrative as testimony assists us in several ways. S. Kent Brown summarizes the value of studying each of the Gospels as individual testimonies: "In the first place, one is invited to treat each Gospel as possessing a certain integrity in its story of the Master. Secondly, one can come to sense how four authors—each from a different background and each needing to address a different audience—met the sacred task of writing about the Savior. Thirdly, one comes to realize that it was the concerns of the evangelists that frequently influenced what they included in their accounts."[2] But reading the Gospels as testimonies has potential pitfalls. One caution is given by Dr. Brown: "The flaw submerged in the modern study of the redactional or editorial activity of the evangelists consists of highlighting the compositional work of each Gospel writer with an unfortunate corresponding de-emphasis on the information that concerns the Savior."[3] It should also be noted that though John brings his own perspective, style, and emphasis to his account, he also wrote by the power of the Holy Ghost and by divine approval (D&C 93:6). His words, as scripture, constitute "the will of the Lord, . . . the mind of the Lord, . . . the word of the Lord, . . . the voice of the Lord, and the power of God unto salvation" (D&C 68:4). In essence, John's words are "the words of Christ" (2 Nephi 33:10).

What is true about John's testimony in general specifically applies to the portrayal of events surrounding the Bread of Life discourse— most of John 6. The sequence of other events in Jesus' life covered in this chapter is essentially the same as the sequence used in the synoptic Gospels (Matthew 14:13–33; Mark 6:31–52; Luke 9:10–17). John, however, approaches the events differently. Instead, he focuses on the pattern of events as a testimony of Jesus Christ.

JOHN'S USE OF SYMBOLISM

John is often cited for his extensive use of symbolism. "Virtually all agree," says C. Wilfred Griggs, "that more than one level of meaning can be found in John's writings, ranging from the obvious 'dictionary' level of meaning to symbolic realms understood only by those with spiritual insight."[4] Symbolism is used in scripture for varying reasons. Elder Bruce R. McConkie suggests that symbolism is used to testify of Jesus Christ in ways that only the faithful and spiritually primed will comprehend. He indicates that one of the many ways scriptures testify of Christ is through the use of "types and shadows, figures and similitudes, their purpose ofttimes being, as it were, to hide that which is 'holy' from the 'dogs' and 'swine' of their day (Matt. 7:6), while at the same time revealing it to those whose hearts were prepared for that light and knowledge which leads to salvation."[5] John's adept use of symbolism underpins his purpose for writing his testimony. John's Gospel is "the account for the saints," declares Elder McConkie. "It is pre-eminently the gospel for the Church, for those who understand the scriptures and their symbolisms and who are concerned with spiritual and eternal things."[6] With a scripturally based and spiritually mature audience as his target, John could divulge his deepest emotions and declare the most profound truths in symbolism. While the prepared Saints would perceive and receive his message, those less prepared could still receive "the lesser portion of the word" (Alma 12:10). Expressed another way, John's style "was essentially gnostic, which means he wished in cryptic fashion to allude to the gospel's deep mysteries without betraying their essence to the unreceptive or as yet uninitiated."[7]

Much of John's symbolism consists of similitudes or likenesses.[8] Elder McConkie states: "To crystallize in our minds the eternal verities which we must accept and believe to be saved, to dramatize their true meaning and import with an impact never to be forgotten, to center our attention on these saving truths, again and again and again, the Lord uses similitudes. Abstract principles may easily be forgotten or their deep meaning overlooked, but visual performances and actual experiences are registered on the mind in such a way as never to be lost."[9] Many of the similitudes recorded in John's testimony are anchored to historical events (the brass serpent, the manna, and so on). Others provide subtle comparisons between the everyday and the divine. Even the casual reader can readily detect recurrent themes of life, light, water, and night that permeate the book. John frequently juxtaposes metaphors, as in the case of light and darkness (John 1:4–5; 3:1–20; 9:35–38, 41). An awareness and understanding of similitudes provides us a valuable tool for digging deeper into John 6.

TYPOLOGY

The symbolism of types closely relates to the concept of similitudes. Joseph Fielding McConkie expresses a concise and encompassing definition of types: "A person, event, or ritual with likeness to another person, event, or ritual of greater importance which is to follow.

The term antitype describes future fulfillment, while typology is the study of types. True types will have noticeable points of resemblance, show evidence of divine appointment, and be prophetic of future events."[10] This is in harmony with the perspective that types are "divinely established models or prerepresentations of corresponding realities."[11] Typology is not the same as allegory. Unlike allegory, typology is rooted in historical reality.[12] Northrop Frye points out that while "allegory is normally a story-myth that finds its 'true' meaning in a conceptual or argumentative translation," typology is grounded in "real people and real events."[13] Nor are typological connections between persons or events considered accidental or arbitrary. George S. Tate writes that typological correspondences "constitute a significant system of intelligible coordinates in the gradual unfolding of God's historical design."[14] In other words, typology is a form of prophetic history presupposing that history follows a divine pattern.

Latter-day Saints should easily grasp the concept of typology. Modern scripture declares that "all things have their likeness, and all things are created and made to bear record" of Jesus Christ (Moses 6:63). The Book of Mormon emphatically announces that "all things which have been given of God from the beginning of the world, unto man, are the typifying of him [Jesus Christ]" (2 Nephi 11:4; cf. Mosiah 3:15; 13:10, 31; Alma 13:16; 25:15; 33:19; 37:45). John's testimony follows the pattern given in the scriptures by revealing Jesus Christ as the fulfillment of types. A sensitivity to typology provides a more profound appreciation and reverence for the Bread of Life sermon and its context.

JOHN AND EXODUS TYPOLOGY

Many instances of typology in John's testimony relate to the Exodus story. The exodus of Israel from Egypt, the miraculous crossing of the Red Sea, the forty years of wandering through the wilderness, and the dramatic entry into the promised land through the River Jordan were such extraordinary events that they became permanently etched into the spirit of all Israel. Much of Israel's perception of history as well as the prophetic framework of understanding the future was shaped by these events.[15] The Exodus, according to Hugh Nibley, "was not only a real event, but also 'a type and a shadow of things,' representing both escape from the wicked world and redemption from the bondage of sin."[16] Old Testament prophets focused on the meaning of the Exodus, often through typology. For example, Isaiah clearly has the Exodus in mind as he prophesies that "the Lord shall set his hand again the second time to recover the remnant of his people." He declares that "the Lord shall utterly destroy the tongue of the Egyptian sea; and with his mighty wind shall he shake his hand over the river, and shall smite it in the seven streams, and make men go over dryshod." Isaiah used additional typology with his prophecy of "an highway for the remnant of his people, which shall be left, from Assyria; like as it was to Israel in the day that he came up out of the land of Egypt" (Isaiah 11:11, 15–16). Important themes that form the Exodus motif resonate throughout the scriptures.[17] "The whole story of Moses and of the Exodus is a very dominant motif" in John's Testimony, according to Raymond E. Brown, and this typology prevails sufficiently that "some scholars have even suggested that the whole organization of the Fourth Gospel was patterned on Exodus."[18] George S. Tate indicates that "it is in the Gospel of John that we encounter the most concentrated Exodus typology."[19] James Plastaras supports that thesis with his statement that "the fourth Gospel presents the ministry, passion, and glorification of Jesus as the Passover mystery. There is hardly a page of this Gospel which does not contain at least one allusion to the exodus story."[20]

John's Gospel contains an extraordinary number of Exodus images.[21] Several examples reveal John's obvious consciousness of Exodus themes: The Baptist's reference to the Savior as "the Lamb of God, which taketh away the sin of the world" (John 1:29) points to the type of the Passover Lamb (Exodus 12:5; 12:21). The Savior's own attestation of himself as the "living water" establishes a connection with the provision of water for a thirsty and grumbling Israel (Exodus 17:3–7; Numbers 20:7–13; 1 Corinthians 10:4). In Numbers 21:4–9, we are told that the "Lord sent fiery serpents among the people" because of their chronic murmuring for the lack of bread and water during their travels. For the safety of his people, Moses was commanded to construct "a fiery serpent, and set it upon a pole." All who would look upon it would live. Moses did as he was commanded by fashioning a bronze serpent and placing it upon a standard. Even persons bitten by poisonous serpents received life as they "beheld the serpent." Centuries later, in a conversation with Nicodemus, Jesus bore witness that "as Moses lifted up the serpent in the wilderness, even so must the Son of man be lifted up: that whosoever believeth in him should not perish, but have eternal life" (John 3:14–15). Repeatedly and consistently, John's record testifies that Jesus was the realization of Exodus typology.

The examples given above disclose both the source and the interpretive framework of John's typology. Jesus Christ was the originator as well as the fulfillment of the typology recorded in John's testimony. John heard the Savior bear witness that the scriptures "testify of me" (John 5:39). As he observed the Master teach, he realized how the scriptures testified of Jesus Christ. John heard Jesus emphatically declare himself to be Jehovah, the very God of Abraham and Moses (Exodus 3:14; John 8:58). The Beloved Disciple comprehended the implications of this truth and could announce: "The same was in the beginning with God. All things were made by him; and without him was not anything made which was made" (JST John 1:2–3). John knew that Jesus Christ, as the creator, the messenger of salvation, and the Redeemer, is not merely involved in our life's story; he *is* the life story (JST John 1:1–5; John 11:25; D&C 93:8). John's use of typology presumes, first, that though man's natural eyes cannot often comprehend it, there is a divine design in history (D&C 58:3–4); and second, that sacred events transcend their mere historical occurrence by typifying Christ and his plan of salvation.

JOHN 6 AND EXODUS TYPOLOGY

John 6 contains a systematically developed Exodus theme with Jesus Christ as the fulfillment of its typology. When examined from a larger perspective, this section of John's testimony clearly shadows the Exodus type. The chart below shows major parallels between the Exodus events and the sequence of John 6. In both cases, a multitude follows a prophet to a place where they are fed miraculously, a deliverance through the sea to safety is miraculously performed; doubt, murmuring, and sign-seeking are rebuked by an exhortation to learn the deeper lessons of what has occurred; and prophets subsequently testify to the reality and meaning of the events.

General Pattern

Exodus of Israel from Egypt	The New Exodus
Israel follows Moses out of bondage into the wilderness by the sea (Exodus 12:38; Numbers 11:4).	Multitude follows Jesus to the other side of the Sea of Galilee (John 6:1–2)

Israel is fed "bread from heaven" (Exodus 16).	The great company is miraculously fed from the five loaves and two fishes (John 6:5–15).
The power of God saves Israel from the Egyptians; they cross the Red Sea on dry ground (Exodus 14–15). Later Israel follows Joshua, crossing the River Jordan on dry ground (Joshua 3).	The disciples fighting the stormy sea are rescued as Jesus walks on the sea to their ship (John 6:16–21).
Discourse from Jehovah on the meaning and significance of the Exodus experience (Exodus 19–20).	Discourse on the meaning and significance of the Bread of Life (John 6:22–65).
Testimony of prophets concerning the significance of the Exodus experience (Exodus 14:31; 15:1–22; Numbers 20:12; Deuteronomy 4:33, 35; Deuteronomy 6; Deuteronomy 26: 5–9; Isaiah 51, 52; 2 Nephi 25:20; 1 Nephi 17).	Peter's testimony that Jesus has the "words of eternal life" (John 6:66–71).

Truly John has caught the spiritual significance of these sacred events. Experiences in this chapter correlate with the Exodus typology, and both sets of sacred events typify salvation through Jesus Christ. In typology, the antitype need not correspond "to the type in all its properties, so as to form an almost photographic copy of it."[22] John does, however, incorporate many corresponding symbols that draw attention to the motif. Some of these specific correspondences are identified as follows:

Specific Images and Details

Exodus of Ancient Israel	The New Exodus
Moses at the "mountain of God" (Exodus 3:1, 12).	Jesus goes into the mountain (John 6:3, 15).
Jehovah multiplies signs and wonders (Exodus 7–11).	People follow because of signs (John 6:2, 26, 30).
Passover instituted by the Lord (Exodus 12).	Passover (John 6:4).
Multitude led by God through the way of the wilderness by the Red Sea (Exodus 12:38; 13:18; Numbers 11:4).	Multitude follows Jesus across the Sea of Galilee (John 6:1–3).

Manna (Exodus 16; Numbers 11; Deuteronomy 8).	Manna (John 6:31, 49, 58).
Manna compared with bread (Exodus 16:15).	Bread (John 6:7, 23).
Manna called bread from heaven (Exodus 16:3–4).	Bread from heaven (John 6:31–35, 41, 48, 50–51, 58).
Gathered according to eating (Exodus 16:16–21).	Gathered fragments; nothing lost (John 6:12).
Prophet like unto Moses (Deuteronomy 18:15–18).	That prophet (John 6:14).
Murmuring (Exodus 15:24; 16:8; 17:3).	Murmuring (John 6:43, 61).
Twelve tribes (Exodus 3:10; 28:21; Numbers 1:44; 34:18; Deuteronomy 13:1).	Twelve baskets; twelve disciples (John 6:12, 13).
Crossing the sea (Exodus 14–15; Joshua 3).	Crossing the sea (John 6:16–21).
Crossing occurred at night (Exodus 14:21).	Crossing at night (John 6:16).
Darkness emphasized (Exodus 14:20).	Darkness emphasized (John 6:17).
East wind (Exodus 14:21).	Great wind (John 6:18).
I AM (Exodus 3:14).	It is I (John 6:20).
Lord saved Israel that day (Exodus 14:30).	Immediately the ship reaches land (John 6:21).

Unveiling connections between typological events stimulates the mind and spirit, but it does not go far enough toward helping us gain scriptural understanding, for developing an analytical framework is worthless without an application. We might go beyond the simple correlations and examine the meaning of these similitudes. As previously noted, all things in the scriptures bear record of and typify Jesus Christ (Moses 6:63; 2 Nephi 11:4), and John writes his book with this same purpose (John 20:31). John quotes the Lord several times in chapter 6 declaring, "I am the bread of life." The multiplication of loaves and fishes, the crossing of the sea, and the manna discourse all reveal that Jesus Christ is our hope for salvation. Once we understand the purpose of John 6 and identify the Exodus theme, we must examine how these things testify of the Lord. We will pay particular attention to how John weaves together the events of his day with the symbols of the Exodus and the emblems of the sacrament of the Lord's Supper to typify Jesus Christ.

THE MULTITUDE FOLLOWS JESUS

The first four verses of John 6 introduce the setting for the subsequent events, as well as offer the first reflection of Exodus typology. John effectively sets this chapter apart from the preceding and subsequent chapters with the use of the phrase "after these things" in the first verse of chapter 6 and again in the beginning of chapter 7.[23] John's narrative indicates that a great multitude followed Jesus across the Sea of Galilee because of the signs they saw (v. 2). Before meeting with the crowd, Jesus "went up into a mountain, and there he sat with his disciples" (v. 3). Significantly, John points out that "the passover, a feast of the Jews, was nigh" (v. 4). These references to the multitudes following the Savior, going up into the mountain, and the Passover, implicitly connect the events of chapter 6 to the ancient Exodus of Israel. Prophets had long understood the sacred meaning of these pivotal events. Moses himself taught that "the Lord brought us out of Egypt with a mighty hand: and the Lord shewed signs and wonders, great and sore, upon Egypt, upon Pharaoh, and upon all his household, before our eyes: and he brought us out from thence, that he might bring us in, to give us the land which he sware unto our fathers. And the Lord commanded us to do all these statutes, to fear the Lord our God, for our good always, that he might preserve us alive, as it is at this day" (Deuteronomy 6:21–24). Joshua also proclaimed that the real lesson to learn from the Exodus is to "fear the Lord, and serve him in sincerity and in truth" (Joshua 24:14). The multitude that followed Christ, in John's account, can be compared with the children of Israel that followed Moses. Like the earlier Israelites of the Exodus, the Judean multitude following Christ are not wholly committed to him but follow because of the signs they saw (v. 2). In both cases, the purpose for leading them into the wilderness is to teach them to trust in the Lord completely (Psalm 78:13–72).

The Exodus pattern may be found in similar stories of wanderers being led through a strange land, a lone and dreary world where tests and trials occur. Hugh Nibley explains: "Now the idea that this life is a pilgrimage through the desert did not originate with the Christians or even the Jews: it has been the religious memory of the human race from the earliest dispensations of the Gospel."[24] Another scholar of antiquity suggests that, in the ancient view, "the desert is the world one passes through. It is nothing in itself, it is barren and inhospitable. It is not meant for people to remain in. One travels through the wilderness as one travels through time. Just like time, so does the desert lead to a new world, to the promised land."[25]

CROSSING THE SEA

A crucial episode of John's chapter 6 narrative is the crossing of the sea. While the other Gospel writers fix this event closely to feeding the five thousand, John sets it off distinctively. It functions as a literal centerpiece, a hinge for the whole chapter. John's focus on the images of the night (v. 16), darkness (v. 17), and the wind (v. 18) emphasize the sea crossing as an Exodus reenaction.

John paints a stirring depiction of people in trouble. His record speaks of the darkness of the night, "and Jesus was not come to them" (v. 17). As Jesus communes with Heavenly Father from the mountain (v. 16), "He [sees] the peril and strugglings of his beloved friends as they [seek] the safety of the western shore of the Galilean lake. They [are] seabound because he had 'constrained' them so to travel. . . . His awareness of their plight must have come by the power of the Spirit rather than the natural eye."[26] As their predicament worsens from "a great wind that blew" (v. 18), Jesus miraculously walks toward the boat on water. The disciples grow afraid (v. 19), but their fears subside with Jesus' simple yet profound assurance: "It is I; be not afraid" (v. 20). Unlike the synoptic writers, John focuses not on the calming of the sea nor on Peter's attempt to walk upon the sea but on safe passage through the sea and the emphasis of the divine name. " 'It is I' evokes remembrance of the passage through the sea in Exodus 14 and recalls to the reader's mind such poetic interpretations of that event as Ps 77:19, which says of Yahweh, 'Thy way was through the sea, thy path through the great waters'; and Ps 29:3, which speaks of 'the voice of the Lord . . . upon the waters.' "[27] In ancient lore, crossing the great waters evokes images of traveling through time or life and traversing from old to new worlds. The story of Noah escaping the destructive floods was thought to teach more than history. Noah and his family survived because of the divinely designed ark. Ark, in Hebrew, is "teba," and according to Rabbinic tradition, it can also mean "word."[28] To the ancients the lesson was quite clear: safe passage through this life depends upon the "word of God."[29] Friedrich Weinreb points out,

"The passage through this world is very much like passing through water, hence . . . a passage through time. And lest we should be drowned in water and in time, God gave us the 'teba', the 'word', which carries us like a ship through the water."[30] Understanding such a view allows certain patterns to emerge. Weinreb notes the similar situations of "the Egyptians perishing in the waters covering them, when biblical Israel, like Noah, gets safely across. Moses also got into a 'teba' and thus was saved in the water. And the passing into the promised land, the world-to-come, with Joshua, takes place through the water that creates a safe passage, through the river 'Jordan.' "[31] The disciples receiving Jesus into their ship and then landing safely compares with Moses and the Israelites crossing the Red Sea by the power of Jehovah.[32] Both accounts typify Jesus Christ as the "Word" with which Israel can safely survive mortality and enter into the eternal land of promise.

The episode of Joshua's crossing the Jordan River into the promised land (Joshua 1–4) carries much of the same symbolism as the crossing of the Red Sea and the crossing of the Sea of Galilee. In some ways, the Joshua account amplifies the others. Joshua, whose name means "Jehovah is salvation" and translates into English from the later Aramaic and Greek as "Jesus,"[33] leads the children of Israel into the promised land by crossing the Jordan River on dry ground. John's subtle literary image portrays Jesus going into the mountain as did Moses; and descending again, as did Joshua, to provide his disciples safe passage to the other side.

THE IMAGE OF BREAD

Much of John 6 focuses on the symbolism of bread and manna. After Jesus feeds the five thousand, the multitude attempts to take him by force and make him their king, causing Jesus to depart alone to a mountain (vv. 14–15). The next day the people finally locate Jesus in Capernaum and inquire, "How camest thou hither?" (JST John 6:25). The Lord without mincing words confronts them with their real motive: "Ye seek me not because ye desire to keep my sayings, neither because ye saw the miracles but because ye did eat of the loaves and were filled" (JST v. 26). Like their ancestors in the wilderness, these people are less interested in obeying the commandments than in eating (Exodus 15:24; 16:2–3). The crowd's concern for "the loaves" may also have been motivated by their messianic expectations. A common tradition of the day anticipated that when the Messiah came, his advent would be identified with a repetition of the Exodus manna miracle.[34]

The Lord speaks to the multitude about eternal aspects of bread instead of the temporal aspects. The people claim that Moses gave them "bread from heaven to eat" (John 6:31). Jesus corrects them, "Moses gave you not that bread from heaven; but my Father giveth you the true bread from heaven" (v. 32). Then he articulates his preeminent point: "The bread of God is he which cometh down from heaven, and giveth life unto the world" (v. 33). The manna of Moses' time is a type of the true bread given of the Father, which is none other than the Son of God. To their request for bread, Jesus unambiguously announces, "I am the bread of life: he that cometh to me shall never hunger; and he that believeth on me shall never thirst" (v. 35). The counterpart images of hunger and thirst are more than rhetorical embellishment; they draw upon the Exodus typology that joined the gift of manna and the gift of water from the rock.[35]

The Jews murmur at that bold declaration. They claim that Jesus is no more that the son of Joseph and Mary, whom they well know (v. 42). Their murmuring likewise follows the Exodus motif. Jesus answers by proclaiming, "No man can come unto me, except he doeth the will of my Father, who hath sent me. And this is the will of him who hath sent me, that ye receive the Son; for the Father beareth record of him; And he who receiveth the testimony, and doeth the will of him who sent me, I will raise up in the resurrection of the just" (JST John 6:44). That is startling news to people committed more to temporal survival and political intrigue than to everlasting life. The Lord reminds them that their "fathers did eat manna in the wilderness, and are dead" (John 6:49) He points out the only way to continue to live: "This is the bread which cometh down from heaven, that a man may eat thereof, and not die. I am the living bread which came down from heaven: if any man eat of this bread, he shall live for ever" (vv. 50–51).

Jesus continues his use of similitudes by adding, "Except ye eat the flesh of the Son of man, and drink his blood, ye have no life in you. Whoso eateth my flesh, and drinketh my blood, hath eternal life; and I will raise him up at the last day. For my flesh is meat indeed, and my blood is drink indeed. He that eateth my flesh, and drinketh my blood, dwelleth in me, and I in him" (vv. 53–56). If taken literally, these words would repulse his Jewish audience. The thought of drinking human blood is altogether abhorrent (Leviticus 17:10–14; cf. Acts

15:29). Even the idea of attaining eternal life by eating human flesh is a shocking notion to his Hellenistic public.[36] But clearly Jesus is not speaking literally, as the context of the discourse reveals. James E. Talmage explains, "There was little excuse for the Jews pretending to understand that our Lord meant an actual eating and drinking of His material flesh and blood. The utterances to which they objected were far more readily understood by them than they are by us on first reading; for the representation of the law and of truth in general as bread, and the acceptance thereof as a process of eating and drinking, were figures in everyday use by the rabbis of that time. Their failure to comprehend the symbolism of Christ's doctrine was an act of will, not the natural consequence of innocent ignorance."[37]

Now in the Bread of Life discourse, the themes of Exodus manna, the unleavened bread of the Passover, the miraculous feeding of the five thousand, and the emblems of the sacrament of the Lord's Supper are woven together in a marvelous way. In each similitude, the bread is provided by God. The bread is not earned but is critical for survival. The preparation and conditions of feeding are only on the Lord's terms. These similitudes also teach how the bread of life can be consumed. Latter-day Saints readily comprehend the symbolism of partaking of "the emblems of the flesh and blood of Christ" (D&C 20:40). For this reason, the Church is commanded to "meet together often to partake of bread and wine in the remembrance of the Lord" (D&C 20:75). Elder McConkie explains, "To eat the flesh and drink the blood of the Son of God is, first, to accept him in the most literal and full sense, with no reservation whatever, as the personal offspring in the flesh of the Eternal Father; and, secondly, it is to keep the commandments of the Son by accepting his gospel, joining his Church, and enduring in obedience and righteousness unto the end."[38] Those who abide these conditions receive the promise of eternal life. That is the essence of what Paul teaches, referring to those who "did all eat the same spiritual meat; and did all drink the same spiritual drink: for they drank of that spiritual Rock that followed them: and that Rock was Christ" (1 Corinthians 10:3–4).

As Jesus finishes his sermon, many are offended by his "hard" teaching (John 6:60). He perceives their thoughts and asks, "What if ye shall see the Son of man ascend up where he was before?" (v. 62). Jesus knows their spiritual blindness and tries to help them see: "It is the spirit that quickeneth; the flesh profiteth nothing: the words that

I speak unto you, they are spirit, and they are life" (v. 63). Like the ancient Israelites, the Lord's audience thought in terms of the flesh (Exodus 16:3). Yet, the Savior's truths can only be understood by the Spirit, as Paul asserts, "For what man knoweth the things of a man, save the spirit of man which is in him? even so the things of God knoweth no man, but the Spirit of God" (1 Corinthians 2:11).

CONCLUSION

The Bread of Life discourse should be studied in the context of the entire sixth chapter of John. Through the use of similitudes, types, and shadows, John bears powerful testimony concerning the divinity of Jesus Christ and the need for mankind to depend on their Lord. The events precipitating the discourse on the bread of life are patterned after Exodus themes. Each scene presented in John 6 portrays Jesus as the way of salvation. The imagery of feeding the five thousand, the crossing of the sea, and the Bread of Life discourse all interlock to form a collage of the Savior. The Exodus pattern and the sacred events of this part of Jesus' Galilean ministry coalesce with images of the sacrament of the Lord's Supper in typifying Jesus as the central figure in sacred history. The actual sermon becomes more understandable and powerful as we see how and why Jesus fused ancient and contemporary symbols to testify of himself.

NOTES

1. Joseph Smith, Jr., *Inspired Version: The Holy Scriptures, A New Corrected Edition* (Independence, Mo.: Herald Publishing House, 1971), p. 1207.

2. S. Kent Brown, "The Four Gospels as Testimonies," *The Eleventh Annual Sidney B. Sperry Symposium*, Provo, Utah: Brigham Young University, 29 Jan. 1983, p. 47.

3. Ibid.

4. C. Wilfred Griggs, "The Apostle John and Christian History," *The Sixth Annual Sidney B. Sperry Symposium*, Provo, Utah: Brigham Young University, 28 Jan. 1978, p. 36.

5. Bruce R. McConkie, *The Promised Messiah: The First Coming of Christ* (Salt Lake City, Utah: Deseret Book Co., 1978), pp. 43–44.

6. Bruce R. McConkie, *Doctrinal New Testament Commentary*, 3 vols. (Salt Lake City, Utah: Bookcraft, 1965), 1:65.

7. Thomas F. Rogers, "The Gospel of John as Literature," *Brigham Young University Studies*, vol. 28, no. 3 (Summer 1988): 68.

8. This paper uses the term *similitudes* according to its definition in the *Oxford English Dictionary*, 2d ed.: "A person or thing resembling, or having the likeness of, some other person or thing; a counterpart or equal; a similarity." Similitudes, defined in this sense, can include metaphors, similies, allegories, parables, types, and other forms of symbolism" (Oxford: Clarendon Press, 15:491).

9. McConkie, *The Promised Messiah*, p. 377.

10. Joseph Fielding McConkie, *Gospel Symbolism* (Salt Lake City, Utah: Bookcraft, 1985), p. 274.

11. Walther Eichrodt, "Is Typological Exegesis an Appropriate Method?" in *Essays on Old Testament Hermeneutics*, ed. C. Westermann (Richmond, Va.: John Knox Press, 1963), p. 225.

12. Ibid., p. 227.

13. Northrop Frye, *The Great Code: The Bible and Literature* (New York: Harcourt Brace Jovanovich, 1982), p. 84.

14. George S. Tate, "The Typology of the Exodus Pattern in the Book of Mormon," in *Literature of Belief*, ed. Neal E. Lambert (Provo, Utah: Religious Studies Center, Brigham Young University, 1981), p. 247.

15. Ibid., p. 248.

16. Hugh Nibley, *An Approach to the Book of Mormon*, 2d ed. (Salt Lake City, Utah: Utah: Deseret Book Co., 1976), p. 116.

17. S. Kent Brown, "The Exodus: Seeing It As a Test, a Testimony, and a Type," *Ensign*, Feb. 1990, p. 2.; Frye, *The Great Code;* Tate, "Typology of the Exodus Pattern," pp. 245–62.

18. Raymond E. Brown, *The Gospel According to John (I-XII)*, Anchor Bible, ed. W. F. Albright and D. N. Freedman (New York: Doubleday, 1966), p. lx.

19. Tate, "The Typology of the Exodus Pattern," p. 256.

20. James Plastaras, *The God of Exodus: The Theology of the Exodus Narratives* (Milwaukee, Wis.: Bruce Publishing, 1966), p. 325.

21. J. J. Enz, "The Book of Exodus As a Literary Type for the Gospel of John," *Journal of Biblical Literature*, 76 (1957): 208–15. Robert Smith, "Exodus Typology in the Fourth Gospel," *Journal of Biblical Literature*, 81 (1962): 329–42.

22. Eichrodt, "Is Typological Exegesis an Appropriate Method?" p. 225.

23. Brown, *The Gospel According to John (I-XII)*, pp. 235–36. Theories of rearrangement have been based upon these verses. The most common suggestion is to reverse chapters 5 and 6. At the end of chapter 4 Jesus is in Cana in Galilee. Having chapter 6 follow would fit better geographically, according to these theories. Chapter 5 could then take Jesus down to Jerusalem, which, it is postulated, would fit better with John 7:1.

There are several problems with the rearrangement theories. One difficulty, already alluded to, is that these theories generally go beyond what the text actually says. Another formidable objection is that there is no early manuscript or textual evidence supporting their suggested order. Additionally, most of the criticism of the current arrangement is based upon the presumption that John's purpose was to set forth a chronological narrative of events. That was probably not the case. Brown sums up the situation by stating, "No rearrangement can solve all the geographical and chronological problems in John, and to rearrange on the basis of geography and chronology is to give undue emphasis to something that does not seem to have been of major importance to the evangelist."

24. Nibley, *An Approach to the Book of Mormon*, p. 116.

25. Friedrich Weinreb, *Roots of the Bible: An Ancient View for a New Outlook*, (Braunton, Great Britain: Merlin Books, Ltd., 1986), p. 125.

26. Bruce R. McConkie, *The Mortal Messiah: From Bethlehem to Calvary*, 4 vols. (Salt Lake City, Utah: Deseret Book Co., 1980), 2:358.

27. Peter F. Ellis, *The Genius of John* (Collegeville, Minn.: Liturgical Press, 1984), pp. 110–11.

28. Weinreb, *Roots of the Bible*, p. 246.

29. This concept was also prevalent among the ancient Nephites. See, for example, Alma 5:3–13.

30. Weinreb, *Roots of the Bible*, p. 248.

31. Ibid., p. 247.

32. One is immediately struck, however, with the differences in the accounts. The Red Sea crossing included the whole company of Israel, but the account in John involved only the disciples of Jesus. Both accounts leave huge multitudes behind: in Exodus the Egyptians are drowned and in John 6 the multitudes are left on the shore. But the differences may suggest that in the final crossing, only true Israel will enter the promised land.

33. *The Illustrated Bible Dictionary* (Wheaton, Ill.: Tyndale House Publishers, 1980), 2:816.

34. McConkie, *Mortal Messiah*, 2:368. Raymond Brown also cites these traditions and concludes, "The expectation grew that the Messiah would come on Passover, and that the manna would begin to fall again on Passover." See Brown, *Gospel According to John* (I-XII), pp. 265–66.

35. Rudolf Schnackenburg, *The Gospel According to St. John*, 2 vols. (New York: Seabury Press, 1980), 2:44.

36. James D. G. Dunn, "John VI—A Eucharistic Discourse?" *New Testament Studies* 17 (1971): 330.

37. James E. Talmage, *Jesus the Christ* (Salt Lake City: Deseret Book Co. , 1967), p. 342.

38. As quoted in McConkie, *Mortal Messiah*, 2:379.

CHAPTER FOURTEEN

The Water Imagery in John's Gospel: Power, Purification, and Pedagogy

Fred E. Woods
Brigham Young University

Spiritual truths are often conveyed through figurative language. The writings of John especially use imagery to unify the structure of the text. More than any other New Testament writer, John was sensitive to the symbolism of water. John's usage of water imagery is striking because other New Testament texts, particulary the Pauline epistles, rarely employ water symbolism. Various derivations of the Greek word *hudōr*[1] (meaning water) appear a total of twenty-four times in his Gospel, while the synoptic Gospels contain only eighteen water references total. Only John included accounts of Christ turning water to wine, healing at the pools of Bethesda and Siloam, washing his disciples' feet, teaching the Samaritan woman at Jacob's well, and discoursing on water at the feast of Tabernacles. On the use of water in the Gospel of John, C. H. Dodd writes, "Thus while water as a simple natural phenomenon . . . provides in itself a suggestive figure, it is the rich accumulation of the symbolic meaning about the figure that gives its main significance to the water-symbol in the gospel."[2] Through the progressive accumulation of this water image, John accomplished his purpose for writing: "But these things are written, that ye might believe that Jesus is the Christ, the Son of God; and that believing ye might have life through his name" (John 20:31).

By his writings, John sought to convince and strengthen the Jewish members' belief that Jesus of Nazareth was the very Jehovah whom they and their fathers had worshipped. He was the Jehovah who created heaven and earth. He was the Jehovah who was the fountain of living water that had sustained their lives. He was the Jehovah who provided spiritual drink to all thirsty souls who desired perpetual pedagogy, or divine instruction. Jesus clearly used water as a vivid symbol to demonstrate his power and to give instruction. John emphasized water imagery to demonstrate the omnipotent power of Jesus and teach us we have a need for purification to receive divine instruction and life eternal. He portrayed Jesus as one who can calm both the waters and a troubled soul. John proclaimed him as the glorified Lord, who stilled the chaotic waves of the sea and also provided peace and order to chaotic lives on condition of purification from sin made available through repentance and ordinances.

POWER OVER WATER

Israel's History

Water is the most significant element in the arid land of Israel, for it sustains life. Because of the importance of water in the desert, Jehovah parted the Red Sea and brought water out of a rock to teach Israel that he had power over water *and* life. Nevertheless, Israel began to forget Jehovah once she reached the land of promise.

Canaanite vegetation, particularly in the north, was rich and the soil fertile. Consequently many Israelites were tempted to ask their Canaanite neighbors, "How does your garden grow?" The Israelites were deceived into thinking the Canaanite storm god Baal regulated the water supply.[3] Thus, the question of who controlled the water became a critical issue, particularly in the northern kingdom. The allegiance of Israel vacillated among many idolatrous gods, but primarily between the two gods who claimed power over water: Baal, the Canaanite storm god, and the Lord Jehovah, who had delivered the Israelites.[4]

Jehovah promised Israel that if they kept his commandments, he would allow them permanent residence in the land of promise (Deuteronomy 11:8–9). He also promised them that he would provide the rain they needed in its proper season (Deuteronomy 11:14). Yet he warned, "Take heed to yourselves, that your heart be not deceived, and ye turn aside, and serve other gods, and worship them; and then the Lord's wrath be kindled against you, and he shut up the heaven, that there be no rain" (Deuteronomy 11:16–17). "The Lord shall bring a nation against thee . . . whose tongue thou shalt not understand" (Deuteronomy 28:49).

Israel, essentially drowning in Baal worship, was taken captive by Assyria in 722 B.C. Although Judah did not succumb to Baalism as quickly as the northern kingdom had, she too sank into its mire and was exiled to Babylon in B.C. 586. When Judah returned from Babylon, however, Baal was extinguished from their lives, as evidenced by the omission of his name in their writings. Although the singular form of Baal as a divine name occurs fifty-eight times in the Old Testament and in the plural form of Baalim eighteen times, neither form is found in writings of the post-exilic period.[5] Furthermore, not one mention of Baal appears in the Apocrypha during the intertestamental period and only one reference appears in the New Testament.[6] The title *Beelzebub* meaning "Lord of the flies" is present seven times in the synoptic Gospels. Beelzebub is a dysphemism which is deliberately distorted to mock Baal-zebul, an epithet for Baal used in the Canaanite literature meaning "exalted," or "prince" Baal.[7] In each of these references Baal-zebul is used as a title for Satan. Thus we can surmise that the Jews no longer were tempted to worship the storm god Baal after their return from Babylon.

These words of Jeremiah must have penetrated the souls of the returning exilic Jews: "Are there any among the vanities [false gods] of the Gentiles that can cause rain? or can the heavens give showers? art not thou he, O Lord our God? therefore we will wait upon thee: for thou hast made all these things" (Jeremiah 14:22).

In the post-exilic period, Ezra and Nehemiah, as well as other priestly leaders, sought spiritually to restore the Jews by renewing emphasis on returning to the law of God. Although the recorded visual display of water miracles ceased, Israel was continually reminded of these miracles. Recitations of the Hebrew literature played a prominent role in reminding Israel of her lawgiver. For example, in the book of Nehemiah we find the children of Israel assembled in sackcloth and ashes in the spirit of fasting. They confessed their sins, and Ezra read from the book of the law of God (Nehemiah 8).[8] The Levites recited the great things the Lord had done for Israel and blessed and praised his holy name: "Thou, even thou, art Lord alone; thou hast made heaven, . . . earth, . . . the seas, and all that is therein" (Nehemiah 9:6). "And shewedst signs and wonders upon Pharaoh, . . . and on all the people of his land. . . . And thou didst divide the sea before them, so that they went through the midst of the sea on the dry land" (Nehemiah 9:10–11).

Central to these verses is the power of the Lord over water and thus over life. This notion is firmly attested throughout the Old

Testament record. Jehovah created the sea, turned the Nile to blood, and parted the Red Sea. Examples from the Apocrypha[9] demonstrate that these miraculous events were remembered during the intertestamental period.[10] The Book of Judith calls God the "creator of waters" (Judith 9:13). The Wisdom of Solomon recalls the Nile river narrative: "Instead of . . . an ever flowing river [the Egyptians received a river], stirred up with filthy blood" (Wisdom of Solomon 11:6). Also in this book God's power over the Red Sea is acclaimed: God's wisdom/power, "brought them over the Red Sea, and led them through deep waters" (Wisdom of Solomon 10:18).

Ecclesiasticus, written by Ben Sirach, connects these examples: "At his [the Lord's] command the waters stood in a heap, and the reservoirs of water at the word he uttered. At his order all that he pleases is done, and there is no one who can interfere with his saving power" (Ecclesiasticus 39:16–18).

Water to Wine

After this long history of miracles, Israel was generally convinced that Jehovah had dominion over all aspects of water. Thus, power to control water became a clear sign of his divine power. The Gospel of John portrays Jesus as the omnipotent, glorified Lord. John wrote to convince all that Jesus of Nazareth was that same Jehovah who controlled water and life. John began his Gospel with echoes of the great works wrought by the premortal Jehovah. "All things were made by him; and without him was not any thing made that was made" (John 1:3). John then informed us that "the Word [Jehovah] was made flesh, and dwelt among us, . . . and we beheld his glory" (John 1:14).

The first public miracle[11] of Jesus occurs in the next chapter, where we witness Jesus turning water to wine at a marriage in Cana (John 2:1–11). Elder Bruce R. McConkie commented, "By turning water into wine, he manifest during the early days of his ministry that he had power over temporal, physical matters."[12] Interestingly, the first plague the Lord brought against Egypt to demonstrate his saving power to the Israelite slaves was turning the Nile water to blood (Exodus 7:19–25). Robert Houston Smith states, "The first Mosaic sign is that of turning water into blood. . . . With it one may justifiably compare Jesus' miraculous changing of water into wine at Cana. . . . Jesus, like Moses, has divine power, with which he changes water into wine, 'the blood of the grape.' But . . . instead of creating death-dealing blood, Jesus creates life-giving wine."[13]

Smith makes a good comparison here, but he does not clarify one important aspect of this miracle. If we read the Exodus account very carefully we find that only "the Egyptians could not drink of the water of the river" (Exodus 7:21). In fact, Josephus informs us that the water "was sweet and fit for drinking to the Hebrews, and no way different from what it naturally used to be."[14] Thus to the Israelites the water served as a dual symbol of death to Egypt and life to Israel.

Some attending the wedding feast believed in Jesus through his first public miracle (John 2:11). John, the only Gospel writer to record this miracle, desired to indicate early that Jesus is indeed Jehovah, or the God of Israel. The question was not which God controls water but rather, is the man Jesus actually Jehovah, who has the power to govern water and thus life? John enlisted the imagery of water and specific water miracles such as the marriage at Cana to reveal that Jesus was indeed the Lord Jehovah who once turned water to blood and who was now come in the flesh as the mortal Messiah, possessing the divine power to turn water into the "blood of the grape" (Deuteronomy 32:14).[15]

Pool of Bethesda

John 5:2–9 is the account of Jesus healing a man at the pool of Bethesda:

"Now there is at Jerusalem by the sheep market a pool, which is called in the Hebrew tongue Bethesda, having five porches. In these lay a great multitude of impotent folk, of blind, halt, withered, waiting for the moving of the water. For an angel went down at a certain season into the pool, and troubled the water: whosoever then first after the troubling of the water stepped in was made whole of whatsoever disease he had. And a certain man was there, which had an infirmity thirty and eight years. When Jesus saw him lie, and knew that he had been now a long time in that case, he saith unto him, Wilt thou be made whole? The impotent man answered him, Sir, I have no man, when the water is troubled, to put me into the pool: but while I am coming, another steppeth down before me. Jesus saith unto him, Rise, take up thy bed, and walk. And immediately the man was made whole, and took up his bed and walked."

Concerning this scriptural account Elder McConkie writes, "No doubt the pool of Bethesda was a mineral spring whose waters had some curative virtue. But any notion that an angel came down and troubled the waters, so that the first person thereafter entering them would be healed, was pure superstition. Healing miracles are not wrought in any such manner."[16]

The focus of this story is neither the infirm man nor the water. The focal point of this story is that Jesus has far greater power than a mineral spring or any of his other creations. He is the creator of heaven and earth, of land and sea, the source of living water and the force behind all life-giving elements. Jesus exclaimed unequivocally, "I am the . . . life" (John 14:6).

Walking on the Sea

After a time, some of the people rationalized away the miracles performed by Jesus and said that he was, at most, a prophet. After all, prophets such as Moses, Joshua, Elijah, and Elisha had all performed miracles demonstrating power over the water. But whose power were they drawing upon?

The scriptures reveal that these miracles were accomplished through the power of the Melchizedek Priesthood. Through modern-day revelation we further understand that "before his [Melchizedek's] day it was called the Holy Priesthood after the Order of the *Son of God*" (D&C 107:3–4). Those prophets performed miracles with this priesthood authority, not in their own name nor in the name of Melchizedek, but in the name of—and with the power of—Jesus Christ, the *Son of God*.

Through this power Moses was able to walk through the parted Red Sea and Joshua, Elijah, and Elisha passed through the River Jordan on dry ground; but was there ever a prophet who walked successfully on water? Peter tried but sank and would have drowned were it not for Jesus who "stretched forth his hand, and caught him" (Matthew 14:31). Yet in the Gospel of John (John 6:16–21) we have the account of Jesus walking twenty-five furlongs on the Sea of Galilee.[17]

Elder Bruce R. McConkie explains that one of the reasons that Jesus walked on the water and calmed the storm was "to bear testimony that he was indeed the promised Messiah, the Son of God, the Incarnate Word, who though made flesh to fulfil the Father's purposes, yet had resident in him the powers of divinity."[18]

At the time of this miraculous phenomenon, perhaps the disciples recalled the words of Job: "[God] . . . treadeth upon the waves of the sea" (Job 9:8). Or maybe they asked the same question that Agur, the son of Jakeh, asked: "Who hath gathered the wind in his fists? who hath bound the waters in a garment?" (Proverbs 30:4). The psalmist also acknowledged, "Thy way is on the sea, and thy path is on the great waters, and thy footsteps are not known" (Psalm 77:19).[19]

Visualizing Jesus walking on the sea, we cannot ignore the powerful imagery and symbolism of the Lord's feet upon the water, for the scriptures bear witness that the earth is the footstool of the Lord.[20] God the Father also informed Satan, "I will put enmity between thee [Satan] and the woman [Eve], between thy seed and her seed [seed of Eve is Christ]; and he [Christ] shall bruise[21] thy head, and thou [Satan] shall bruise his heel" (Moses 4:21). Thus Jesus Christ has the power to put Satan's force of death, darkness, and doom beneath his feet.

The image of chaotic waters and the unruly sea serpent are often used in scripture to represent the battle against the powers of Satan that must be brought under control by the power of Jehovah.[22] By walking on the water, Jesus demonstrated that he possessed the power to conquer the Adversary; at the same time he illustrated the way whereby he and his disciples might subdue all enemies under their feet and conquer death and hell. From the Psalmist we read, "Thou madest him [man] to have dominion over the works of thy hands; thou hast put all things under his feet" (Psalm 8:6).

PURIFICATION THROUGH WATER

We have thus witnessed how water provides us with a dual symbol of both life and death. In the realm of ritual, water is used in ordinances such as baptism and the washing of feet to bring order to chaos or to purify and spiritually renew life. Brigham Young made the following statement about purification through water:

"In the beginning God cursed the earth; but did he curse all things pertaining to it? No, he did not curse the water, but he blessed it.[23] Pure water is cleansing—it serves to purify; and you are aware that the ancient Saints were very tenacious with regard to their purification by water. From the beginning the Lord instituted water for that purpose among others. I do not mean from the beginning of this earth alone . . . water has been the means of purification in every world that has been organized out of the immensity of matter."[24]

The Ordinance of Baptism

Water is a life-giving substance in the ordinance of baptism. And Jesus, by his use of water in his miracles, reminded us that he has power over our salvation as well as over the elements. "Baptism" is derived from a Greek word meaning to dip or to immerse,[25] but the history of baptism is obscure in the Old Testament, because of alterations in the original text. Joseph Smith said that, "Ignorant translators, careless transcribers, and designing and corrupt priests have committed many errors."[26] Nephi explained, "Many parts which are plain and precious; and also many covenants of the Lord have they taken away" (1 Nephi 13:26); however, Nephi also foretold a biblical restoration that would occur from other books that would come forth to "establish the truth of the first" (1 Nephi 13:39–40).[27] From these latter-day records we learn that the first man to be baptized was Adam (Moses 6:64–65) and that the ordinance of baptism was taught by ancient patriarchs and prophets. For example, Enoch explained that the Lord gave unto him, "a commandment that I should baptize" (Moses 7:11). Noah preached, "Believe and repent of your sins and be baptized in the name of Jesus Christ, the Son of God, even as our fathers" (Moses 8:24). By the time of Abraham the people had already strayed from this ordinance. God told Abraham, "My people have gone astray from my precepts, and have not kept mine ordinances, which I gave to their fathers; And they have not observed . . . the burial, or baptism wherewith I commanded them; but have turned from the commandment, and taken unto themselves the washing of children, and the blood of sprinkling; and have said that the blood of righteous Abel was shed for sins" (JST Genesis 17:4–7). Already the people had forgotten that baptism must be performed in the name of Jesus Christ, by immersion, and only for accountable persons.

In the days of Moses, the Melchizedek Priesthood ordinances were taken from Israel generally as a whole. The preparatory gospel of repentance and the ordinance of baptism continued, however, until the days of John the Baptist, who himself was baptized as a child (D&C 84:25–28). John the Baptist was never criticized for performing baptisms by the Pharisees of his day because the practice of immersion in water wasn't new to them. The Pharisees did say to Jesus, however, "Why will ye not receive us with our baptism, seeing we keep the whole law?" (JST Matthew 9:18).

Clearly the Pharisees as well as other Jewish sects had confused and distorted the ordinance of baptism by immersion for the remission of sins with other Mosaic rituals of purification as well as their own additions to the law.[28] This apostate syncretism seems to be present in Apocryphal literature from the book of Judith, which dates between 150–125 B.C.[29] The text states that Judith "washed herself at the spring, . . . and when she was come up from the water, she prayed the Lord God of Israel to make her way straight" (Judith 12:7–9). Josephus also indicates that the baptisms performed by John the Baptist were "not to beg for pardons for sins committed, but for the purification of the body."[30]

Baptism in the Gospel of John

John discussed baptism in the powerful introductory chapter of his Gospel. He recorded the event of the baptism of Jesus by John the Baptist in the River Jordan. In Joseph Smith's translation of John 1:29–34 we read as follows:

"Behold the Lamb of God, who taketh away the sin of the world . . . This is he of whom I said; After me cometh a man who is preferred before me; for he was before me, and I knew him, and that he should be manifest to Israel; therefore am I come baptizing with water. And John bare record, saying; When he was baptized of me, I saw the Spirit descending from heaven like a dove, and it abode upon him. . . . And I saw and bear record that it was the Son of God. These things were done in Bethabara,[31] beyond Jordan where John was baptizing."

Concerning this location, Elder Russell M. Nelson asks,

"Is it significant that this sacred ordinance was performed in virtually the lowest body of fresh water on the planet? Could He have selected a better place to symbolize the humble depths to which He went and from which He rose? By example, He taught us that He literally descended beneath all things to rise above all things. Surely, being baptized after the manner of His baptism signifies that through our obedience and effort we, too, can come from the depths to ascend to lofty heights of our own destiny."[32]

Elder Nelson also asks, "Could it be that Christ chose this location for His baptism in the River Jordan as a silent commemoration of the crossing of those faithful Israelites under Joshua's direction so many years before, as well as a symbol that baptism is a spiritual crossing into the kingdom of God?"[33]

This question merits a resounding yes! For Jesus so testified, "Behold, all things have their likeness, and all things are created and made to bear witness of me, both things which are temporal, and things which are spiritual, . . . things which are on the earth, and things which are in the earth" (Moses 6:63).

Israel's crossing through the River Jordan should also be viewed as a symbol of the need for baptism to journey to the promised land, or celestial kingdom. Joshua 3:13 and 16 says that the waters were "cut off." The Hebrew verbal root in these passages is *k-r-t*, the same root meaning to "cut a covenant." Also, we read in Joshua 4:1 that the people were, "clean passed over Jordan." Joshua 5:1 informs us that the children of Israel were circumcised. The concepts of baptism, covenant, and circumcision are very closely connected within the covenant of Abraham.[34] Paul even viewed the Israelite crossing of the Red Sea as a symbol for the ordinance of baptism (1 Corinthians 10:1–2).

The concept of baptism surfaced when Nicodemus came to talk to Jesus by night. Jesus said to Nicodemus, "Except a man be born again, he cannot see the kingdom of God" (John 3:3).[35] Nicodemus, misunderstanding Jesus, thought he was speaking of being physically reborn. Jesus then clarified, "Except a man be born of water and of the Spirit, he cannot enter into the kingdom of God" (John 3:5). Joseph Smith further explained this purpose, "It is one thing to see the kingdom of God, and another to enter into it. We must have a change of heart to see the kingdom of God, and subscribe to the articles of adoption to enter therein."[36] One of these specific requirements is baptism by water; however, water in and of itself does not spiritually cleanse a person. Brigham Young once asked this rhetorical question, "Has water, in itself, any virtue to wash away sin? Certainly not; but the Lord says, 'If the sinner will repent of his sins, and go down into the waters of baptism, and there be buried in the likeness of being put into the earth and buried, and again be delivered from the water, in the likeness of being born—if in the sincerity of his heart he will do this, his sins shall be washed away.' "[37] Thus baptism without repentance avails nothing.

The Gospel of John tells of a man born blind who was sincere in heart and thus was able to see the kingdom of God on earth. In John 9 we read that Jesus anointed the eyes of a blind man with clay and then told him, "Go, wash in the pool of Siloam. . . . He went . . . and washed, and came away seeing" (John 9:7). Because the hearts of the

Pharisees were unchanged, they remained spiritually blind, while the blind man went away seeing both temporally and spiritually. This story not only teaches the importance of faith and obedience but also alludes to baptism and the importance of being washed clean through ordinances.[38] Water clearly plays a crucial symbolic role as a representation of new life. And because the Lord demonstrated his power over water, he showed us that he has power to cleanse us and give us new life.

PEDAGOGY THROUGH WATER IMAGERY

Jacob's Well

The Greek words *hudōr zōn,* meaning "living water," are contained twice in the Gospel of John (John 4:10; 7:38). In the Joseph Smith Translation of John, Jesus journeyed to a city of Sychar, where he offered a woman living water:

"Now Jacob's well was there. Jesus therefore being wearied with his journey, sat thus on the well: and it was about the sixth hour. There cometh a woman of Samaria to draw water: Jesus saith unto her, Give me to drink. The woman of Samaria saith unto him, How is it that thou being a Jew, asketh drink of me, which am a woman of Samaria? for the Jews have no dealings with the Samaritans. Jesus answered and said unto her, if thou knewest the gift of God, and who it is that saith unto thee, Give me to drink; thou wouldest have asked of him, and he would have given thee living water. Whosoever shall drink of this well shall thirst again: But whosoever drinketh of the water that I shall give him shall never thirst;[39] but the water that I shall give him shall be in him a well of water springing up into everlasting life" (JST John 4:6–7, 9–10, 13–14).

This account shows us another facet of John's water imagery. The living water that Jesus referred to here is divine revelation that flows from him and leads to eternal life. At the conclusion of this encounter, "The woman then left her waterpot, and went her way into the city, and saith to the men, Come, see a man, which told me all things that ever I did: is not this the Christ?" (John 4:28–29). The woman left her stagnant, apostate teachings at the well, like her water pot,[40] and went forth with a well of living water within.

The use of water symbolism for instruction is attested to throughout John's writings[41] as well as in other roughly contemporary Jewish literature. For example, in the Babylonian Talmud, the Rabbis refer to water as "Torah," which means "divine instruction." In *'Abodah Zarah* R. (Rabbi) Johanan said on behalf of R. (Rabbi) Bana'h: "what is meant by 'water' is Torah, as it is said, Oh ye who are thirsty come to the water."[42] The Mishnah's instruction to "drink in their [Sages'] words with thirst" (Aboth 1:4).[43] From the apocryphal literature dated near to the time of the writings of John, we also have God's instruction to Ezra the Scribe: "Ezra, open your mouth and drink what I give, what I give you to drink. And I opened my mouth, and behold a full cup was offered me. It was full of what looked like water . . . And I took it, and drank, and when I had drank it my heart gushed forth understanding and wisdom grew in my breast" (2 Esdras 14:38–40).

The Feast of Tabernacles

In Joseph Smith's translation of John 7:37–39, we encounter another water narrative, the second reference to "living water" in the Gospel of John:

"In the great last day, that great day of the feast, Jesus stood and cried saying, If any man thirst, let him come unto me and drink. He that believeth on me, as the scripture hath said,[44] out of his belly[45] shall flow rivers of living water. (But this he spake of the Spirit, which they that believe on him should receive; for the Holy Ghost was promised unto them who believe, after that Jesus was glorified.)"

The feast referred to here is the feast of Booths, which recalled Israel's sojourn in the wilderness and celebrated the gathering of all the fruits of the annual Israelite harvest at the close of the agricultural year. It is also known in the Bible as the feast of Tabernacles or the feast of Ingathering (Ezra 23:16; Leviticus 27:34).[46] The feast symbolizes the gathering of the human harvest of souls in the millennial day. Elder Bruce R. McConkie writes, "Above all other occasions it was one for rejoicing, bearing testimony, and praising the Lord. In the full sense, it is the Feast of Jehovah, the one Mosaic celebration which . . . shall be restored when Jehovah comes to reign personally upon the earth for a thousand years."[47]

Ceremonial rituals were said to be added to the feast of Tabernacles in the post-Exilic period.[48] Such additions included the illumination of the temple and the pouring out of the water of Siloam on the temple altar. According to Elder McConkie, if that is so, "it is an indication of continuing revelation to the Lord's people; or, it may be that the rites, though not mentioned in Holy Writ, were part of the ceremonies from the beginning.[49] In any event they were a vital part of valid and approved performances in the day of Jesus. He was acquainted with them and used them for his own purposes."[50] When the priest poured water on the altar, Jesus was at the appropriate place and time to declare these penetrating words: "If any man thirst, let him come unto me, and drink. He that believeth on me . . . out of his belly shall flow rivers of living water" (John 7:37–38). "It was as though he said: 'This feast is designed to point your attention to me and the salvation which I bring. Now I have come; if ye will believe in me, ye shall be saved; and then from you, by the power of the Spirit, shall also go forth living water.' "[51] "According to Rabbi bar-Kahana (c. A.D. 130) the feast [of Tabernacles] holds within itself the promise of the Messiah. . . . Again, the tractate on this feast in the Jerusalem Talmud explains the name of the [water] ceremony by referring to the Isaian te[x]t . . . explaining the name 'Place of Drawing' from the fact that it was 'from there that they drew the Holy Spirit.' "[52] Most Jews, however, rejected the message of Jesus to "draw water out of the wells of salvation" (Isaiah 12:3). Instead they forsook "the fountain of living waters, and hewed them out cisterns, broken cisterns, that [could] hold no water" (Jeremiah 2:13).

CONCLUSION

Through the imagery of water, the apostle John revealed the power and purposes of the great Jehovah, even Jesus Christ. Today this same Jesus promises that "unto him that keepeth my commandments I will give the mysteries of my kingdom, and the same shall be in him a well of living water, springing up unto everlasting life" (D&C 63:23). These mysteries are made known to the righteous, who absorb and apply the written and oral words of God's servants and partake of the sacred truths within the House of the Lord. In these latter days, the Lord has once again blessed thirsting Saints with those mysteries. A common feature of many temples is a beautiful fountain of water at its doors. The flowing of water seems to symbolize the knowledge available within, the personal purity necessary to obtain it, and the heavenly power associated with it. In the Dead Sea Scrolls, we are told that the teachers of lies withhold the drink of knowledge from the thirsty. (IQH 4:25–26.) Yet the Spirit testifies today as it did in John's day that the teacher of truth, even Jesus Christ, who once thirsted like no other (John 19:28), has made it possible for us to drink and never thirst again.

NOTES

1. Leonard Goppelt, *"hudōr,"* in *Theological Dictionary of the New Testament,* ed. Gerhard Kittel, trans. Geoffrey W. Bromily, 10 vols. (Grand Rapids, Mich.: William B. Eerdmans Publishing Co., 1982), 1:322.

2. C. H. Dodd, *The Interpretation of the Fourth Gospel* (Cambridge: Cambridge University Press, 1953), p. 138.

3. H. H. Guthrie in his article "Hadad" in the *Interpreter's Dictionary of the Bible,* 2:507, informs us that the name *Baal* is a title. The proper name was *Hadad,* which means "thunderer" in Akkadin. For further information regarding Baal, see the article by John Gray entitled "Baal" in *Interpreter's Dictionary of the Bible,* 1:328–29.

4. The many water miracles recorded in the Old Testament seem to have functioned as a polemic against the Canaanite storm god, Baal.

5. M. J. Mulder, *"ba'al,"* in the *Theological Dictionary of the Old Testament,* ed. G. Johannes Botterweck and Helmer Ringren, trans. John T. Willis, 10 vols. (Grand Rapids, Mich.: William B. Eerdmans Publishing Co., 1975), 2:192.

6. In Romans 11:4, Paul paraphrases 1 Kings 19:18l where the Lord tells Elijah that seven thousand souls have not bowed to Baal.

7. See the word *zebub* in William L. Holladay, *A Concise Hebrew and Aramaic Lexicon of the Old Testament* (Grand Rapids, Mich.: William B. Eerdmans Publishing Co., 1982), p. 86.

8. At this time the figurative usage of water seems apparent, shown by the fact that the people were gathered at the *water gate* to hear the word of God (Nehemiah 8:1). On another occasion when Ezra read from the Law there was a *great rain* (Ezra 10:9). This evidence suggests that water was used as a symbol for divine instruction. When Israel was reminded of God's power over the water, she was also told that God gave his Spirit to instruct Israel and that he also gave them water for thirst (Nehemiah 9:20).

9. The Apocrypha is a collection of fourteen books written during the intertestamental period and that were once positioned between the Old and the New Testaments of the English Bible. When Joseph Smith was involved with his translation of the Bible and came upon the Apocrypha in his English Bible, he asked the Lord if he should translate it. The Lord responded "There are many things contained therein that are true, and it is mostly translated correctly; There are many things contained therein that are not true, which are interpolations by the hands of men. Verily, I say unto you, that it is not needful that the Apocrypha should be translated. Therefore, whoso readeth it, let him understand, for the Spirit manifesteth truth; And whoso is enlightened by the Spirit shall obtain benefit therefrom" (D&C 91:1–5).

10. These translations of the Apocrypha are from *The Apocrypha: An American Translation,* trans. Edgar J. Goodspeed, with intro. by Moses Hadas (New York: Vintage Books, 1959).

11. I use the word *public* here, because Jesus may have performed private or

personal miracles before this time. Elder McConkie thus states, "We cannot avoid the conclusion that between Jesus' twelfth and thirtieth years there were many marvelous and miraculous things of which Mary knew. There is no reason to believe there was a spiritual drought of eighteen years, a period when all that was divine and heaven-guided should be obscured" (Bruce R. McConkie, *The Mortal Messiah: From Bethlehem to Calvary*, 4 vols. [Salt Lake City: Deseret Book Co., 1979–81], 1:452). He also wrote that "Indeed, Mary's appeal to him at the wedding celebration for aid carries an inference of her prior knowledge of his miraculous abilities" (Bruce R. McConkie, *Doctrinal New Testament Commentary*, 3 vols. [Salt Lake City, Utah: Bookcraft, 1977], 1:137).

   12. McConkie, *Doctrinal New Testament Commentary*, 1:136.

   13. Robert Houston Smith, "Exodus Typology in the Fourth Gospel," *Journal of Biblical Literature* 81 (1962): 334–35.

   14. Josephus, Antiquities of the Jews, 14:1, in *Complete Works*, trans. William Whiston (Grand Rapids, Mich.: Kregel Publications, 1978), p. 61.

   15. On the idea that the turning of water into wine was a demonstration that Jesus was the Messiah, we have the following recorded Messianic prophecy from 2 Baruch 29:3, 5–6: "And it will happen that when . . . the Anointed One will begin to be revealed . . . on one vine will be a thousand branches, and one branch will produce a thousand clusters, and one cluster will produce a thousand grapes, and one grape a cor of wine." "2 [Syriac Apocalypse of] Baruch," trans. A. F. Klijn, in James H. Charlesworth, *The Old Testament Pseudepigrapha*, 2 vols. (Garden City, N.Y.: Doubleday, 1983), 1:630.

   16. McConkie, *Doctrinal New Testament Commentary*, 1:188. It should also be noted that Raymond E. Brown, a prominent Catholic scholar on the Gospel of John, suggests a similar view. He omits verse 4 in his translation and interprets this verse as a later gloss. He states, "That it is a gloss is indicated not only by the poor textual attestation, but also by the presence of seven non-Johannine words in one sentence. This ancient gloss, however, may well reflect with accuracy a popular tradition about the pool. The bubbling of the water (vs 7), caused perhaps by an intermittent spring, was thought to have healing power; and this may well have been attributed in the popular imagination to supernatural powers." *Anchor Bible* (Garden City, N.Y.: Doubleday, 1966), 29:207.

   17. O. R. Sellers, in his article entitled "Furlong," in *Interpreter's Dictionary of the Bible* (Nashville, Tenn.: Abingdon Press), 2:330, informs us that a furlong is 220 yards long (1/8th of a mile). Thus twenty-five furlongs would be just over three miles. The LDS Bible Dictionary explains that the Sea of Galilee is twelve and a half miles long and seven and a half miles wide (p. 677). This would indicate that the disciples of Jesus were near the middle of the sea and that Jesus had traveled quite a distance.

   18. McConkie, *Doctrinal New Testament Commentary*, 1:347.

   19. This is my own translation from the Hebrew text. The Hebrew preposition *b* used twice in this verse is translated "in" by the KJV at both places. The preposition *be* can also be translated as "on," which is the translation that I prefer. Thus "Thy way is *on* the sea, and thy path is *on* the great waters."

20. See, for example, 1 Nephi 17:39; Isaiah 66:1; Matthew 5:35; D&C 38:17; Moses 6:9, 44; Abraham 2:7.

21. In Genesis 3:15, footnote *c* of the LDS Bible, we are informed that the word *bruise* in Hebrew can also be translated "crush." Thus I would extrapolate from these two verses that although Satan may bruise the feet of Christ and his disciples, the power of Jesus Christ can crush the head of Satan.

22. Various works have been written on this topic. The most recent are Mary Wakeman, *God's Battle with the Sea Monster* (1973); Carola Kloo, *Yhwh's Battle with the Sea* (1986); and finally John Day, *God's Conflict with the Dragon and the Sea* (1985). Day's index of passages cited (pp. 214–21) contains an exhaustive treatment of all the references in the Old Testament that deal with the conflict between God and the sea or sea monster, which typifies Satan. This theme is strongly attested in John's writings in the book of Revelation. (See, for example, Revelation 8:8–11; 11:6; 12:3; 13:1–8; 14:7; 16:3–4.)

23. In D&C 61:14 we are told that "Behold, I the Lord, in the beginning blessed the waters; but in the last days, by the mouth of my servant John, I cursed the waters." This same John is the author of the Gospel of John, the Epistles of John, and the book of Revelation. In the book of Revelation the cursed waters are a prominent theme that occurs shortly before the second coming of Jesus Christ.

24. Brigham Young, in *Journal of Discourses*, 26 vols. (London: Latter-day Saints' Book Depot, 1855–86), 7:162.

25. Walter Bauer, *A Greek-English Lexicon of the New Testament and other Early Christian Literature*, trans. William F. Arndtand, F. Wilbur Gingrich, 2d ed. (Chicago: University of Chicago Press, 1958), p. 131.

26. Joseph Smith, *Teachings of the Prophet Joseph Smith*, sel. Joseph Fielding Smith (Salt Lake City: Deseret Book Co., 1976), p. 32.

27. These other books would include our modern-day scriptures such as the Doctrine and Covenants, Book of Mormon, and the Pearl of Great Price.

28. For example, the Essenes practiced ritual purification in a small pool of water called a *mikvah*. Many of these small ritual baths appear at Qumran. For a discussion of this issue, see Frank Moore Cross, *The Ancient Library of Qumran and Modern Biblical Studies*, Jr. (Garden City, N.Y.: Anchor Books, 1961), pp. 67–68. It should be clearly understood that these ritual baths were not done by proper priesthood authority in the name of Jesus Christ for the remission of sins. Nevertheless, as new members did enter the Qumran community, they were immersed in water for purification from the contamination of the outside world. Water rituals of immersion were also used for cleanliness before the community ate their daily meals, which they considered sacred. They also bathed after physically relieving themselves. Any contact with a person who was not a member of the sect as well as any contact with a member considered of a lower caste required a ritual bath. Emil Schurer, *The History of the Jewish People in the Age of Jesus Christ*, ed. Geza Vermes, Fergus Millar, and Matthew Black, 3 vols. (Edinburgh: T&T Clark, Ltd., 1979), 1:569, 582.

29. P. Winter, "Judith, Book of," in *Interpreter's Dictionary of the Bible*, 2:1025.

30. Josephus, Antiquities of the Jews, 18:117; quoted from "The Johannine

Paraclete and the Qumran Scrolls," by A. R. C. Leaney, from *John and Qumran*, ed. James H. Charlesworth (London: Geoffrey Chapman Publishers, 1972), p. 52.

31. Bethabara is attested in the Medeba map mosaic on the west bank of the Jordan River (Rudolph Schnackenburg, *The Gospel According to John*, 3 vols., trans. Kevin Smith [New York: Herder and Herder, 1968], 1:296).

32. Russell M. Nelson, "Why This Holy Land," *Ensign*, Dec. 1989, p. 15.

33. Ibid.

34. See, for example, JST Genesis 17:11.

35. Joseph Smith taught that "being born again, comes by the Spirit of God through ordinances" (*Teachings of the Prophet Joseph Smith*, p. 162.)

36. *Teachings of the Prophet Joseph Smith*, p. 328.

37. *Journal of Discourses*, 2:4.

38. It is of interest to note that the Lord told Enoch, who was not physically blind, "Anoint thine eyes with clay and wash them and thou shalt see" (Moses 6:35). The element of clay seems to symbolize the natural man who must wash (be cleansed), in order to see the things of God.

39. In the Bread of Life sermon that Jesus gave at Capernaum, he also stated, "he that believeth on me shall never thirst" (John 6:35).

40. Peter, in fact, refers to apostate teachings as "wells without water" (2 Peter 2:17).

41. See, for example, Revelation 7:17; 14:2; 19:5 & 6; 22:1, 7. John seems to be heavily influenced by Ezekiel's writings as evidenced by the book of Revelation. Of sixty-five New Testament references from Ezekiel, forty-eight are mentioned in the book of Revelation. For a treatment of the water motif in Ezekiel that seems to have influenced John's writings on living water see the author's article "The Waters Which Make Glad the City of God," in *A Witness of Jesus Christ: The 1989 Sperry Symposium on the Old Testament*, ed. Richard D. Draper (Salt Lake City, Utah: Deseret Book Co.), pp. 281–98.

42. *The Babylonian Talmud: Seder Nezikin*, 4 vols., ed. Rabbi Dr. I. Epstein (London: Soncino Press, 1935), 4:22. Note also that Rabbi Johanan quotes from Isaiah 55:1, which states, "Everyone that thirsteth, come ye to the water." It should be noted here that although the Rabbis drank the Law, they did not partake of the fountain of living waters, even Jesus Christ (Jeremiah 2:13).

43. *The Mishnah*, trans. Herbert Danby (Oxford: Oxford University Press, 1933), p. 446.

44. K. Barret in "The Old Testament in the Fourth Gospel," *Journal of Theological Studies*, vol. 48, (1947), p. 156, writes concerning John 7:38: "No commentator has succeeded in explaining satisfactorily the source of the quotation." Elder McConkie observes that "no single Old Testament passage promises that living water shall flow from the disciples to others. Jesus is either quoting a prophecy which has not been preserved for us or he is combining such statements as those found in Isaiah 44:3, 55:1 and 58:11, in such a way as to give an interpretive rendition of them" (McConkie, *Doctrinal New Testament Commentary*, 1:446).

45. Raymond Brown informs us that other scholars have suggested that "from his belly" has actually been translated too literally from the Aramaic. "The same

Aramaic expression, *min giwweh*, can mean 'from within him' and 'from his belly' "
(*Anchor Bible: The Gospel According to John,* 29:323).

46. J. Coert Rylaarsdam, "Booths, Feast of," *Interpreter's Dictionary of the Bible* 1:455–88.

47. Bruce R. McConkie, *Promised Messiah: The First Coming of Christ* (Salt Lake City, Utah: Deseret Book Co., 1978), pp. 432–33.

48. For a full discussion of the origin and development of the feast of Tabernacles, see George McRae's article entitled "The Meaning and Evolution of the Feast of Tabernacles," *Catholic Biblical Quarterly,* vol. 22 (1960), pp. 251–76.

49. Elder James Talmage commented that this ceremonial ritual could be understood in two different ways. "It may have been with reference to the bringing of waters from the pool, *or* to the omission of the ceremony from the ritualistic procedure of the great day, that Jesus cried aloud, If any man thirst . . . " *Jesus the Christ* (Salt Lake City, Utah: Deseret Book Co., 1976), p. 403.

50. McConkie, *The Mortal Messiah,* 1:178–79.

51. McConkie, *Promised Messiah,* p. 434.

52. J. Blenkinsopp, "The Quenching of Thirst: Reflections on the Utterance in the Temple, John 7:37–39," *Scripture* (1960) 12:47.

Index

Left hand, those on the, of God, 16–17, 19
Leprosy, 28–29, 125
Lewis, C. S., 23–24
Lindsay, Richard P., 162
Luke, 84–85, 89–96: emphasizes spiritual dimension of Jesus' life, 89
Luther, Martin, 27

Marcus, Joel, 74
Mark, 84–86
Mammon, 154
Marriage, higher law of, 3–4
McConkie, Bruce R.: on lessons of parables, 9, 16; on miracles, 23; on the four Gospels, 83; on wordly ease, 150, 154–56; on Savior's teachings in Jerusalem, 168–69; on symbolism, 174–75; on water, 192, 193–94; on the Feast of Jehovah, 200; on continuing revelation, 200–201
McConkie, Joseph Fielding, 175–76
Medical practitioners, 118–23
Medical theories, early, 118–19
Medicine: in the time of Christ, 113–23; Old Testament, 116–17; Greek, 117–18
Melchizedek Priesthood: miracles through power of, 194; ordinances, 196
Messiah-kingship issue, 74
Messiahship, divine, 165–67
Messianic symbolism in Jewish feasts, 168
Millenial day, 138
Miracles, 23–37; role of, in God's work, 24; involving cancer, 29; involving sight, 30; involving deafness, 30; involving touching, 30–31; of raising the dead, 31–32; of casting out evil spirits, 32, 102–5; of nature, 32–33; of food, 33–35; of passing unseen, 35; modern, 36–37; through the power of the priesthood, 194
Miracles of Jesus the Messiah, The, 26
Money, value of, 151–52

Montefiore, C. G., 58
Moses, 101, 168. See also Law of Moses
Mount of Olives, 8. See also Olivet sermon
Mount of the Transfiguration, 6–7
Multitude follows Jesus, 181–82

Natural History, 120–21
Nelson, Russell M., 197
Neoplatonism, 45
Nephi, 110; and the quest for riches, 156
Nibley, Hugh, 176, 181
Nicodemus, 198

Oaks, Dallin H., 171
Old Testament medicine, 116–17
Olivet sermon, 8–20
Oppressiveness, sin of, 17
Outer darkness, 14–15, 19

Packard, Noah, 30
Parables: in the Olivet sermon, 8; as stories, 56; of the lost sheep, 57–58, 142–44; of the lost coin, 58; of the prodigal son, 58–60; of the two debtors, 60–61; of the good Samaritan, 61–63; of the vineyard, 63–64; of the Pharisee and the tax collector, 64–65; of the unjust steward, 65–66, 152–57; of the great banquet, 66; of the foolish rich man, 149–52; of the rich man and Lazarus, 157–160
Passion narratives, 69–79; Matthew's, 70–73; Mark's, 73–75; Luke's, 75–77; John's, 77–79
Passover, 102; lamb, 144–45
Paul, 138; on riches, 150–51
Perdition, Sons of. See Sons of Perdition
Persecution, of members of the Church, 84–85
Peter: as eyewitness, 4–5; denial of, 73,74; and testimony of Christ's messiahship, 86, 88; walks on water, 109–10

Pharisee and the tax collector, parable
  of the, 64–65
Philastratus, 123
Pilate, 71–72, 74, 78–79
Plague, 192
Plastaras, James, 177
Pliny, 120–21
Poor, the, 158–59
Possessed man, 102–5
Pratt, Parley P., 28
Prayer: form and content of, 3; need
  for, 94
Priesthood authority, 143
Prodigal son, parable of the, 58–60
Purification, need for, 190

Quail, miracle of the, 34–35

Rasmussen, Dennis, 125–26
Reconciliation of differences, 2
Repent, those who refuse to, 19
Repentance, 12–13: requires suffering,
  15; and condition of souls, 108–9
Restoration, 111
Resurrection: Lord's physical, 40–41,
  42–45, 53; witness of the, 46–47
Rich man: parable of the foolish, 149–
  52; and Lazarus, 157–60
Role, of Jesus Christ, 85

Sacrifice, infinite, 106
Samaritan, the good, 61–63, 66; as a
  healer, 124
Samaritans, 5, 62
Savior. See Jesus Christ
Scott, B. B., 63
Scourging, 75
Second Coming, 9, 13: sign of the, 20
Self-delusion, 11
Sermon on the Mount: spirit of the
  New Testament in the, 2–3;
  spiritual reinforcing of the, 7; and
  wordly goods, 150
Serpent as a symbol, 131–32
Severson, Hack, 36
Sheep, parable of the lost, 57–58
Shakespeare, Suzanne, 29
Sheep as symbols, 139–40
Sheep and goats, parable of, 15–18

Shelley, Harry Rowe, 142
Shepherds, 57–58; the Good, 140–44
Sight, restoring of, 30
Simon, 60
Sin, unpardonable, 20
Sins, Christ forgives, 61
Slander, 18
Smith, George A., 28
Smith, John Henry, 28
Smith, Joseph: on understanding
  parables, 9; vision of, 111; on
  translation, 196; on the kingdom of
  God, 198
Smith, Joseph F., 130
Smith, Lucy Mack, 30
Smith, Robert Houston, 192
Snow, Lorenzo, 31
Sons of Perdition, 17
Sonship of Christ, 163–65
Spinoza, 23
Spiritual body, 46
Spiritual wickedness in the name of
  Christ, 20
Steward, parable of the unjust, 65–66,
  152–57
Stewardship, 13
Suffering, 88–89
Surety, Savior as a, 1
Swearing, 2
Symbolism: in the Old Testament, 99–
  100; John's use of, 174–75
Symbols, the Savior's use of animals
  as, 129–46
Synopsis, 69
Synoptic Gospels, 70

Tabernacles, feast of, 169
Talents, parable of the, 13–15
Talmage, James E., on miracles, 24,
  26; on parables, 149, 154, 157; on
  bread of life, 185
Talmud, Babylonian, water in the,
  199–200
Tarry, Charles C., 65
Tate, George S., 177
Telestial kindgom, 15
Temples and water, 201
Testament, a better, 1, 4, 7